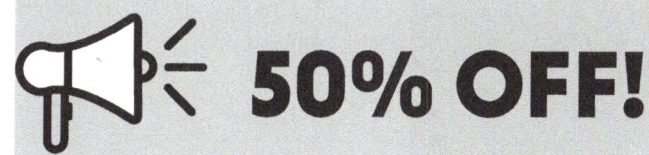 **50% OFF!**

GRE Online Test Prep Course

We consider it an honor and a privilege that you chose our GRE Study Guide. As a way of showing our appreciation and to help us better serve you, we have partnered with Mometrix Test Preparation to offer you 50% off their online GRE Prep Course.

Mometrix has structured their online course to perfectly complement your printed study guide. Many GRE courses are needlessly expensive and don't deliver enough value. With their course, you get access to the best GRE prep material, and you only pay half price.

WHAT'S IN THE GRE TEST PREP COURSE?

- **GRE Study Guide**: Get access to content that complements your study guide.
- **Progress Tracker**: Their customized course allows you to check off content you have studied or feel confident with.
- **600+ Practice Questions**: With 600+ practice questions and lesson reviews, you can test yourself again and again to build confidence.
- **GRE Flashcards**: Their course includes a flashcard mode consisting of over 543 content cards to help you study.

TO RECEIVE THIS DISCOUNT, VISIT THE WEBSITE AT

link.mometrix.com/gre

USE THE DISCOUNT CODE:
STARTSTUDYING

IF YOU HAVE ANY QUESTIONS OR CONCERNS, PLEASE CONTACT MOMETRIX AT SUPPORT@MOMETRIX.COM

Free DVD Free DVD

Essential Test Tips Video from Trivium Test Prep

Dear Customer,

Thank you for purchasing from Trivium Test Prep! Whether you're looking to join the military, get into college, or advance your career, we're honored to be a part of your journey.

To show our appreciation (and to help you relieve a little of that test-prep stress), we're offering a **FREE *Essential Test Tips* Video** by Trivium Test Prep. Our video includes 35 test preparation strategies that will help keep you calm and collected before and during your big exam. All we ask is that you email us your feedback and describe your experience with our product. Amazing, awful, or just so-so: we want to hear what you have to say!

To receive your **FREE Video**, please email us at 5star@ triviumtestprep.com. Include "Free 5 Star" in the subject line and the following information in your email:

1. The title of the product you purchased.
2. Your rating from 1 – 5 (with 5 being the best).
3. Your feedback about the product, including how our materials helped you meet your goals and ways in which we can improve our products.
4. Your full name and shipping address so we can send your **FREE *Essential Test Tips* Video**.

If you have any questions or concerns please feel free to contact us directly at 5star@triviumtestprep.com.

Thank you, and good luck with your studies!

GRE Prep Book 2025-2026
5 Practice Tests and GRE Study Guide
[2nd Edition]

G. T. McDivitt

Copyright ©2025 Trivium Test Prep

ISBN-13: 9781637988688

ALL RIGHTS RESERVED. By purchase of this book, you have been licensed on copy for personal use only. No part of this work may be reproduced, redistributed, or used in any form or by any means without prior written permission of the publisher and copyright owner. Trivium Test Prep; Accepted, Inc.; Cirrus Test Prep; and Ascencia Test Prep are all imprints of Trivium Test Prep, LLC.

ETS was not involved in the creation or production of this product, is not in any way affiliated with Accepted, Inc., and does not sponsor or endorse this product.

Image(s) used under license from Shutterstock.com

Online Resources

Accepted, Inc. includes online resources with the purchase of this study guide to help you fully prepare for your GRE exam.

Flash Cards

Accepted flash cards allow you to review important terms easily on your computer or smartphone.

From Stress to Success

Watch "From Stress to Success," a brief but insightful YouTube video that offers the tips, tricks, and secrets experts use to score higher on the exam.

Cheat Sheets

Review the core skills you need to master the exam with easy-to-read Cheat Sheets.

Feedback

Let us know what you think!

Access these materials at: acceptedinc.com/gre-online-resources

Table of Contents

INTRODUCTION 1

ANALYTICAL WRITING 3
    STRUCTURING THE ESSAY 3
    WRITING A THESIS STATEMENT 4
    WRITING WELL 6
    PRACTICE ESSAY 7
    PROMPT 8

VERBAL REASONING 9
    PARTS OF SPEECH 10
    CONSTRUCTING SENTENCES 14
    PUNCTUATION 16
    POINT OF VIEW 18
    ACTIVE AND PASSIVE VOICE 19
    TRANSITIONS 19
    WORDINESS AND REDUNDANCY 20
    WORD STRUCTURE 21
    TEXT COMPLETION AND SENTENCE EQUIVALENCE 23
    ANSWER KEY 25

READING COMPREHENSION 28
    THE MAIN IDEA 29
    SUPPORTING DETAILS 32
    TEXT STRUCTURE 34
    THE AUTHOR'S PURPOSE 34
    FACTS VS. OPINIONS 35
    DRAWING CONCLUSIONS 36
    COMPARING PASSAGES 37
    ANSWER KEY 40

NUMBERS AND OPERATIONS 42
    INTRODUCTION TO QUANTITATIVE REASONING 42
    NUMBERS 44
    BASIC OPERATIONS 47
    FRACTIONS AND DECIMALS 51
    RATIOS, PROPORTIONS, AND PERCENTS 53
    WORKING WITH LARGE AND SMALL NUMBERS 55
    ANSWER KEY 57

ALGEBRA 59
    ALGEBRAIC EXPRESSIONS 59
    LINEAR EQUATIONS 61
    LINEAR INEQUALITIES 66
    QUADRATIC EQUATIONS 68
    FUNCTIONS 72
    ARITHMETIC AND GEOMETRIC SEQUENCES 75
    SOLVING WORD PROBLEMS 76

  Answer Key 78

GEOMETRY 83
  Units of Measurement 83
  Lines and Angles 85
  Perimeter and Area 86
  Properties of Two-Dimensional Shapes 87
  Properties of Three-Dimensional Shapes 92
  Congruency and Similarity 94
  Right Triangles and the Pythagorean Theorem 95
  Answer Key 96

DATA ANALYSIS 98
  Statistics 98
  Measures of Central Tendency 99
  Measures of Dispersion 101
  Data Presentation 101
  Counting Principles 104
  Set Theory 106
  Probability 107
  Answer Key 109

GRE PRACTICE TEST #1 111
  Analytical Writing 111
  Quantitative Reasoning 1 111
  Quantitative Reasoning 2 113
  Verbal Reasoning 1 116
  Verbal Reasoning 2 119

GRE PRACTICE TEST #1 ANSWER KEY 124
  Analyze and Issue: Sample Essay 124
  Quantitative Reasoning 1 Answer Key 125
  Quantitative Reasoning 2 Answer Key 126
  Verbal Reasoning 1 Answer Key 129
  Verbal Reasoning 2 Answer Key 130

GRE PRACTICE TEST #2 132
  Analytical Writing 132
  Quantitative Reasoning 1 132
  Quantitative Reasoning 2 135
  Verbal Reasoning 1 139
  Verbal Reasoning 2 142

GRE PRACTICE TEST #2 ANSWER KEY 147
  Analyze an Issue: Sample Essay 147
  Quantitative Reasoning 1 Answer Key 147
  Quantitative Reasoning 2 Answer Key 149
  Verbal Reasoning 1 Answer Key 151
  Verbal Reasoning 2 Answer Key 152

GRE PRACTICE TEST #3 154
  Analytical Writing 154
  Analyze an Issue: Sample Essay 154

- Quantitative Reasoning 1 155
- Quantitative Reasoning 2 157
- Verbal Reasoning 1 160
- Verbal Reasoning 2 164

GRE PRACTICE TEST #3 ANSWER KEY 168
- Quantitative Reasoning 1 168
- Quantitative Reasoning 2 169
- Verbal Reasoning 1 171
- Verbal Reasoning 2 172

GRE PRACTICE TEST #4 174
- Analytical Writing 174
- Analyze an Issue: Sample Essay 174
- Quantitative Reasoning 1 175
- Quantitative Reasoning 2 177
- Verbal Reasoning 1 180
- Verbal Reasoning 2 183

GRE PRACTICE TEST #4 ANSWER KEY 187
- Quantitative Reasoning 1 187
- Quantitative Reasoning 2 189
- Verbal Reasoning 1 191
- Verbal Reasoning 2 192

GRE PRACTICE TEST #5 194
- Analytical Writing 194
- Analyze an Issue: Sample Essay 194
- Quantitative Reasoning 1 195
- Quantitative Reasoning 2 197
- Verbal Reasoning 1 200
- Verbal Reasoning 2 203

GRE PRACTICE TEST #5 ANSWER KEY 207
- Quantitative Reasoning 1 207
- Quantitative Reasoning 2 208
- Verbal Reasoning 1 210
- Verbal Reasoning 2 211

INTRODUCTION

Congratulations on choosing to take the GRE! By purchasing this book, you've taken the first step toward your graduate school career. This guide will provide you with a detailed overview of the GRE so you will know exactly what to expect on test day. We'll take you through all of the concepts covered on the exam and give you the opportunity to test your knowledge with practice questions. Even if it's been a while since you took a major test, don't worry; we'll make sure you're more than ready!

What is the GRE?

The GRE (Graduate Record Examinations) is developed by Educational Testing Service (ETS). The GRE assesses your reasoning, critical thinking, and analytical writing abilities. Universities use your GRE score to help determine if you're ready to tackle graduate-level material.

What's on the GRE?

The GRE consists of three sections: Verbal Reasoning, Quantitative Reasoning, and Analytical Writing. The Analytical Writing portion appears first; sections following Analytical Writing may appear in any order. Verbal Reasoning and Quantitative Reasoning are each broken up into two sections of twenty questions each.

The Analytical Writing section asks you to write an essay in response to an issue.

Verbal Reasoning questions are multiple-choice. There are three types of Verbal Reasoning questions:

- ▶ Text Completion
- ▶ Sentence Equivalence
- ▶ Reading Comprehension

Quantitative Reasoning questions are multiple-choice and grid-in. A calculator will be available on-screen during the Quantitative Reasoning sections. There are three types of Quantitative Reasoning questions:

- ▶ Quantitative Comparisons
- ▶ Problem Solving
- ▶ Data Interpretation

Each test section has a time limit (as specified in the following table), for a total of 54 scored questions. Expect to spend one hour and fifty-eight minutes taking the test.

Section	Description	Time
Analytical Writing	One "Analyze an Issue" writing task	30 minutes
Quantitative Reasoning: Section 1	12 questions	21 minutes
Quantitative Reasoning: Section 2	15 questions	26 minutes
Verbal Reasoning: Section 1	12 questions	18 minutes
Verbal Reasoning: Section 2	15 questions	23 minutes
Total	**54 questions**	**1 hour and 58 minutes**

How is the GRE Scored?

Each question on the GRE is worth one point. There is no guess penalty, meaning there is no penalty for choosing an incorrect answer. So be sure to guess if you do not know the answer to a question.

The Verbal Reasoning and Quantitative Reasoning sections are section-adaptive. In **section-adaptive testing**, if you do well on the first Verbal Reasoning section, the second Verbal Reasoning section will be slightly harder. The same goes for Quantitative Reasoning.

The total number of questions you answer correctly is your raw score. Scoring considers the difficulty level of the questions you address. This score will then be scaled from 130 – 170. Analytical Writing is scored separately on a scale of 0 – 6.

How is the GRE Administered?

The GRE is a computer-based test offered at Prometric testing centers throughout the year. On the day of your test, arrive early and be sure to bring proper identification and your admission ticket. You are required to put away all personal belongings before the test begins. Cell phones and other electronic, photographic, recording, or listening devices are not permitted in the testing center at all. In some cases, GRE testing is available at home. For more details on what to expect on testing day, check with ETS.

About This Guide

This guide will help you master the most important test topics and develop critical test-taking skills. We have built features into our books to prepare you for your tests and increase your score. Along with a detailed summary of the format, content, and scoring of the GRE, we offer an in-depth overview of the content knowledge required to pass the exam. In the review you'll find sidebars that provide interesting information, highlight key concepts, and review content so that you can solidify your understanding of the exam's concepts. You can also test your knowledge with sample questions throughout the text and practice questions that reflect the content and format of the exams. We're pleased you've chosen Accepted, Inc. to be a part of your academic journey!

Analytical Writing

On the Analytical Writing section of the GRE, you will be required to read a short passage and write an essay analyzing the author's argument. The passage will address an issue from science, art, or civics and provide different viewpoints and a range of supporting evidence. Your job will be to describe how the author presents his or her argument. Your essay should include a discussion of the following:

- ▶ the author's main argument
- ▶ the structure of the passage
- ▶ the evidence the author uses to support his or her claim
- ▶ the rhetorical elements (e.g., metaphors, word choice, or appeals to emotion and authority) used by the author

You should not discuss your own opinion or reactions to the passage in your essay. Your only task is to objectively analyze the author's argument, not to discuss how you personally feel about either the topic or the effectiveness of the passage.

Structuring the Essay

There are a few different ways to organize an essay, but some basics apply no matter what the style.

Essays may differ in how they present an idea, but they all have the same basic parts—introduction, body, and conclusion. The most common essay types are persuasive essays and expository essays:

- ▶ A persuasive essay takes a position on an issue and attempts to show the reader why it is correct.
- ▶ An expository essay explains different aspects of an issue without necessarily taking a side.

Introductions

The introduction is where your argument or idea is presented. Usually, the introductory paragraph ends with a **THESIS STATEMENT**, which clearly sets forth the position or point the essay will prove. The introduction is a good place to bring up complexities, counterarguments, and context, all of which will help the reader understand the reasoning behind your position on the issue at hand. Later, revisit those issues and wrap all of them up in the conclusion.

Example

Below is an example of an introduction. Note that it provides some context for the argument, acknowledges an opposing perspective, and gives the reader a good idea of the issue's complexities. In the last few lines, pay attention to the thesis statement, which clearly states the author's position.

Technology has changed immensely in recent years, but today's generation barely notices—high school students are already experienced with the internet, computers, apps, cameras, cell phones, and more. Teenagers must learn to use these tools safely and responsibly. Opponents of 1:1 technology programs might argue that students will be distracted or misuse the technology, but that is exactly why schools must teach them to use it. By providing students with technology, schools can help them apply it positively by creating projects with other students, communicating with teachers and classmates, and conducting research for class projects. In a world where technology is improving and changing at a phenomenal rate, schools have a responsibility to teach students how to navigate that technology safely and effectively; providing each student with a laptop or tablet is one way to help them do that.

The Body Paragraphs

The body of an essay consists of a series of structured paragraphs. It may be organized by

- ▶ creating paragraphs that describe or explain each reason that is given in your thesis;
- ▶ addressing the issue as a problem and offering a solution in a separate paragraph;
- ▶ telling a story that demonstrates your point (make sure to break it into paragraphs around related ideas); or
- ▶ comparing and contrasting the merits of two opposing sides of the issue (make sure to draw a conclusion about which is better at the end).

Each paragraph must be structurally consistent, beginning with a topic sentence to introduce the main idea, followed by supporting ideas and examples. No extra ideas unrelated to the paragraph's focus should appear. Transition words and phrases should be used to connect body paragraphs and improve the flow and readability of your essay.

The *Providing Supporting Evidence* section contains an example of a paragraph that is internally consistent and explains one of the main reasons given in the example introduction. Your essay should have one or more paragraphs like this to form the main body.

Conclusions

In order to end your essay smoothly, a conclusion should be written that reminds the reader why these topics are being discussed in the first place. To craft the conclusion, refer to the ideas in the introduction and thesis statement. Be sure that you do not simply restate your ideas; the purpose of the conclusion is to reinforce your argument.

Example

Below is a sample conclusion paragraph that could go with the introduction above. Notice that this conclusion talks about the same topics as the introduction (changing technology and the responsibility of schools), but it does not simply rewrite the thesis.

As technology continues to change, teens will need to adapt to it. Schools already teach young people myriad academic and life skills, so it makes sense that they would also teach students how to use technology appropriately. Providing students with their own devices is one part of that important task, and schools should be supporting it.

Writing a Thesis Statement

The **THESIS**, or **THESIS STATEMENT**, is central to the structure and meaning of an essay. It presents the writer's argument, or position on an issue; in other words, it tells readers specifically what you think and what you will discuss. A strong, direct thesis statement is key to the organization of any essay. The thesis statement is typically located at the end of the introductory paragraph. Writing a good thesis statement is as simple as stating your idea and why you think it is true or correct.

Example

The Prompt

Many high schools have begun to adopt 1:1 technology programs, meaning that each school provides every student with a computing device such as a laptop or tablet. Educators who support these initiatives say that the technology allows for more dynamic collaboration and that students need to learn technology skills to compete in the job market. On the other hand, opponents cite increased distraction and the dangers of cyber-bullying or unsupervised internet use as reasons not to provide students with such devices.

In your essay, take a position on this question. You may write about either one of the two points of view given, or you may present a different point of view on this question. Use specific reasons and examples to support your position.

Possible thesis statements:

Providing technology to every student is good for education because it allows students to learn important skills such as typing, web design, and video editing; it also gives students more opportunities to work cooperatively with their classmates and teachers.

I disagree with the idea that schools should provide technology to students because most students will simply be distracted by the free access to games and websites when they should be studying or doing homework.

In a world where technology is improving and changing at a phenomenal rate, schools have a responsibility to teach students how to navigate that technology safely and effectively; providing each student with a laptop or tablet is one way to help them do that.

Providing Supporting Evidence

Your essay requires not only structured, organized paragraphs; it must also provide specific evidence that supports your arguments. Whenever you make a general statement, follow it up with specific examples that will help to convince the reader that your argument has merit. These specific examples do not bring new ideas to the paragraph; rather, they explain or defend the general ideas that have already been stated. The following are some examples of general statements and specific statements that provide more detailed support:

- ▶ **GENERAL**: Students may get distracted online or access harmful websites.

- ▶ **SPECIFIC**: Some students spend too much time using chat features or social media, or they get caught up in online games. Others spend time reading websites that have nothing to do with an assignment.

- ▶ **SPECIFIC**: Teens often think they are hidden behind their computer screens. If teenagers give out personal information such as age or location on a website, it can lead to dangerous strangers seeking them out.

- ▶ **GENERAL**: Schools can teach students how to use technology appropriately and expose them to new tools.

- ▶ **SPECIFIC**: Schools can help students learn to use technology to work on class projects, communicate with classmates and teachers, and carry out research for classwork.

▶ **SPECIFIC**: Providing students with laptops or tablets will allow them to get lots of practice using technology and programs at home, and only school districts can ensure that these tools are distributed widely, especially to students who may not have them at home.

Example

Below is an example of a structured paragraph that uses specific supporting ideas. The following paragraph supports the thesis introduced above (see Introductions*).*

Providing students with their own laptop or tablet will allow them to explore new programs and software in class with teachers and classmates and practice using the device at home. In schools without laptops for students, classes have to visit computer labs where they share old computers that are often missing keys or that run so slowly they are hardly powered on before class ends. When a teacher tries to show students how to use a new tool or website, students must scramble to follow along and have no time to explore the new feature. If they can take laptops home instead, students can do things like practice editing video clips or photographs until they are perfect. They can email classmates or use shared files to collaborate even after school. If schools expect students to learn these skills, it is the responsibility of the schools to provide students with enough opportunities to practice them.

This paragraph has some general statements:

"... their own laptop or tablet will allow them to explore new programs and software... and to practice..."

"... it is the schools' responsibility to provide... enough opportunities... "

It also has some specific examples to back up the general statements:

"... computers... run so slowly they are hardly powered on... students must scramble to follow along and have no time to explore... "

"They can email classmates or use shared files to collaborate... "

Writing Well

Transitions

Transitions are words, phrases, and ideas that help connect ideas throughout a text. They should be used between sentences and between paragraphs. Some common transitions include *then, next, in other words, as well, and in addition to*. Be creative with your transitions, and make sure you understand what the transition you are using shows about the relationship between the ideas. For instance, the transition *although* implies that there is some contradiction between the first and second ideas.

Syntax

The way you write sentences is important to maintaining the reader's interest. Try to begin sentences differently. Make some sentences long and some sentences short. Write simple sentences. Write complex sentences that have complex ideas in them. Readers appreciate variety.

There are four basic types of sentences: simple, compound, complex, and compound-complex. Try to use some of each type. Be sure that your sentences make sense, though—it is better to have clear and simple writing that a reader can understand than to have complex, confusing syntax that does not clearly express the idea.

Word Choice and Tone

The words you choose influence the impression you make on readers. Use words that are specific, direct, and appropriate to the task. For instance, a formal text may benefit from complex sentences and impressive vocabulary, while it may be more appropriate to use simple vocabulary and sentences in writing intended for a young audience. Make use of strong vocabulary; avoid using vague, general words such as *good*, *bad*, *very*, or *a lot*. However, make sure that you are comfortable with the vocabulary you choose: if you are unsure about a word's meaning or its use in the context of your essay, do not use it at all.

Editing, Revising, and Proofreading

When writing a timed essay, you will not have very much time to follow the steps described in this chapter. Spend any time you have left after writing the essay to look it over and check for spelling and grammar mistakes that may interfere with a reader's understanding. Common mistakes to look out for include: subject/verb disagreement, pronoun/antecedent disagreement, comma splices, run-ons, and sentence fragments (phrases or dependent clauses unconnected to an independent clause).

Practice Essay

Read the passage from John F. Kennedy's commencement address at American University in 1963, "A Strategy of Peace," and then write an essay based on the prompt.

As you read the passage below, consider how John F. Kennedy uses the following:

- ▶ evidence, such as facts or examples, to support claims
- ▶ reasoning to develop ideas and to connect claims and evidence
- ▶ stylistic or persuasive elements, such as word choice or appeals to emotion, to add power to the ideas expressed

Adapted from the Commencement Address given by John F. Kennedy at American University on June 10, 1963.

I have, therefore, chosen this time and place to discuss a topic on which ignorance too often abounds and the truth is too rarely perceived. And that is the most important topic on Earth: peace. What kind of peace do I mean and what kind of a peace do we seek? Not a Pax Americana enforced on the world by American weapons of war. Not the peace of the grave or the security of the slave. I am talking about genuine peace, the kind of peace that makes life on Earth worth living, and the kind that enables men and nations to grow, and to hope, and build a better life for their children; not merely peace for Americans but peace for all men and women, not merely peace in our time but peace in all time.

I speak of peace because of the new face of war. Total war makes no sense in an age where great powers can maintain large and relatively invulnerable nuclear forces and refuse to surrender without resort to those forces. It makes no sense in an age where a single nuclear weapon contains almost ten times the explosive force delivered by all the allied air forces in the Second World War.

It makes no sense in an age when the deadly poisons produced by a nuclear exchange would be carried by wind and water and soil and seed to the far corners of the globe and to generations yet unborn.

Today the expenditure of billions of dollars every year on weapons acquired for the purpose of making sure we never need them is essential to the keeping of peace. But surely the acquisition of such idle stockpiles which can only destroy and never create is not the only, much less the most efficient, means of assuring peace. I speak of peace, therefore, as the necessary, rational end of rational men. I realize the pursuit of peace is not as dramatic as the pursuit of war, and frequently the words of the pursuers fall on deaf ears. But we have no more urgent task.

Some say that it is useless to speak of peace or world law or world disarmament, and that it will be useless until the leaders of the Soviet Union adopt a more enlightened attitude. I hope they do. I believe we can help them do it. But I also believe that we must reexamine our own attitudes, as individuals and as a Nation, for our attitude is as essential as theirs.

And every graduate of this school, every thoughtful citizen who despairs of war and wishes to bring peace, should begin by looking inward, by examining his own attitude towards the possibilities of peace, towards the Soviet Union, towards the course of the Cold War, and towards freedom and peace here at home.

First examine our attitude towards peace itself. Too many of us think it is impossible. Too many think it is unreal. But that is a dangerous, defeatist belief. It leads to the conclusion that war is inevitable, that mankind is doomed, that we are gripped by forces we cannot control. We need not accept that view. Our problems are manmade; therefore, they can be solved by man. And man can be as big as he wants.

No problem of human destiny is beyond human beings. Man's reason and spirit have often solved the seemingly unsolvable, and we believe they can do it again. I am not referring to the absolute, infinite concept of universal peace and good will of which some fantasies and fanatics dream. I do not deny the value of hopes and dreams but we merely invite discouragement and incredulity by making that our only and immediate goal.

Let us focus instead on a more practical, more attainable peace, based not on a sudden revolution in human nature but on a gradual evolution in human institutions, on a series of concrete actions and effective agreements which are in the interest of all concerned. There is no single, simple key to this peace; no grand or magic formula to be adopted by one or two powers. Genuine peace must be the product of many nations, the sum of many acts. It must be dynamic, not static, changing to meet the challenge of each new generation. For peace is a process, a way of solving problems.

Prompt

Write an essay explaining how John F. Kennedy builds his argument to convince his audience that peace between the United States and Soviet Union will come about not through a "Pax Americana" obtained in an American victory in a nuclear war, but through a fundamental shift in the human attitude towards peace. In your essay, explain how he uses the techniques and elements listed above to strengthen his argument; be sure to focus on the most relevant ones. Remember not to discuss whether you agree with Kennedy or not; analyze his argument and explain it to your audience instead.

Verbal Reasoning

VERBAL REASONING questions focus on understanding written media, evaluating ideas, synthesizing concepts, and recognizing relationships and trends in a text. You will need to analyze written concepts and understand relationships between words. There are twenty questions on each Verbal Reasoning section and three types of Verbal Reasoning questions:

- ▶ Text Completion
- ▶ Sentence Equivalence
- ▶ Reading Comprehension

TEXT COMPLETION QUESTIONS ask you to complete a sentence or passage using a word, words, or phrase. There are six Text Completion questions on each Verbal Reasoning section.

Text Completion Question Format

Even though the desert doesn't seem like an ideal place for _____, many animals and insects live there.
- A) racing
- B) dehydration
- C) water
- D) habitation
- E) congruence

Option D is correct.

Habitation means abode or home. Animals and insects make their homes or habitats in the desert.

SENTENCE EQUIVALENCE questions ask you to choose TWO correct answers to create two sentences that differ in wording but align in meaning. There are about four Sentence Equivalence questions on each Verbal Reasoning section.

Sentence Equivalence Question Format

The veterinarian faced a _____; she needed to operate on the wounded animal, but the animal wasn't in stable condition and might not make it through surgery.
- A) prospect
- B) chance
- C) dilemma
- D) disagreement
- E) predicament

Options C (dilemma) and E (predicament) are correct.

A *dilemma* is a difficult choice; a *predicament* is a difficult situation.

Parts of Speech

The first step in getting ready for the Verbal Reasoning Test is to review parts of speech and the rules that accompany them. The good news is that you have been using these rules since you first began to speak; even if you do not know a lot of the technical terms, many of these rules may be familiar to you.

Nouns and Pronouns

NOUNS are people, places, or things. For example, in the sentence, "The hospital was very clean," the noun is *hospital*; it is a place. Pronouns replace nouns and make sentences sound less repetitive. Take the sentence, "Sam stayed home from school because Sam was not feeling well." The word *Sam* appears twice in the same sentence. To avoid repetition and improve the sentence, use a pronoun instead: "Sam stayed at home because *he* did not feel well."

Because pronouns take the place of nouns, they need to agree both in number and gender with the noun they replace. A plural noun therefore needs a plural pronoun, and a feminine noun needs a feminine pronoun. In the first sentence of this paragraph, for example, the plural pronoun *they* replaces the plural noun *pronouns*. Questions on the test may cover pronoun agreement, so it is good to get comfortable identifying pronouns.

Quick Review

Singular pronouns:
- ▶ I, me, mine, my
- ▶ you, your, yours
- ▶ he, him, his
- ▶ she, her, hers
- ▶ it, its

Plural pronouns:
- ▶ we, us, our, ours
- ▶ they, them, their, theirs

Quick Review

If the subject is separated from the verb, cross out the phrases between them to make conjugation easier.

Practice Questions

1. Which of the following sentences is correct?
   A) If a student forgets their homework, it is considered incomplete.
   B) If a student forgets his or her homework, it is considered incomplete.

2. Which of the following sentences is correct?
   A) Everybody will receive their paychecks promptly.
   B) Everybody will receive his or her paycheck promptly.

3. Which of the following sentences is correct?
   A) When a nurse begins work at a hospital, you should wash your hands.
   B) When a nurse begins work at a hospital, he or she should wash his or her hands.

4. Which of the following sentences is correct?
   A) After the teacher spoke to the student, she realized her mistake.
   B) After speaking to the student, the teacher realized her own mistake.

Verbs

A **VERB** is the action of a sentence: verbs *do* things. A verb must be conjugated to match the context of the sentence; this can sometimes be tricky because English has many irregular verbs. For example, *run* is an action verb in the present tense that becomes *ran* in the past tense; the linking verb *is* (which describes a state of being) becomes *was* in the past tense.

Conjugation of the Verb *To Be*			
	Past	Present	Future
Singular	was	is	will be
Plural	were	are	will be

Verb tense must make sense in the context of the sentence. For example, the sentence, "I was baking cookies and eat some dough" probably sounds strange. That is because the two verbs *was baking* and *eat* are in different tenses. *Was baking* occurred in the past; *eat*, on the other hand, occurs in the present. To correct this error, conjugate *eat* in the past tense: *I was baking cookies and ate some dough*.

Quick Review

Think of the subject and the verb as sharing a single *s*. If the noun ends with an *s*, the verb should not and vice versa

Like pronouns, verbs must agree in number with the noun to which they refer. In the example above, the verb *was* refers back to the singular *I*. If the subject of the sentence were plural, it would need to be modified to read *They were baking cookies and ate some dough*. Note that the verb *ate* does not change form; this is common for verbs in the past tense.

Practice Questions

5. Which of the following sentences is correct?
    A) The cat chase the ball while the dogs runs in the yard.
    B) The cat chases the ball while the dogs run in the yard.

6. Which of the following sentences is correct?
    A) The cars that had been recalled by the manufacturer was returned within a few months.
    B) The cars that had been recalled by the manufacturer were returned within a few months.

7. Which of the following sentences is correct?
    A) The deer hid in the trees.
    B) The deer are not all the same size.

8. Which of the following sentences is correct?
    A) Either the patient or her parents complete her discharge paperwork.
    B) Neither the nurse nor her boss was scheduled to take a vacation.

9. Which of the following sentences is correct?
    A) Because it will rain during the party last night, we had to move the tables inside.
    B) Because it rained during the party last night, we had to move the tables inside.

Other Parts of Speech

ADJECTIVES are words that describe a noun. Take the sentence, "The boy hit the ball." If you want to know more about the noun *ball*, then you could use an adjective to describe it: "The boy hit the red ball." An adjective simply provides more information about a noun in a sentence.

Like adjectives, **ADVERBS** provide more information about a part of a sentence. Adverbs can describe verbs, adjectives, and even other adverbs. For example, in the sentence, "The doctor had recently hired a new employee," the adverb *recently* tells us more about how the action *hired* took place. Often (but not always) adverbs end in *-ly*. Remember that adverbs can never describe nouns—only adjectives can.

Adjectives, adverbs, and **MODIFYING PHRASES** (groups of words that together modify another word) should always be placed as close as possible to the words they modify. Separating words from their modifiers can result in incorrect or confusing sentences.

Practice Questions

10. Which of the following sentences is correct?
    A) Running through the hall, the bell rang and the student knew she was late.
    B) Running through the hall, the student heard the bell ring and knew she was late.

11. Which sentence below is correct?
    A) The terrifyingly lion's loud roar scared the zoo's visitors.
    B) The lion's terrifyingly loud roar scared the zoo's visitors.

Other Parts of Speech

PREPOSITIONS generally help describe relationships in space and time; they may express the location of a noun or pronoun in relation to other words and phrases in a sentence. For example, in the sentence, "The nurse parked her car in a parking garage," the preposition *in* describes the position of the car in relation to the garage. The noun that follows the preposition is called its "object." In the example above, the object of the preposition *in* is the noun *parking garage*.

Did You Know?

Other prepositions include after, between, by, during, of, on, to, and with.

CONJUNCTIONS connect words, phrases, and clauses. The conjunctions summarized in the acronym *FANBOYS*—for, and, nor, but, or, yet, so—are called **COORDINATING CONJUNCTIONS** and are used to join independent clauses. For example, in the sentence, "The nurse prepared the patient for surgery, and the doctor performed the surgery," the conjunction *and* joins the two independent clauses together. **SUBORDINATING CONJUNCTIONS**, like *although, because,* and *if,* join together an independent and dependent clause. In the sentence, "She had to ride the subway because her car was broken," the conjunction *because* joins together the two clauses. (Independent and dependent clauses are covered in more detail later in this chapter.)

Quick Review

See the "Phrases and Clauses" section for more information on independent and dependent clauses.

INTERJECTIONS, like *wow* and *hey*, express emotion and are most commonly used in conversation and casual writing. They are often followed by *exclamation points*.

Constructing Sentences

Phrases and Clauses

A **PHRASE** is a group of words acting together that contain either a subject or verb, but not both. Phrases can be constructed from several different parts of speech. For example, a prepositional phrase includes a preposition and the object of that preposition (e.g., *under the table*), and a verb phrase includes the main verb and any helping verbs (e.g., *had been running*). Phrases cannot stand alone as sentences.

A **CLAUSE** is a group of words that contains both a subject and a verb. There are two types of clauses: **INDEPENDENT CLAUSES** can stand alone as sentences, and **DEPENDENT CLAUSES** cannot stand alone. Again, dependent clauses are recognizable as they begin with subordinating conjunctions.

Practice Question

12. Classify each of the following as a phrase, independent clause, or dependent clause:
    1) I have always wanted to drive a bright red sports car
    2) under the bright sky filled with stars
    3) because my sister is running late

Types of Sentences

A sentence can be classified as simple, compound, complex, or compound-complex based on the type and number of clauses it has.

Sentence Type	Number of Independent Clauses	Number of Dependent Clauses
Simple	1	0
Compound	2+	0
Complex	1	1+
Compound-complex	2+	1+

A **SIMPLE SENTENCE** consists of only one independent clause. Because there are no dependent clauses in a simple sentence, it can be as short as two words—a subject and a verb (e.g., *I ran.*). However, a simple sentence may also contain prepositions, adjectives, and adverbs. Even though these additions can extend the length of a simple sentence, it is still considered a simple sentence as long as it does not contain any dependent clauses.

COMPOUND SENTENCES have two or more independent clauses and no dependent clauses. Usually, a comma and a coordinating conjunction (*for, and, nor, but, or, yet,* and *so*) join the independent clauses, though semicolons can be used as well. For example, the sentence, "My computer broke, so I took it to be repaired" is compound.

Did You Know?

Joining two independent clauses with only a comma and no coordinating conjunction is a punctuation error called a comma splice—be on the lookout for these.

COMPLEX SENTENCES have one independent clause and at least one dependent clause. In the complex sentence, "If you lie down with dogs, you'll wake up with fleas," the first clause is dependent (because of the subordinating conjunction *if*), and the second is independent.

COMPOUND-COMPLEX SENTENCES have two or more independent clauses and at least one dependent clause. For example, the sentence, "City traffic frustrates David because the streets are congested, so he is seeking an alternate route home," is compound-complex. "City traffic frustrates David" is an independent clause, as is "he is seeking an alternate route home"; however, the subordinating conjunction *because* indicates that "because the streets are so congested" is a dependent clause.

Practice Questions

13. Classify the following sentence: *San Francisco is one of my favorite places in the United States.*
    A) a simple sentence
    B) a compound sentence
    C) a complex sentence
    D) a compound-complex sentence

14. Classify the following sentence: *I love listening to the radio in the car because I enjoy loud music on the open road.*
    A) a simple sentence
    B) a compound sentence
    C) a complex sentence
    D) a compound-complex sentence

15. Classify the following sentence: *I wanted to get a dog, but I got a fish because my roommate is allergic to pet dander.*
    A) a simple sentence
    B) a compound sentence
    C) a complex sentence
    D) a compound-complex sentence

16. Classify the following sentence: *The game was canceled, but we will still practice on Saturday.*
    A) a simple sentence
    B) a compound sentence
    C) a complex sentence
    D) a compound-complex sentence

Clause Placement

In addition to the classifications above, sentences can also be defined by the location of the main clause. In a **PERIODIC SENTENCE**, the main idea of the sentence is held until the end. In a **CUMULATIVE SENTENCE**, the independent clause comes first, and any modifying words or clauses follow it. (Note that this type of classification—periodic or cumulative—is not used in place of the simple, compound, complex, or compound-complex classifications. A sentence can be both cumulative and complex, for example.)

Practice Questions

17. Classify the following sentence: *The GED, the TASC, the SAT, the ACT—this dizzying array of exams proved no match for the determined students.*
    A) a cumulative sentence
    B) a periodic sentence

18. Classify the following sentence: *Jessica was well prepared for the test, for she had studied for weeks, taken practice exams, and reviewed the material with other students.*
    A) a cumulative sentence
    B) a periodic sentence

Punctuation

The basic rules for using the major punctuation marks are given in Table 2.3.

Punctuation	Purpose	Example
Period	ending sentences	Periods go at the end of complete sentences.
Question mark	ending questions	What's the best way to end a sentence?
Exclamation point	indicating interjections or commands; ending sentences that show extreme emotion	Help! I'll never understand how to use punctuation!
Comma	joining two independent clauses (always with a coordinating conjunction)	Commas can be used to join independent clauses, but they must always be followed by a coordinating conjunction in order to avoid a comma splice.
Comma	setting apart introductory and nonessential words and phrases	Commas, when used properly, set apart extra information in a sentence.
Comma	separating three or more items in a list	My favorite punctuation marks include the colon, semicolon, and period.
Semicolon	joining together two independent clauses (never with a conjunction)	I love semicolons; they make sentences so concise!
Colon	introducing a list, explanation, or definition	When I see a colon I know what to expect: more information.
Apostrophe	form contractions	It's amazing how many people can't use apostrophes correctly.
Apostrophe	show possession	The students' grammar books are out of date, but the school's principal cannot order new ones yet.
Quotation marks	indicate a direct quote	I said to her, "Tell me more about parentheses."

Practice Questions

19. Which of the following sentences is correct?
    A) Her roommate asked her to pick up milk, and a watermelon from the grocery store.
    B) Her roommate asked her to pick up milk and a watermelon from the grocery store.

20. Which of the following sentences is correct?
    A) The softball coach—who had been in the job for only a year, quit unexpectedly on Friday.
    B) The softball coach—who had been in the job for only a year—quit unexpectedly on Friday.
    C) The softball coach, who had been in the job for only a year, quit unexpectedly on Friday.

21. Which of the following sentences is correct?
    A) I'd like to order a hamburger, with extra cheese, but my friend says I should get a fruit salad instead.
    B) I'd like to order a hamburger with extra cheese, but my friend says I should get a fruit salad instead.

Point of View

A sentence's **POINT OF VIEW** s the perspective from which it is written. Point of view is described as either first, second, or third person.

Person	Pronouns	Who's acting?	Example
first	I, we	the writer	I take my time when shopping for shoes.
second	you	the reader	You prefer to shop online.
third	he, she, it, they	the subject	She buys shoes from her cousin's store.

First-person perspective appears when the writer's personal experiences, feelings, and opinions are an important element of the text. Second-person perspective is used when the author directly addresses the reader. Third-person perspective is most common in formal and academic writing; it creates distance between the writer and the reader. A sentence's point of view must remain consistent.

Practice Question

22. Which of the following sentences is correct?
    A) If someone wants to be a professional athlete, you have to practice often.
    B) If you want to be a professional athlete, you have to practice often.
    C) If someone wants to be a professional athlete, he or she has to practice often.

Active and Passive Voice

Sentences can be written in active voice or passive voice. **ACTIVE VOICE** means that the subjects of the sentences are performing the action of the sentence. In a sentence written in **PASSIVE VOICE**, the subjects are being acted on. The sentence, "Justin wrecked my car" is in the active voice because the subject (*Justin*) is doing the action (*wrecked*). The sentence can be rewritten in passive voice by using a "to be" verb: "My car was wrecked by Justin." Now the subject of the sentence (*car*) is being acted on. It is also possible to write the sentence so that the person performing the action is not identified: "My car was wrecked."

Generally, good writing will avoid using passive voice; however, when it is unclear who or what performed the action of the sentence, passive voice may be the only option.

Practice Question

23. Rewrite the following sentence in active voice: *I was hit with a stick by my brother.*

24. Rewrite the following sentence in passive voice: *My roommate made coffee this morning.*

Transitions

TRANSITIONS connect two ideas and explain the logical relationship between them. For example, the transition *because* tells you that two things have a cause-and-effect relationship, while the transitional phrase *on the other hand* introduces a contradictory idea. On the Verbal Reasoning Test, you may need to identify the best transition for a particular sentence, and you will definitely need to make good use of transitions in the Analytical Writing component.

Transition Type	Examples
Cause and effect	as a result, because, consequently, due to, if/then, so, therefore, thus
Similarity	also, likewise, similar, between
Contrast	but, however, in contrast, on the other hand, nevertheless, on the contrary, yet
Concluding	briefly, finally, in conclusion, in summary, to conclude

Transition Type	Examples
Addition	additionally, also, as well, further, furthermore, in addition, moreover
Examples	in other words, for example, for instance, to illustrate
Time	after, before, currently, later, recently, since, subsequently, then, while

Practice Questions
Choose the transition word or words that would best fit in the blank.

25. Clara's car breaks down frequently, _____ she decided to buy a new one.
    A) however
    B) for example
    C) while
    D) therefore

26. Chad scored more points than any other player on his team. _____, he is often late to practice, so his coach won't let him play in the game Saturday.
    A) However
    B) For example
    C) While
    D) Therefore

27. Miguel will often eat his lunch outside. _____, on Wednesday he took his sandwich to the park across from his office.
    A) However
    B) For example
    C) While
    D) Therefore

28. Alex set the table _____ the lasagna finished baking in the oven.
    A) however
    B) for example
    C) while
    D) therefore

Wordiness and Redundancy

Sometimes sentences that are grammatically correct can still be confusing or poorly written. Often this problem arises when sentences are wordy or contain redundant phrasing (i.e., when several words with similar meanings are used). Such phrases are used to make the writing seem more serious or academic when actually they can confuse the reader. On the test, you might be asked to clarify—or even remove—such phrases. Some examples of excessive wordiness and redundancy include the following:

- I'll meet you in the *place where I parked my car.* →I'll meet you in the *parking lot.*
- *The point I am trying to make is that* the study was flawed. The study was flawed.
- A memo was sent out *concerning the matter of* dishes left in the sink. →A memo was sent out *about* dishes left in the sink.
- The email was *brief and to the point.* →The email was *terse.*
- I don't think I'll ever *understand or comprehend* Italian operas. →I don't think I'll ever *understand* Italian operas.

Practice Questions

Rewrite each of the following sentences to eliminate wordiness and redundancy.

29. The game was canceled due to the fact that a bad storm was predicted.

30. The possibility exists that we will have a party for my mother's birthday.

31. With the exception of our new puppy, all of our dogs have received their vaccinations.

32. We threw away the broken microwave that didn't work.

33. It was an unexpected surprise when we won the raffle.

Word Structure

Vocabulary is a big part of many exams, but you do not have to memorize long lists of words to do well. Instead, you can use word structure to figure out the definition of words. Many words can be broken down into three main parts to help determine their meaning:

- prefix
- root
- suffix

PREFIXES are elements added to the beginning of a word, and **SUFFIXES** are elements added to the end of the word; together they are known as **AFFIXES**. They carry assigned meanings and can be attached to a word to completely change the word's meaning or to enhance the word's original meaning.

Let us use the word *prefix* as an example: *Fix* means "to place something securely," and *pre–* means "before." Therefore, "*prefix*" means "to place something before or in front of."

Now let's look at a suffix: in the word *fearful, fear* is the root word. The suffix *–ful* means "full of." Thus, "*fearful*" means "being full of fear or being afraid."

The **ROOT** is what is left when you take away the prefixes and suffixes from a word. For example, in the word *unclear*, if you take away the prefix *un–*, you have the root *clear*.

Roots are not always recognizable words because they often come from Latin or Greek words, such as *nat*, a Latin root meaning "born." The word *native*, which means "a person born in a referenced place," comes from this root.

21

Table 2.6. shows some common affixes and root words. (A more thorough list with detailed examples is in the appendix.)

Table 2.6. Common Affixes and Root Words		
Prefixes	**Root Words**	**Suffixes**
a–, an–, im–, in–, un– (without, not)	ambi (both)	–able, –ible (capable)
ab– (away from)	aud (to hear)	–dom (quality)
ante– (before)	bell (combative)	–en (made of)
anti– (against)	bene (good)	–ful (full of)
bi–, di– (two)	contra (against)	–ian (related to)
dis– (not, apart)	dys (bad, impaired)	–ine (nature of)
ex– (out)	equ (equal)	–ment (act of)
micro– (small)	morph (shape)	
omni– (all)		
over– (excessively)		
pre– (before)		
re– (again)		
sym– (with)		
uni– (single)		

Practice Questions

Select the answer that most closely matches the definition of the given word.

34. BELLICOSE
    A) misbehaved
    B) friendly
    C) scared
    D) aggressive

35. REJUVENATED
    A) established
    B) invigorated
    C) improved
    D) motivated

36. CIRCUMSPECT
    A) round
    B) guarded
    C) dominant
    D) winding

37. CONCURRENT
    A) surging
    B) splashy
    C) sophisticated
    D) simultaneous

38. PATRIARCH
    A) patriotic person
    B) wise counselor
    C) male leader
    D) mother figure

Text Completion and Sentence Equivalence

Sentence completion questions will give you a sentence with one, two, or three words missing. You will need to choose the word(s) that best complete the sentence.

Sentence Completion Question Format

Once Jaelyn learned the code, she was able to _____ its meaning.
    A) endure
    B) modify
    C) misunderstand
    D) decipher

Option D is correct.

To answer the question, think about the context of the sentence. Once Jaelyn has learned the code, she will understand its meaning. So, we need a word that means "to understand."

Using your knowledge of roots and prefixes, you can figure out what "decipher" means: The prefix *de–* means "to undo." The root word *cipher* means "secret" or "code." Thus the word *decipher* means "to understand" or "to figure out."

CONTEXT CLUES can be used to solve sentence completion questions. To use context clues, look for words in the sentence that tell you what kind of word will go in the blank.

RESTATEMENT CLUES state the definition of a word in the sentence. The definition is often set apart from the rest of the sentence by a comma, parentheses, or a colon. This structure is common in sentence completion questions. Let's use the following sentence as an example: Teachers should understand the basics of cognition, how students apply new information to other settings.

The meaning of *cognition* is restated following the comma as the ability to "apply new information to other settings." In sentence completion questions, look for parts of the sentence that might restate the meaning of the missing word.

CONTRAST CLUES include the opposite meaning of a word. Words like *but*, *on the other hand*, and *however* are tip-offs that a sentence contains a contrast clue. For example, "The teacher offered remedial materials to the struggling student, but the student wanted to read more advanced books."

The word *remedial* is contrasted with "more advanced," so the definition of *remedial* is "basic" or "general."

POSITIVE/NEGATIVE CLUES tell you whether a word has a positive or negative meaning. For example, "The teaching assistant suggested offering enrichment to the student who had quickly mastered the required curriculum."

The positive descriptions *quickly* and *mastered* suggest that "enrichment" has a positive meaning.

Practice Questions

39. The dog was _____ in the face of danger, braving the fire to save the girl trapped inside the building.
    A) overwhelmed
    B) dauntless
    C) imaginative
    D) startled

40. Beth did not spend any time preparing for the test, but Tyrone kept a _____ study schedule.
    A) rigorous
    B) unprecedented
    C) analytical
    D) strange

41. Because she was an _____ runner, Georgette was a _____ opponent on the racetrack.
    A) avid...formidable
    B) exotic...challenging
    C) accomplished...weak
    D) ungainly...gullible

42. The editor preferred a _____ writing style, so he cut 500 words from the article.
    A) descriptive
    B) graceful
    C) friendly
    D) terse

43. Michael's upbeat personality _____ the tension in the room, and the party continued happily.
    A) created
    B) diminished
    C) elided
    D) exaggerated

Answer Key

1. B: *Student* is a singular noun, but *their* is a plural pronoun, making the first sentence grammatically incorrect. To correct it, replace *their* with the singular pronoun *his* or *her*.

2. B: *Everybody* is a singular noun, but *their* is a plural pronoun; the first sentence is grammatically incorrect. To correct it, replace *their* with the singular pronoun *his* or *her*.

3. B: This sentence begins in third-person perspective and finishes in second-person perspective. To correct it, ensure the sentence finishes with third-person perspective.

4. B, C: This sentence refers to a teacher and a student. But to whom does *she* refer, the teacher or the student? To improve clarity, use specific names or rewrite the sentence so that the pronoun antecedent is clear.

5. B: *Cat* is singular, so it takes a singular verb (which confusingly ends with an s); *dogs* is plural, so it needs a plural verb.

6. B: Sometimes the subject and verb are separated by clauses or phrases. Here, the subject *cars* is separated from the verb phrase *were returned*, making it more difficult to conjugate the verb correctly; this results in a number error.

7. A, B: The subject of these sentences is a collective noun, which describes a group of people or things. This noun can be singular if it is referring to the group as a whole or plural if it refers to each item in the group as a separate entity.

8. A, B: When the subject contains two or more nouns connected by *and*, that subject is plural and requires a plural verb. Singular subjects joined by *or, either/or, neither/nor*, or *not only/but also* remain singular; when these words join plural and singular subjects, the verb should match the closest subject.

9. B: All the verb tenses in a sentence need to agree both with each other and with the other information in the sentence. In the first sentence, the tense does not match the other information in the sentence: *last night* indicates the past (rained) not the future (will rain).

10. B: The phrase *running through the hall* should be placed next to *student*, the noun it modifies.

11. B: While the lion may indeed be terrifying, the word *terrifyingly* is an adverb and so can only modify a verb, an adjective or another adverb, not the noun *lion*. In the second sentence, *terrifyingly* is modifying the adjective *loud*, telling us more about the loudness of the lion's roar—so loud, it was terrifying.

12. Number 1 is an independent clause: it has a subject (*I*), a verb (*have wanted*), and no subordinating conjunction. Number 2 is a phrase made up of a preposition (*under*), its object (*sky*), and words that modify sky (*bright, filled with stars*), but it lacks a conjugated verb. Number 3 is a dependent clause: it has a subject (*sister*), a verb (*is running*), and a subordinating conjunction (*because*).

13. A: Although the sentence is lengthy, it is simple because it contains only one subject and verb (*San Francisco... is*) modified by additional phrases.

14. C: The sentence has one independent clause ("*I love... car*") and one dependent clause ("*because I... road*"), so it is complex.

15. D: This sentence has three clauses: two independent ("*I wanted... dog*" and "*I got a fish*") and one dependent ("*because my... dander*"), so it is a compound-complex sentence.

16. B: This sentence is made up of two independent clauses joined by a conjunction (*but*), so it is compound.

17. B: In this sentence the main independent clause—"*this...students*"—is held until the very end, so it is periodic. Furthermore, despite its length the sentence is simple because it has only one subject (*dizzying array*) and verb (*proved*).

18. A: Here, the main clause "*Jessica... test*" begins the sentence; the other clauses modify the main clause, providing more information about the main idea and resulting in a cumulative sentence. In addition, the sentence is compound as it links two independent clauses together with a comma and the coordinating conjunction *for*.

19. B: Commas are only needed when joining three items in a series; this sentence only has two (milk and watermelon).

20. B, C: When setting apart nonessential words and phrases, you can use either dashes or commas, but not both.

21. B: Prepositional phrases are usually essential to the meaning of the sentence, so they do not need to be set apart with commas. Here, the prepositional phrase *with extra cheese* helps the reader understand that the speaker wants a particularly unhealthy meal; however, the friend is encouraging a healthier option. Removing the prepositional phrase would limit the contrast between the burger and the salad. Note that the second comma remains because it is separating two independent clauses.

22. B, C: In the first sentence, the person shifts from third (*someone*) to second (*you*). It needs to be rewritten to be consistent.

23. First, identify the person or object performing the action (usually given in a prepositional phrase—here, *by my brother*) and make it the subject; the subject of the original sentence (*I*) becomes the object. Remove the *to be* verb: *My brother hit me with a stick.*

24. Here, the object (*coffee*) becomes the subject; move the original subject (*my roommate*) to a prepositional phrase at the end of the sentence. Add the *to be* verb: *The coffee was made this morning by my roommate.*

25. D: The sentence is describing a cause (*her car breaks down*) and an effect (*she'll buy a new one*), so the correct transition is *therefore*.

26. A: The sentence includes a contrast: it would make sense for Chad to play in the game, but he isn't, so the best transition is *however*.

27. B: In the sentence, the clause after the transition is an example, so the best transition is *for example*.

28. C: In the sentence, two things are occurring at the same time, so the best transition is *while*.

29. The game was canceled because a bad storm was predicted.

Replace the long phrase *due to the fact that* with the much shorter *because*.

30. We might have a party for my mother's birthday.

By rearranging the sentence, we can replace the phrase *the possibility exists that* with the word *might*.

31. All of our dogs have been vaccinated except our new puppy.

The sentence can be rearranged to replace *with the exception of* with *except*. The phrase *receive their vaccinations* has also been shortened to *been vaccinated*.

32. We threw away the broken microwave.

If something is broken that means it does not work, so the phrase *that didn't work* can be removed.

33. It was a surprise when we won the raffle.

By definition, a surprise is always unexpected, so the word *unexpected* can be removed.

34. D: The prefix *belli–* means "combative" or "warlike." The word choice closest in meaning is *aggressive*.

35. B: The root word *juven* means "young" and the prefix *re–* means "again," so *rejuvenate* means "to be made young again."

36. B: The root word *circum* means "around," and the root word *specere* means "to look," so a *circumspect* person looks cautiously around herself and is guarded.

37. D: The prefix *con–* means "with or together," and the root word *concurrere* means "to run together." Two or more *concurrent* events happen at the same time, or simultaneously.

38. C: The root word *pater* means "father," and the root word *arkhein* means "to rule," so a patriarch is a man who leads his family.

39. B: Demonstrating bravery in the face of danger would be *fearless*. The restatement clue (*braving*) tells you exactly what the word means.

40. A: The word *but* functions here as a contrast clue that tells us that Tyrone studied in a different way from Beth. If Beth did not study hard, then Tyrone did. The best answer, therefore, is *rigorous*.

41. A: The word *because* suggests the two words in the blanks have a cause-and-effect relationship. Only option A fits. *Avid* means "enthusiastic," and *formidable* means "impressive." An avid runner is likely to be a formidable opponent in a race—an impressive runner, difficult to beat.

42. D: The clue here is "cut 500 words." *Terse* means "few words," so if the editor preferred a terse writing style, he would cut words from the article.

43. B: The sentence contains several positive clues ("upbeat," "happily"). The only answer option that creates a positive sentence is *diminished*, which means to "to make less."

Reading Comprehension

In **READING COMPREHENSION QUESTIONS**, you will be asked to read passages that cover a range of topics. Excerpts from works on science, history, social studies, and humanities are common. Each passage or set of passages will be followed by one to six questions that cover the following topics:

- ▶ the main idea of a passage
- ▶ the role of supporting details in a passage
- ▶ adding supporting details to a passage
- ▶ the structure of a passage
- ▶ the author's purpose
- ▶ logical inferences that can be drawn from a passage
- ▶ comparing passages
- ▶ vocabulary and figurative language

There are five Reading Comprehension passages and ten questions on each Verbal Reasoning section. Each passage is followed by one to six questions.

Reading Comprehension Question Format

Between November 15 and December 21, 1864, Major General William Tecumseh Sherman marched Union troops from the recently captured city of Atlanta to the port of Savannah. The goal was not only to capture the port city and secure Georgia for the Union, but also to destroy the Confederacy's infrastructure and demoralize its people. Sherman and his troops destroyed rail lines and burned buildings and fields. They packed only twenty days' worth of rations, foraging for the rest of their supplies from farms along the way. By the time they reached Savannah, they had destroyed 300 miles of railroad; countless cotton gins and mills; seized 4,000 mules; 13,000 head of cattle; 9.5 million pounds of corn; and 10.5 million pounds of fodder. Sherman estimated his troops inflicted $100 million in damages.

It can be inferred from the passage that the Confederacy
- A) strongly resisted the actions of Sherman's troops.
- B) was greatly weakened by the destruction.
- C) used Sherman's March as a rallying point.
- D) was relatively unaffected by the march.
- E) relied heavily on the port of Savannah.

Option B is correct.

The author describes the level of destruction in detail, suggesting it had a significant negative impact on the Confederacy.

The Main Idea

The main idea of a text is the author's purpose in writing a book, article, story, etc. Being able to identify and understand the main idea is a critical skill necessary to comprehend and appreciate what you are reading.

Consider a political election. A candidate is running for office and plans to deliver a speech asserting her position on tax reform. The topic of the speech—tax reform—is clear to voters, and probably of interest to many. However, imagine that the candidate believes that taxes should be lowered. She is likely to assert this argument in her speech, supporting it with examples proving why lowering taxes would benefit the public and how it could be accomplished. While the topic of the speech would be tax reform, the benefit of lowering taxes would be the main idea. Other candidates may have different perspectives on the topic; they may believe that higher taxes are necessary, or that current taxes are adequate. It is likely that their speeches, while on the same topic of tax reform, would have different main ideas—different arguments likewise supported by different examples. Determining what a speaker, writer, or text is asserting about a specific issue will reveal the **MAIN IDEA**.

Quick Review

Topic: The subject of the passage.

Theme: An idea or concept the author refers to repeatedly.

Main idea: The argument the writer is making about the topic.

The exam may also ask about a passage's **THEME**, which is similar to—but distinct from—its topic. While a **TOPIC** is usually a specific *person*, *place*, *thing*, or *issue*, the theme is an *idea* or *concept* that the author refers back to frequently. Examples of common themes include ideas like the importance of family, the dangers of technology, and the beauty of nature.

There will be many questions on the exam that require you to differentiate between the topic, theme, and main idea of a passage. Let's look at an example:

Babe Didrikson Zaharias, one of the most decorated female athletes of the twentieth century, is an inspiration for everyone. Born in 1911 in Beaumont, Texas, Zaharias lived in a time when women were considered second class to men, but she never let that stop her from becoming a champion. Babe was one of seven children in a poor immigrant family, and was competitive from an early age. As a child she excelled at most things she tried, especially sports, which continued into high school and beyond. After high school, Babe played amateur basketball for two years, and soon after began training in track and field. Despite the fact that women were only allowed to enter in three events, Babe represented the United States in the 1932 Los Angeles Olympics, and won two gold medals and one silver for track and field events.

In the early 1930s, Babe began playing golf which earned her a legacy. The first tournament she entered was a men's only tournament; however, she did not make the cut to play. Playing golf as an amateur was the only option for a woman at this time, since there was no professional women's league. Babe played as an amateur for a little over a decade, until she turned pro in 1947 for the Ladies Professional Golf Association (LPGA) of which she was a founding member. During her career as a golfer, Babe won eighty-two tournaments, amateur and professional, including the US Women's Open, All-American Open, and British Women's Open. In 1953, Babe was diagnosed with cancer, but fourteen weeks later, she played in a tournament. That year she won her third US Women's Open. However, by 1955, she didn't have the physicality to compete anymore, and she died of the disease in 1956.

The topic of this passage is obviously Babe Zaharias—the whole passage describes events from her life. Determining the main idea, however, requires a little more analysis. The passage describes Babe

Zaharias' life, but the main idea of the paragraph is what it says about her life. To figure out the main idea, consider what the writer is saying about Babe Zaharias. The writer is saying that she's someone to admire—that's the main idea and what unites all the information in the paragraph. Lastly, what might the theme of the passage be? The writer refers to several broad concepts, including never giving up and overcoming the odds, both of which could be themes of the passage.

There are two major indicators of the main idea of a paragraph or passage:

▶ It is a general idea and applies to all the more specific ideas in the passage. Every other sentence in a paragraph should be able to relate in some way to the main idea.

▶ It asserts a specific viewpoint that the author supports with facts, opinions, or other details. In other words, the main idea takes a stand.

Practice Question

It's easy to puzzle over the landscapes of our solar system's distant planets—how could we ever know what those far-flung places really look like? However, scientists utilize a number of tools to visualize the surfaces of many planets. The topography of Venus, for example, has been explored by several space probes, including the Russian Venera landers and NASA's Magellan orbiter. These craft used imaging and radar to map the surface of the planet, identifying a whole host of features including volcanoes, craters, and a complex system of channels. Mars has likewise been mapped by space probes, including the famous Mars Rovers, which are automated vehicles that actually landed on the planet's surface. These rovers have been used by NASA and other space agencies to study the geology, climate, and possible biology of the planet.

In addition to these long-range probes, NASA has also used its series of orbiting telescopes to study distant planets. These four massively powerful telescopes include the famous Hubble Space Telescope as well as the Compton Gamma Ray Observatory, Chandra X-Ray Observatory, and the Spitzer Space Telescope. These allow scientists to examine planets using not only visible light but also infrared and near-infrared light, ultraviolet light, x-rays and gamma rays.

Powerful telescopes aren't just found in space: NASA makes use of Earth-bound telescopes as well. Scientists at the National Radio Astronomy Observatory in Charlottesville, VA, have spent decades using radio imaging to build an incredibly detailed portrait of Venus' surface. In fact, Earth-bound telescopes offer a distinct advantage over orbiting telescopes because they allow scientists to capture data from a fixed point, which in turn allows them to effectively compare data collected over a long period of time.

1. Which of the following sentences best describes the main idea of the passage?
    A) It's impossible to know what the surfaces of other planets are really like.
    B) Telescopes are an important tool for scientists studying planets in our solar system.
    C) Venus' surface has many of the same features as Earth's surface, including volcanoes, craters, and channels.
    D) Scientists use a variety of advanced technologies to study the surface of the planets in our solar system.

Topic and Summary Sentences

The main idea of a paragraph usually appears within the topic sentence. The **TOPIC SENTENCE** introduces the main idea to readers; it indicates not only the topic of a passage, but also the writer's perspective on the topic.

Notice, for example, how the first sentence in the text about Babe Zaharias states the main idea: "*Babe Didrikson Zaharias, one of the most decorated female athletes of the twentieth century, is an inspiration for everyone.*"

Even though paragraphs generally begin with topic sentences due to their introductory nature, on occasion writers build up to the topic sentence by using supporting details in order to generate interest or build an argument. Be alert for paragraphs when writers do not include a clear topic sentence at all; even without a clear topic sentence, a paragraph will still have a main idea. You may also see a **SUMMARY SENTENCE** at the end of a passage. As its name suggests, this sentence sums up the passage, often by restating the main idea and the author's key evidence that supports it.

Practice Question

The Constitution of the United States establishes a series of limits to rein in centralized power. Separation of powers distributes federal authority among three competing branches: the executive, the legislative, and the judicial. Checks and balances allow the branches to check the usurpation of power by any one branch. States' rights are protected under the Constitution from too much encroachment by the federal government. Enumeration of powers names the specific and few powers the federal government has. These four restrictions have helped sustain the American republic for over two centuries.

2. In the above paragraph, what are the topic and summary sentences?

Implied Main Idea

A paragraph without a clear topic sentence still has a main idea; however, it is implied rather than clearly stated. Determining the implied main idea requires some detective work: you will need to look at the author's word choice and tone in addition to the content of the passage.

Practice Questions

One of my summer reading books was *Mockingjay*. Though it's several hundred pages long, I read it in just a few days. I was captivated by the adventures of the main character and the complicated plot of the book. However, I felt like the ending didn't reflect the excitement of the story. Given what a powerful personality the main character has, I felt like the ending didn't do her justice.

3. Even without a clear topic sentence, this paragraph has a main idea. What is the writer's perspective on the book—what is the writer saying about it?
   A) *Mockingjay* is a terrific novel.
   B) *Mockingjay* is disappointing.
   C) *Mockingjay* is full of suspense.
   D) *Mockingjay* is a lousy novel.

Read the following paragraph:

Fortunately, none of Alyssa's coworkers have ever seen inside the large filing drawer in her desk. Disguised by the meticulous neatness of the rest of her workspace, the drawer betrayed no sign of the chaos within. To even open it, she had to struggle for several minutes with the enormous pile of junk jamming the drawer, until it would suddenly give way, and papers, folders, and candy wrappers spilled out onto the floor. It was an organizational nightmare, with torn notes and spreadsheets haphazardly thrown on top of each other and melted candy smeared across pages. She was worried the odor would soon waft to her coworkers' desks, revealing her secret.

4. Which sentence best describes the main idea of the paragraph above?
    A) Alyssa wishes she could move to a new desk.
    B) Alyssa wishes she had her own office.
    C) Alyssa is glad none of her coworkers know about her messy drawer.
    D) Alyssa is sad because she doesn't have any coworkers.

Supporting Details

SUPPORTING DETAILS provide more support for the author's main idea. For instance, in the Babe Zaharias example, the writer makes the general assertion that "*Babe Didrikson Zaharias, one of the most decorated female athletes of the twentieth century, is an inspiration for everyone.*" The rest of the paragraph provides supporting details with facts showing why she is an inspiration: the names of the challenges she overcame, and the specific years she competed in the Olympics.

Be alert for **SIGNAL WORDS**, which indicate supporting details and can therefore be helpful in identifying supporting details. Signal words can also help you rule out sentences that are not the main idea or topic sentence—if a sentence begins with one of these phrases, it will likely be too specific to be a main idea.

Questions on the exam will ask you to find details that support a particular idea and explain why a particular detail was included in the passage. In order to answer these questions, you must have a solid understanding of the passage's main idea. With this knowledge, you can determine how a supporting detail fits in with the larger structure of the passage.

Practice Questions

It's easy to puzzle over the landscapes of our solar system's distant planets—how could we ever know what those far-flung places really look like? However, scientists utilize a number of tools to visualize the surfaces of many planets. The topography of Venus, for example, has been explored by several space probes, including the Russian Venera landers and NASA's Magellan orbiter. These craft used imaging and radar to map the surface of the planet, identifying a whole host of features including volcanoes, craters, and a complex system of channels. Mars has likewise been mapped by space probes, including the famous Mars Rovers, which are automated vehicles that actually landed on the planet's surface. These rovers have been used by NASA and other space agencies to study the geology, climate, and possible biology of the planet.

In addition to these long-range probes, NASA has also used its series of orbiting telescopes to study distant planets. These four massively powerful telescopes include the famous Hubble Space Telescope as well as the Compton Gamma Ray Observatory, Chandra X-Ray Observatory, and the Spitzer Space Telescope. These allow scientists to examine planets using not only visible light but also infrared and near-infrared light, ultraviolet light, x-rays and gamma rays.

Powerful telescopes aren't just found in space: NASA makes use of Earth-bound telescopes as well. Scientists at the National Radio Astronomy Observatory in Charlottesville, VA, have spent decades using radio imaging to build an incredibly detailed portrait of Venus' surface. In fact, Earth-bound telescopes offer a distinct advantage over orbiting telescopes because they allow scientists to capture data from a fixed point, which in turn allows them to effectively compare data collected over a long period of time.

5. Which sentence from the text best develops the idea that scientists make use of many different technologies to study the surfaces of other planets?
   A) These rovers have been used by NASA and other space agencies to study the geology, climate, and possible biology of the planet.
   B) It's easy to puzzle over the landscapes of our solar system's distant planets—how could we ever know what those far-flung places really look like?
   C) In addition to these long-range probes, NASA has also used its series of orbiting telescopes to study distant planets.
   D) These craft used imaging and radar to map the surface of the planet, identifying a whole host of features including volcanoes, craters, and a complex system of channels.

6. If true, which sentence could be added to the passage above to support the author's argument that scientists use many different technologies to study the surface of planets?
   A) Because the Earth's atmosphere blocks X-rays, gamma rays, and infrared radiation, NASA needed to put telescopes in orbit above the atmosphere.
   B) In 2015, NASA released a map of Venus which was created by compiling images from orbiting telescopes and long-range space probes.
   C) NASA is currently using the Curiosity and Opportunity rovers to look for signs of ancient life on Mars.
   D) NASA has spent over $2.5 billion to build, launch, and repair the Hubble Space Telescope.

7. Which of the following is the most likely reason for which the author includes the detail that Earth-bound telescopes offer a distinct advantage over orbiting telescopes because they allow scientists to capture data from a fixed point?
   A) to explain why it has taken scientists so long to map the surface of Venus
   B) to suggest that Earth-bound telescopes are the most important equipment used by NASA scientists
   C) to prove that orbiting telescopes will soon be replaced by Earth-bound telescopes
   D) to demonstrate why NASA scientists rely on many different types of scientific equipment

Text Structure

Authors can structure passages in a number of different ways. These distinct organizational patterns, referred to as **TEXT STRUCTURE**, use the logical relationships between ideas to improve the readability and coherence of a text. The following are the most common ways in which passages are organized:

- ▶ **PROBLEM-SOLUTION**: The author presents a problem and then discusses a solution.

- ▶ **COMPARE-CONTRAST**: The author presents two situations and then discusses their similarities and differences.

- ▶ **CAUSE-EFFECT**: The author presents an action and then discusses the resulting effects.

- ▶ **DESCRIPTIVE**: The author describes an idea, object, person, or other item in detail.

Practice Question

The issue of public transportation has begun to haunt the fast-growing cities of the southern United States. Unlike their northern counterparts, cities like Atlanta, Dallas, and Houston have long promoted growth out and not up—these are cities full of sprawling suburbs and single-family homes, not densely concentrated skyscrapers and apartments. What to do then, when all those suburbanites need to get into the central business districts for work? For a long time it seemed highways were the twenty-lane wide expanses of concrete that would allow commuters to move from home to work and back again. But these modern miracles have become time-sucking, pollution-spewing nightmares. They may not like it, but it's time for these cities to turn toward public transport like trains and buses if they are to remain livable.

8. The organization of this passage can best be described as
   A) a comparison of two similar ideas.
   B) a description of a place.
   C) a discussion of several effects all related to the same cause.
   D) a discussion of a problem followed by the suggestion of a solution.

The Author's Purpose

Authors always have a purpose when they write a text. The purpose could be to entertain, inform, explain, or persuade. A short story, for example, is meant to entertain, while an online news article would be designed to inform the public about a current event. Each of these different types of writing has a specific name:

- ▶ **NARRATIVE WRITING** tells a story (e.g., novel, short story, play).

- ▶ **EXPOSITORY WRITING** informs people (e.g., newspaper and magazine articles).

▶ **TECHNICAL WRITING** explains something (e.g., product manual, directions).

▶ **PERSUASIVE WRITING** tries to convince the reader of something (e.g., opinion column on a blog).

Did You Know?

When reading, pay attention to the following: characters, people, and their titles; dates; places; main ideas; quotations; and italics.

On the exam, you may be asked to categorize a passage as one of these types, either by specifically naming it as such or by identifying its general purpose.

You may also be asked about primary and secondary sources. These terms describe not the writing itself but the author's relationship to what is being written. A **PRIMARY SOURCE** is an unaltered piece of writing that was composed during the time when the events being described took place; these texts are often written by the people directly involved. A **SECONDARY SOURCE** might address the same topic but provide extra commentary or analysis. These texts are written by outside observers and may even be composed after the event. For example, a book written by a political candidate to inform people about his or her stand on an issue is a primary source. An online article written by a journalist analyzing how that candidate's position will affect the election is a secondary source; a book by a historian about that election would also be a secondary source.

Practice Question

Elizabeth closed her eyes and braced herself on the armrests that divided her from her fellow passengers. Take-off was always the worst part for her. The revving of the engines, the way her stomach dropped as the plane lurched upward; it made her feel sick. Then, she had to watch the world fade away beneath her, getting smaller and smaller until it was just her and the clouds hurtling through the sky. Sometimes (but only sometimes) it just had to be endured, though. She focused on the thought of her sister's smiling face and her new baby nephew as the plane slowly pulled onto the runway.

9. This passage is reflective of which type of writing?
    A) narrative
    B) expository
    C) technical
    D) persuasive

Facts vs. Opinions

On the exam, you might be asked to identify a statement in a passage as either a fact or an opinion, so you will need to know the difference between the two. A **FACT** is a statement or thought that can be proven to be true. The statement, "*Wednesday comes after Tuesday*" is a fact—you can point to a calendar to prove it.

Helpful Hint:

Keep an eye out for answer options that may be facts but which are not stated or discussed in the passage.

In contrast, an **OPINION** is an assumption that is not based in fact and cannot be proven to be true. The assertion that television is more entertaining than feature films is an opinion—people will disagree on this, and there's no reference you can use to prove or disprove it.

Practice Question

Exercise is critical for healthy development in children. Today, there is an epidemic of unhealthy children in the United States who will face health problems in adulthood due to poor diet and lack of exercise during their childhoods. This is a problem for all Americans, especially with the rising cost of health care.

It is vital that school systems and parents encourage their children to engage in a minimum of thirty minutes of cardiovascular exercise each day, mildly increasing their heart rate for a sustained period. This is proven to decrease the likelihood of developmental diabetes, obesity, and a multitude of other health problems. Children also need a proper diet rich in fruits and vegetables so that they can grow and develop physically, as well as learn healthy eating habits early on.

10. Which of the following is a fact in the passage, not an opinion?
    A) Fruits and vegetables are the best way to help children be healthy.
    B) Children today are lazier than they were in previous generations.
    C) The risk of diabetes in children is reduced by physical activity.
    D) Children should engage in thirty minutes of exercise a day.

Drawing Conclusions

In addition to understanding the main idea and factual content of a passage, you'll also be asked to take your analysis one step further and anticipate what other information could logically be added to the passage. In a nonfiction passage, for example, you might be asked which statement the author of the passage would agree with. In an excerpt from a fictional work, you might be asked to anticipate what a character would do next.

To answer these questions, you must have a solid understanding of the topic, theme, and main idea of the passage; armed with this information, you can figure out which of the answer options best fits within those criteria (or alternatively, which ones do not). For example, if the author of the passage is advocating for safer working conditions in textile factories, any supporting details that would be added to the passage should support that idea. You might add sentences that contain information about the number of accidents that occur in textile factories or that outline a new plan for fire safety.

Practice Questions

Today, there is an epidemic of unhealthy children in the United States who will face health problems in adulthood due to poor diet and lack of exercise during their childhoods. This is a problem for all Americans, as adults with chronic health issues are adding to the rising cost of health care. A child who grows up living an unhealthy lifestyle is likely to become an adult who does the same.

Because exercise is critical for healthy development in children, it is vital that school systems and parents encourage their children to engage in a minimum of thirty minutes of cardiovascular exercise each day. Even this small amount of exercise has been proven to decrease the likelihood that young people will develop diabetes, obesity, and other health issues as adults. In addition to exercise, children need a proper diet rich in fruits and vegetables so that they can grow and develop physically. Starting a good diet early also teaches children healthy eating habits they will carry into adulthood.

11. The author of this passage would most likely agree with which statement?
    A) Parents are solely responsible for the health of their children.
    B) Children who do not want to exercise should not be made to.
    C) Improved childhood nutrition will help lower the amount Americans spend on health care.
    D) It's not important to teach children healthy eating habits because they will learn them as adults.

Elizabeth closed her eyes and braced herself on the armrests that divided her from her fellow passengers. Take-off was always the worst part for her. The revving of the engines, the way her stomach dropped as the plane lurched upward; it made her feel sick. Then, she had to watch the world fade away beneath her, getting smaller and smaller until it was just her and the clouds hurtling through the sky. Sometimes (but only sometimes) it just had to be endured, though. She focused on the thought of her sister's smiling face and her new baby nephew as the plane slowly pulled onto the runway.

12. Which of the following is Elizabeth least likely to do in the future?
    A) Take a flight to her brother's wedding.
    B) Apply for a job as a flight attendant.
    C) Never board an airplane again.
    D) Get sick on an airplane.

Analyzing Words

As you no doubt know, determining the meaning of a word can be more complicated than just looking in a dictionary. A word might have more than one **DENOTATION**, or definition; which one the author intends can only be judged by examining the surrounding text. For example, the word *quack* can refer to the sound a duck makes, or to a person who publicly pretends to have a qualification which he or she does not actually possess.

A word may also have different **CONNOTATIONS**, which are the implied meanings and emotions a word evokes in the reader. For example, a cubicle is simply a walled desk in an office, but for many the word implies a constrictive, uninspiring workplace. Connotations can vary greatly between cultures and even between individuals.

Lastly, authors might employ **FIGURATIVE LANGUAGE**, which is the use of a word to imply something other than the word's literal definition. This is often done by comparing two things. If you say, "*I felt like a butterfly when I got a new haircut*," the listener knows you did not resemble an insect but instead felt beautiful and transformed.

Comparing Passages

In addition to analyzing single passages, the exam may require you to compare two passages. Usually, these passages will discuss the same topic, and it will be your task to identify the similarities and differences between the authors' main ideas, supporting details, and tones.

Practice Questions

Read Passages One and Two, and then answer the questions which follow.

Passage One

Today, there is an epidemic of unhealthy children in the United States who will face health problems in adulthood due to poor diet and lack of exercise during their childhoods: in 2012, the Centers for Disease Control found that 18 percent of students aged 6 – 11 are obese. This is a problem for all Americans, as adults with chronic health issues are adding to the rising cost of health care. A child who grows up living an unhealthy lifestyle is likely to become an adult who does the same.

Because exercise is critical for healthy development in children, it is vital that school systems and parents encourage their children to engage in a minimum of thirty minutes of cardiovascular exercise each day. Even this small amount of exercise has been proven to decrease the likelihood that young people will develop diabetes, obesity, and other health issues as adults. In addition to exercise, children need a proper diet rich in fruits and vegetables so that they can grow and develop physically. Starting a good diet early also teaches children healthy eating habits they will carry into adulthood.

Passage Two

When was the last time you took a good, hard look at a school lunch? For many adults, it's probably been years—decades even—since they last thought about students' midday meals. If they did stop to ponder, they might picture something reasonably wholesome if not very exciting: a peanut butter and jelly sandwich paired with an apple, or a traditional plate of meat, potatoes, and veggies. At worst, they may think kids are making do with some pizza and a carton of milk.

The truth, though, is that many students aren't even getting the meager nutrients offered up by a simple slice of pizza. Instead, schools are serving up heaping helpings of previously frozen, recently fried delicacies like French fries and chicken nuggets. These high-carb, low-protein options are usually paired with a limp, flavorless, straight-from-the-freezer vegetable that quickly gets tossed in the trash. And that carton of milk? It's probably a sugar-filled chocolate sludge, or it's been replaced with a student's favorite high-calorie soda.

"So what," you might ask. "Kids like to eat junk food—it's a habit they'll grow out of soon enough. Besides, parents can always pack lunches for students looking for something better." But is that really the lesson we want to be teaching our kids? Many of those children aren't going to grow out of bad habits; they're going to reach adulthood thinking that ketchup is a vegetable. And students in low-income families are particularly impacted by the sad state of school food. These parents rely on schools to provide a warm, nutritious meal because they don't have the time or money to prepare food at home. Do we really want to be punishing these children with soggy meat patties and salt-soaked potato chips?

13. Both authors are arguing for the importance of improving childhood nutrition. How do the authors' strategies differ?
    A) Passage 1 presents several competing viewpoints while Passage 2 offers a single argument.
    B) Passage 1 uses scientific data while Passage 2 uses figurative language.
    C) Passage 1 is descriptive while Passage 2 uses a cause-effect structure.
    D) Passage 1 has a friendly tone while the tone of Passage 2 is angry.

14. Both authors argue that
    A) children should learn healthy eating habits at a young age.
    B) low-income students are disproportionately affected by the low-quality food offered in schools.
    C) teaching children about good nutrition will lower their chances of developing diabetes as adults.
    D) schools should provide children an opportunity to exercise every day.

Answer Key

1. D: Option A can be eliminated because it directly contradicts the rest of the passage, which goes into detail about how scientists have learned about the surfaces of other planets. Options B and C can also be eliminated because they offer only specific details from the passage; while both choices contain details from the passage, neither is general enough to encompass the passage as a whole. Only option D provides an assertion that is both supported by the passage's content and general enough to cover the entire passage.

2. The topic sentence is the first sentence in the paragraph. It introduces the topic of discussion, in this case the constitutional limits on centralized power. The summary sentence is the last sentence in the paragraph. It sums up the information that was just presented: here, that constitutional limits have helped sustain the United States of America for over two hundred years.

3. B: The process of elimination will reveal the correct answer if it is not immediately clear. While the paragraph begins with positive commentary on the book—"I was captivated by the adventures of the main character and the complicated plot of the book"—this positive idea is followed by the contradictory transition word *however*. Option A cannot be the correct answer because the author concludes that the novel was poor. Likewise, option D cannot be correct because it does not encompass all the ideas in the paragraph; despite the negative conclusion, the author enjoyed most of the book. The main idea should be able to encompass all of the thoughts in a paragraph; option D does not apply to the beginning of this paragraph. Finally, option C is too specific; it could only apply to the brief description of the plot and adventures of the main character. That leaves option B as the best answer choice. The author initially enjoyed the book but was disappointed by the ending, which seemed unworthy of the exciting plot and character.

4. C: The paragraph begins by indicating her gratitude that her coworkers do not know about her drawer ("Fortunately, none of Alyssa's coworkers have ever seen inside the large filing drawer in her desk."). Notice also how the drawer is described: "it was an organizational nightmare," and it apparently doesn't even function properly: "to even open the drawer, she had to struggle for several minutes... ." The writer reveals that it even has an odor, with old candy inside. Alyssa is clearly ashamed of her drawer and fearful of being judged by her coworkers about it.

5. C: You're looking for details from the passage that support the main idea—scientists make use of many different technologies to study the surfaces of other planets. Option A includes a specific detail about rovers but does not offer any details that support the idea of multiple technologies being used. Similarly, option D provides another specific detail about space probes. Option B does not provide any supporting details; it simply introduces the topic of the passage. Only option C provides a detail that directly supports the author's assertion that scientists use multiple technologies to study the planets.

6. B: Options C and D can be eliminated because they do not address the topic of studying the surface of planets. Option A can also be eliminated because it only addresses a single technology. Only option B would add support to the author's claim about the importance of using multiple technologies.

7. D: Only option D relates directly to the author's main argument. The author does not mention how long it has taken to map the surface of Venus (option A), nor does he say that one technology is more important than the others (option B). Although the advantages of using Earth-bound telescopes are provided in detail, the author's argument is that many technologies are being used at the same time, so there's no reason to think that orbiting telescopes will be replaced (option C).

8. D: Answer option C can be excluded because the author provides no root cause or a list of effects. From there this question gets tricky because the passage contains structures similar to those described above. For example, it compares two things (cities in the North and South) and describes a place (a sprawling city); however, if you look at the overall organization of the passage, you can see that it starts by presenting a problem (transportation) and then presents a solution (trains and buses), making option D the only choice that encompasses the entire passage.

9. A: The passage is telling a story—we meet Elizabeth and learn about her fear of flying—so it is a narrative text (option A). There is no factual information presented or explained, nor is the author trying to persuade the reader of anything.

10. C: Option B can be discarded immediately because it is negative (recall that particularly negative answer statements are generally wrong) and is not discussed anywhere in the passage. Answer options A and D are both opinions—the author is promoting exercise, fruits, and vegetables as a way to make children healthy. (Notice that these incorrect answer options contain words that hint at being an opinion, such as *best*, *should*, or other comparisons.) Option C, on the other hand, is a simple fact stated by the author; it appears in the passage with the word *proven*, indicating that you do not just need to take the author's word for it.

11. C: The author would most likely support option C—he mentions in the first paragraph that poor diets are adding to the rising cost of health care. The main idea of the passage is that nutrition and exercise are important for children, so option B does not make sense—the author would likely support measures to encourage children to exercise. Answer options A and D can also be eliminated because they are directly contradicted in the text. The author specifically mentions the role of school systems, so he does not believe parents are solely responsible for their children's health. He also specifically states that children who grow up with unhealthy eating habits will become adults with unhealthy eating habits, which contradicts answer option D.

12. B: It is clear from the passage that Elizabeth hates flying but is willing to endure it for the sake of visiting her family. Thus, it seems likely that she would be willing to get on a plane for her brother's wedding, making answer options A and C incorrect. The passage also explicitly tells us that she feels sick on planes, so option D is likely to happen. We can however infer that she would not enjoy being on an airplane for work, so she is very unlikely to apply for a job as a flight attendant (option B).

13. B: The first author uses scientific facts ("the Centers for Disease Control found…" and "Even this small amount of exercise has been proven…") to back up his argument, while the second author uses figurative language ("fried delicacies" and the metaphor "sugar-filled chocolate sludge"), so the correct answer option is B. Option A is incorrect because the first author does not present any opposing viewpoints. Option C is incorrect because Passage 2 does not have a cause-effect structure. And while the author of the second passage could be described as angry, the first author is not particularly friendly, so answer option D can be eliminated as well.

14. A: Both authors argue that children should learn healthy eating habits at a young age (option A). The author of Passage 1 states that a child who grows up living an unhealthy lifestyle is likely to become an adult who does the same, and the author of Passage 2 states that many of those children are not going to grow out of bad habits—both of these sentences argue that it is necessary to teach children about nutrition early in life. Answer options C and D are mentioned only by the author of Passage 1, and answer option B is only discussed in Passage 2.

Numbers and Operations

Introduction to Quantitative Reasoning

QUANTITATIVE REASONING questions focus on mathematical reasoning and quantitative thinking. You will need to perform calculations and think about the relationships between mathematical concepts. There are three types of Quantitative Reasoning questions:

- ▶ Quantitative Comparisons
- ▶ Problem-solving
- ▶ Data Interpretation

For **QUANTITATIVE COMPARISON** questions, you will be asked to compare two quantities and choose which one is greater. The answer options for these questions are always the same. There are about seven Quantitative Comparison questions on each Quantitative Reasoning section.

Example

Column A   Column B

x^3 x^{-3}

A) The quantity in Column A is greater.
B) The quantity in Column B is greater.
C) The two quantities are equal.
D) The relationship cannot be determined from the information given.

Option D is correct.

The greater value cannot be determined without knowing the sign and value of x. For example, if $x = 4$, then Column A is the greater value. If $x = \frac{1}{4}$ then Column B is the greater value.

PROBLEM-SOLVING QUESTIONS ask you to solve a word problem. There are about ten Problem-solving questions in each Quantitative Reasoning section.

Example

The dosage for a particular medication is proportional to the weight of the patient. If the dosage for a patient weighing 60 kg is 90 mg, what is the dosage for a patient weighing 80 kg?

A) 60 mg
B) 90 mg
C) 1200 mg
D) 7200 mg

Option C is correct.

Write a proportion using x for the missing value.

$$\frac{60 \text{ kg}}{90 \text{ mg}} = \frac{80 \text{ kg}}{x \text{ mg}}$$

Cross multiply.

$$60(x) = 80(90)$$

Divide by 60.

$$60x = 7200$$

$$x = 1200$$

The proper dosage is **1200 mg**.

DATA INTERPRETATION questions ask you to interpret visual data. Expect to see charts, graphs, or other visual media. There are about three Data Interpretation questions on each Quantitative Reasoning section.

Example

The graph below shows Company X's profits for the years 2010 to 2013. How much more profit did Company X make in 2013 than in 2012?

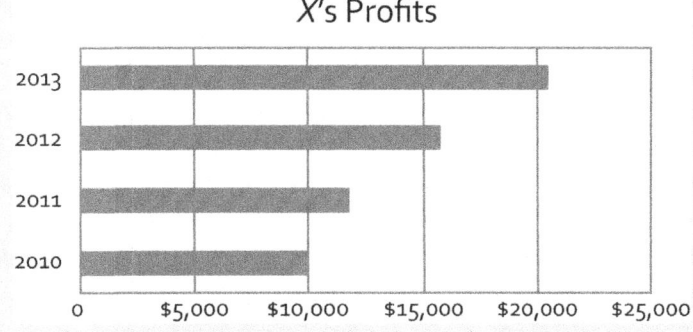

A) $1,000
B) $2,000
C) $5,000
D) $10,000

tion C is correct.

Find Company X's profits for 2012 and 2013 on the bar graph:

$$2012 \text{ profit} \approx \$15,000$$

$$2013 \text{ profit} \approx \$20,000$$

Subtract to find the change in profit:

$$\$20,000 - \$15,000 = \$5,000$$

Questions are multiple-choice or numeric entry. Multiple-choice questions may have one or more correct answers. If there is only one correct answer, there will be ovals next to the answer choices. If there is more than one correct answer, there will be squares next to the answer choices. Numeric-entry questions require you to enter your answer into an on-screen box.

An on-screen calculator will be available during the Quantitative Reasoning sections. You may not use the calculator on your tablet or phone.

Numbers

Types of Numbers

Numbers are classified based on their properties.

Table 4.1. Types of Numbers		
Type of Number	**Description**	**Examples**
Natural number	a number greater than zero that does not contain a decimal or fractional part	{1, 2, 3, 4,...}
Whole numbers	natural numbers and the number zero	{0, 1, 2, 3, 4,...}
Integers	all whole numbers and their opposites	{..., −4, −3, −2, −1, 0, 1, 2, 3, 4,...}
Rational number	can be represented as a quotient of two integers (fraction) with a denominator that is not zero; any decimal part must terminate or resolve into a repeating pattern	$-12, \frac{3}{4}, 0.36, 7.777...,$
Irrational number	cannot be represented as fraction; an irrational decimal never ends and never resolves into a repeating pattern	$-\sqrt{7}, \pi, 0.34567989135...$
Real number	can be represented by a point on a number line	All rational and irrational numbers

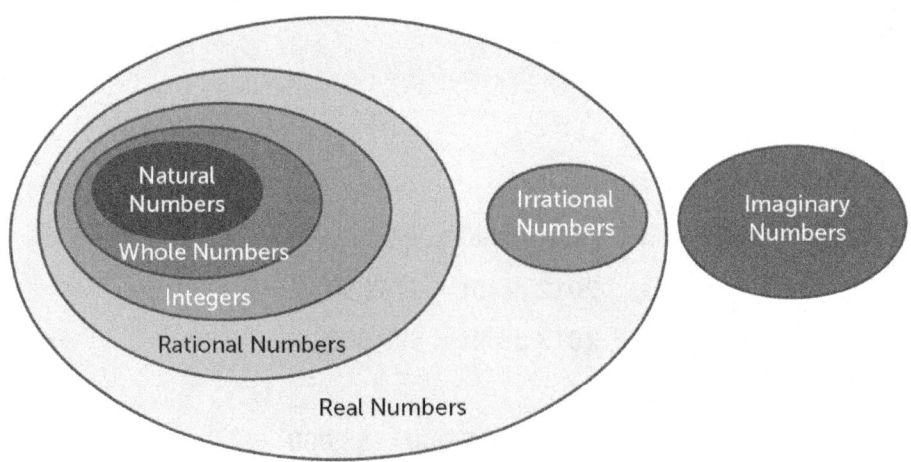

Figure 4.1. Types of Numbers

Every natural number (except 1) is either prime or composite. A **PRIME NUMBER** is a natural number greater than 1 that can only be divided evenly by 1 and itself. For example, 7 is a prime number because it can only be divided by the numbers 1 and 7.

A **COMPOSITE NUMBER** is a natural number greater than 1 that can be evenly divided by at least one other number besides 1 and itself. For example, 6 is a composite number because it can be divided evenly by 1, 2, 3, and 6.

Helpful Hint

Factors are numbers that are multiplied by each other.

Helpful Hint

If a real number is a natural number (e.g., 50), then it is also an integer, a whole number, and a rational number.

Composite numbers can be factored into prime factors using **FACTOR TREES**. For example, 54 factors as 2 × 27, then 27 factors as 3 × 9, and 9 factors as 3 × 3, as shown below. The prime factorization of 54 is 2 × 3 × 3 × 3.

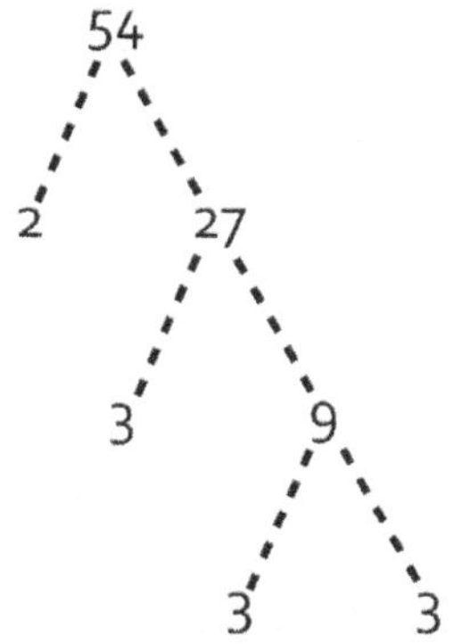

Figure 4.2. Factor Tree

Practice Question

Classify the number as natural, whole, integer, rational, or irrational. (The number may have more than one classification.)

1. 72
    A) natural
    B) whole
    C) integer
    D) rational
    E) irrational

Exponents and Radicals

Exponential expressions, such as 5^3, contain a base and an exponent. The **EXPONENT** indicates how many times to use the **BASE** as a factor.

In the expression 5^3, 5 is the base and 3 is the exponent. The value of 5^3 is found by multiplying 5 by itself 3 times: $5^3 = 5 \times 5 \times 5 = 125$.

Rules for working with exponents are described in Table 4.2.

Table 4.2. Operations with Exponents	
Rule	Example
$a^0 = 1$	$5^0 = 1$
$a^{-n} = \dfrac{1}{a^n}$	$5^{-3} = \dfrac{1}{5^3}$
$a^m a^n = a^{m+n}$	$5^3 5^4 = 5^{3+4} = 5^7$
$(a^m)^n = a^{mn}$	$(5^3)^4 = 5^{3(4)} = 5^{12}$
$\dfrac{a^m}{a^n} = a^{m-n}$	$\dfrac{5^4}{5^3} = 5^{4-3} = 5^1$
$(ab)^n = a^n b^n$	$(5 \times 6)^3 = 5^3 6^3$
$\left(\dfrac{a}{b}\right)^n = \dfrac{a^n}{b^n}$	$\left(\dfrac{5}{6}\right)^3 = \dfrac{5^3}{6^3}$
$\left(\dfrac{a}{b}\right)^{-n} = \left(\dfrac{b}{a}\right)^n$	$\left(\dfrac{5}{6}\right)^{-3} = \left(\dfrac{6}{5}\right)^3$
$\dfrac{a^{-m}}{b^{-n}} = \dfrac{b^n}{a^m}$	$\dfrac{5^{-3}}{6^{-4}} = \dfrac{6^4}{5^3}$

Finding the **ROOT** of a number is the inverse of raising a number to a power. Roots are named for the power on the base:

- ▶ 5 is the **SQUARE ROOT** of 25 because $5^2 = 25$
- ▶ 5 is the **CUBE ROOT** of 125 because $5^3 = 125$
- ▶ 5 is the **FOURTH ROOT** of 625, because $5^4 = 625$

The symbol for finding the root of a number is the radical: $\sqrt{}$. The number under the radical is called the **RADICAND**. By itself, the radical indicates a square root. Other numbers can be included in front of the radical to indicate different roots.

$$\sqrt{36} = 6 \leftrightarrow 6^2 = 36$$

$$\sqrt[4]{1{,}296} = 6 \leftrightarrow 6^4 = 1{,}296$$

Rules for working with radicals are described in Table 4.3.

Table 4.3. Operations with Radicals	
Rule	Example
$\sqrt[b]{ac} = \sqrt[b]{a}\sqrt[b]{c}$	$\sqrt[3]{81} = \sqrt[3]{27}\sqrt[3]{3} = 3\sqrt[3]{3}$
$\sqrt[b]{\dfrac{a}{c}} = \dfrac{\sqrt[b]{a}}{\sqrt[b]{c}}$	$\sqrt{\dfrac{4}{81}} = \dfrac{\sqrt{4}}{\sqrt{81}} = \dfrac{2}{9}$
$\sqrt[b]{a^c} = \left(\sqrt[b]{a}\right)^c = a^{\frac{c}{b}}$	$\sqrt[3]{6^2} = \left(\sqrt[3]{6}\right)^2 = 6^{\frac{2}{3}}$

Practice Question

2. Which of the following values is equivalent to $\sqrt{48}$?
    A) $16\sqrt{3}$
    B) $4\sqrt{3}$
    C) $3\sqrt{4}$
    D) $2\sqrt{12}$

Basic Operations

Arithmetic Operations

The four basic arithmetic operations are addition, subtraction, multiplication, and division:

▶ **ADD** to combine two or more quantities ($6 + 5 = 11$).

▶ **SUBTRACT** to find the difference of two or more quantities ($10 - 3 = 7$).

▶ **MULTIPLY** to add a quantity multiple times ($4 \times 3 = 12 \leftrightarrow 3 + 3 + 3 + 3 = 12$).

▶ **DIVIDE** to determine how many times one quantity goes into another ($10 \div 2 = 5$).

Word problems contain **clue words** that help determine which operation to use (see Table 4.4.).

Table 4.4. Operations Word Problems		
Operation	Clue Words	Example
Addition	sum, together, (in) total, all, in addition, increased, give	Leslie has 3 pencils. If her teacher **gives** her 2 pencils, how many does she now have **in total**? $3 + 2 = 5$ pencils
Subtraction	minus, less than, take away, decreased, difference, how many left, how many more/less	Sean has 12 cookies. His sister **takes** 2 cookies. **How many** cookies does Sean have **left**? $12 - 2 = 10$ cookies
Multiplication	product, times, of, each/every, groups of, twice	A hospital department has 10 patient rooms. If **each** room holds 2 patients, how many patients can stay in the department? $10 \times 2 = 20$ patients
Division	divided, per, each/every, distributed, average, how many for each	A teacher has 150 stickers to **distribute** to her class of 25 students. If each student gets the same number of stickers, **how many** stickers will **each** student get? $150 \div 25 = 6$ stickers

Practice Question

3. A case of pencils contains 10 boxes. Each box contains 150 pencils. How many pencils are in the case?
   - A) 15
   - B) 160
   - C) 1,500
   - D) 16,000

Positive and Negative Numbers

POSITIVE NUMBERS are greater than zero, and **NEGATIVE NUMBERS** are less than zero. Use the rules in Table 4.5. to determine the sign of the answer when performing operations with positive and negative numbers.

Table 4.5. Operations with Positive and Negative Numbers	
Addition	**Multiplication and Division**
positive + positive = positive $4 + 5 = 9$	positive × positive = positive $5 \times 3 = 15$
negative + negative = negative $-4 + (-5) = -9 \rightarrow -4 - 5 = -9$	negative × negative = positive $-6 \times (-5) = 30$
negative + positive = sign of the larger number $-15 + 9 = -6$	negative × positive = negative $-5 \times 4 = -20$

Subtraction is the same as adding a negative value.

$$5 - 7 = 5 + (-7) = -2$$

A **NUMBER LINE** shows numbers increasing from left to right (usually with zero in the middle). When adding positive and negative numbers, a number line can be used to find the sign of the answer. When adding a positive number, count to the right. When adding a negative number, count to the left.

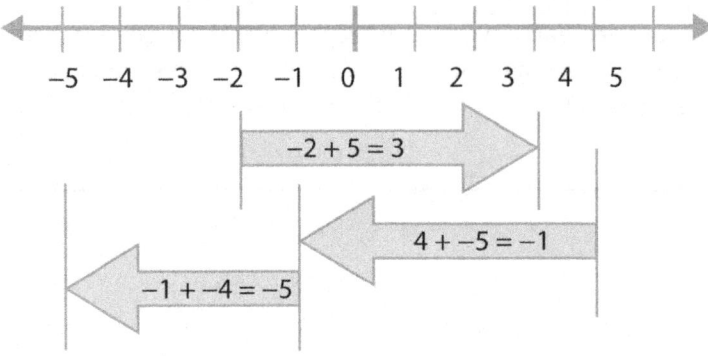

Figure 4.3. Adding Positive and Negative Numbers

Practice Question

4. One day in January, the low temperature was −7°F. During the day, the temperature rose 15 degrees. What was the high temperature for that day?
   A) −23°F
   B) −8°F
   C) 8°F
   D) 23°F

Order of Operations

Operations in a mathematical expression are always performed in a specific order, which is described by the acronym *PEMDAS*:

1. Parentheses
2. Exponents
3. Multiplication
4. Division
5. Addition
6. Subtraction

Perform the operations within parentheses first, and then address any exponents. After those steps, perform all multiplication and division. These are carried out from left to right as they appear in the problem. Finally, do all required addition and subtraction, also from left to right as each operation appears in the problem.

Simplify the expression $(3^2 − 2)2 + (4)5^3$.

Parentheses $(3^2 − 2)2 + (4)5^3$
$= (9 − 2)2 + (4)5^3$
$= 7 \cdot 2 + (4)5^3$

Exponents $= 49 + (4)125$

Multiplication and division $= 49 + 500$

Addition and subtraction $= 549$

Helpful Hint

When working with complicated expressions, underline or highlight the operation being performed in each step to avoid confusion.

Practice Question

5. Simplify: $2(7 − 9) + 4 \times 10$
   A) 0
   B) 36
   C) 44
   D) 160

Comparison of Rational Numbers

Rational numbers can be ordered from least to greatest, or greatest to least, by placing the numbers in the order in which they appear on a number line:

Helpful Hint

Drawing a number line can help when comparing numbers. The final list should be ordered from left to right (least to greatest) or right to left (greatest to least) on the line.

▶ When comparing a set of fractions try to convert each value to an equivalent fraction with a common denominator. Then, it is only necessary to compare the numerators of each fraction.

▶ When working with numbers in multiple forms (for example, a group that contains fractions and decimals), convert the values so that the set contains only fractions or only decimals.

▶ When ordering negative numbers, remember that the negative number with the greatest absolute value is furthest from 0 and is therefore the least number. (For example, −75 is less than −25.)

Example

Order the numbers from least to greatest: $\frac{3}{8}, -0.75, -1\frac{3}{5}, \frac{5}{4}, 0.6, -0.2$

Convert each fraction to a decimal:

$$\frac{3}{8} = 0.375$$

$$-\frac{13}{5} = -1.6$$

$$\frac{5}{4} = 1.25$$

Plot each decimal value on a number line.

−1.6 − 0.75 −.2 .375 0.6 1.25

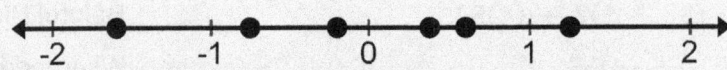

Order from least to greatest (left to right on the number line) using the original given values.

$$-1\frac{3}{5}, -0.75, -0.2, \frac{3}{8}, 0.6, \frac{5}{4}$$

Practice Question

6. Andre welded together 3 pieces of metal pipe, measuring 26.5 inches, 18.9 inches, and 35.1 inches. How long was the welded pipe?
   A) 10.3 inches
   B) 27.5 inches
   C) 42.7 inches
   D) 80.5 inches

Fractions and Decimals

Fractions

A **FRACTION** represents parts of a whole. The top number of a fraction, called the **NUMERATOR**, indicates how many equal-sized parts are present. The bottom number of a fraction, called the **DENOMINATOR**, indicates how many equal-sized parts make a whole.

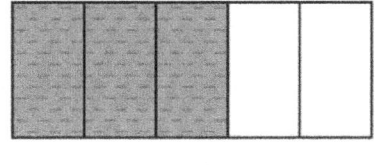

Figure 4.4. Parts of Fractions

Fractions have several forms:

- ▶ **PROPER FRACTION**: the numerator is less than the denominator
- ▶ **IMPROPER FRACTION**: the numerator is greater than or equal to the denominator
- ▶ **MIXED NUMBER**: the combination of a whole number and a fraction

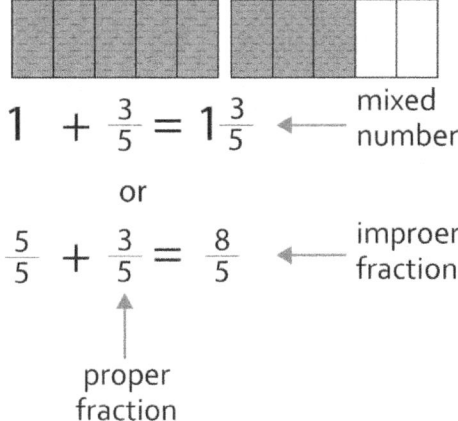

Figure 4.5. Types of Fractions

Improper fractions can be converted to mixed numbers by dividing. (In fact, the fraction bar is also a division symbol.)

$$\frac{14}{3} = 14 \div 3 = 4 = 4\frac{2}{3}$$

To convert a mixed number to a fraction, multiply the whole number by the denominator of the fraction, and add the numerator. The result becomes the numerator of the improper fraction; the denominator remains the same.

$$5\frac{2}{3} = \frac{(5 \times 3) + 2}{3} = \frac{17}{3}$$

To **MULTIPLY FRACTIONS**, multiply numerators and multiply denominators. Reduce the product to lowest terms. To **DIVIDE FRACTIONS**, multiply the first fraction by the reciprocal of the second fraction.

When multiplying and dividing mixed numbers, the mixed numbers must be converted to improper fractions.

$$\frac{a}{b} \times \frac{c}{d} = \frac{ac}{bd}$$

$$\frac{a}{b} \div \frac{c}{d} = \left(\frac{a}{b}\right)\left(\frac{d}{c}\right) = \frac{ad}{bc}$$

Adding or subtracting fractions requires a common denominator. To find a **COMMON DENOMINATOR**, multiply the denominators of the fractions. Then, add the numerators and keep the denominator the same to find the sum.

Helpful Hint

The reciprocal of a fraction is just the fraction with the top and bottom numbers switched.

$$\frac{a}{b} + \frac{c}{b} = \frac{a+c}{b}$$

$$\frac{a}{b} - \frac{c}{b} = \frac{a-c}{b}$$

Practice Question

7. Which of the following quantities is the greatest?
   A) $2\frac{3}{4}$
   B) $\frac{26}{16}$
   C) $3\frac{1}{2}$
   D) $\frac{35}{8}$

Decimals

In the base-10 system, each digit (the numeric symbols 0 – 9) in a number is worth 10 times as much as the number to the right of it. For example, in the number 321 each digit has a different value based on its position: 321 = 300 + 20 + 1. The value of each place is called **PLACE VALUE**.

Table 4.6. Place Value Chart									
1,000,000	100,000	10,000	1,000	100	10	1		1/10	1/100
10^6	10^5	10^4	10^3	10^2	10^1	10^0	.	10^{-1}	10^{-2}
millions	hundred thousands	ten thousands	thousands	hundreds	tens	ones	decimal	tenths	hundredths

To convert a decimal number to a fraction, write the digits in the numerator and write the place value of the final digit in the denominator. Reduce to lowest terms, if necessary.

$$0.096 = \frac{96}{1,000} = \frac{96 \div 4}{1,000 \div 4} = \frac{23}{250}$$

To convert a fraction to a decimal, divide the numerator by the denominator.

$$\frac{5}{8} = 5 \div 8 = 0.625$$

Practice Question

8. Which of the following numbers is equivalent to 0.45?
   A) $\frac{9}{100}$
   B) $\frac{45}{1,000}$
   C) $\frac{9}{20}$
   D) $\frac{4}{5}$

Ratios, Proportions, and Percents

Ratios and Proportions

A **RATIO** is a comparison of two quantities. For example, if a class consists of 15 women and 10 men, the ratio of women to men is 15 to 10. This ratio can also be written as 15: 10 or $\frac{15}{10}$. Ratios, like fractions, can be reduced by dividing by common factors.

A **PROPORTION** is a statement that two ratios are equal. For example, the proportion $\frac{5}{10} = \frac{7}{14}$ is true because both ratios are equal to $\frac{1}{2}$.

The **CROSS PRODUCT** is found by multiplying the numerator of one fraction by the denominator of the other (*across* the equal sign).

$$\frac{a}{b} = \frac{c}{d} \rightarrow ad = bc$$

The fact that the cross products of proportions are equal can be used to solve proportions in which one of the values is missing. Use x to represent the missing value, then cross multiply and solve.

$$\frac{5}{x} = \frac{7}{14}$$
$$5(14) = x(7)$$
$$70 = 7x$$
$$x = 10$$

Practice Question

9. In a theater, there are 4,500 lower-level seats and 2,000 upper-level seats. What is the ratio of lower-level seats to total seats?

   A) $\frac{4}{13}$

   B) $\frac{4}{9}$

   C) $\frac{9}{13}$

   D) $\frac{9}{4}$

Percents

A **PERCENT** (or percentage) means *per hundred* and is expressed with the percent symbol (%). For example, 54% means 54 out of 100. Percentages are converted to decimals by moving the decimal point two places to the left.

$$54\% = 0.54$$

Percentages can be solved by setting up a proportion.

$$\frac{\text{part}}{\text{whole}} = \frac{\%}{100}$$

PERCENT CHANGE involves a change from an original amount. Often percent change problems appear as word problems that include discounts, growth, or markups.

In order to solve percent change problems, it is necessary to identify the percent change (as a decimal), the amount of change, and the original amount. (Keep in mind that one of these will be the value being solved for.) These values can then be substituted in the equations below.

$$\text{amount of change} = \text{original amount} \times \text{percent change}$$

$$\text{percent change} = \frac{\text{amount of change}}{\text{original amount}}$$

$$\text{original amount} = \frac{\text{amount of change}}{\text{percent change}}$$

Practice Question

10. On Tuesday, a radiology clinic had 80% of patients come in for their scheduled appointments. If they saw 16 patients, how many scheduled appointments did the clinic have on Tuesday?

    A) 11

    B) 12

    C) 20

    D) 22

Working with Large and Small Numbers

Scientific Notation

SCIENTIFIC NOTATION is a method of representing very large and very small numbers in the form $a \times 10^n$, where a is a value between 1 and 10, and n is a nonzero integer. For example, the number 927,000,000 is written in scientific notation as 9.27×10^8. The rules of exponents are used to perform operations with numbers in scientific notation.

▶ When adding and subtracting numbers in scientific notation, write all numbers with the same n value and add or subtract the a values.

▶ When multiplying numbers in scientific notation, multiply the a values and add the n values (exponents).

▶ To divide numbers in scientific notation, divide the a values and subtract the n values (exponents).

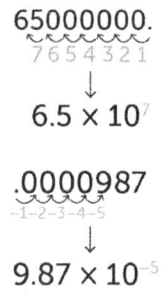

Figure 4.6. Scientific Notation

Practice Question

11. Write the number 4,520,000 in scientific notation.
    A) 452×10^4
    B) 4.52×10^5
    C) 4.52×10^6
    D) 0.452×10^7

Rounding and Estimation

ESTIMATION is the process of rounding numbers before performing operations to make operations easier. Estimation can be used to check work or when an exact answer is not necessary.

To **ROUND** a number, first identify the digit in the specified place value. Then look at the digit one place to the right. If that digit is 4 or less, keep the digit in the specified place value the same. If that digit is 5 or more, add 1 to the digit in the specified place value. All the digits to the right of the specified place value become zeros.

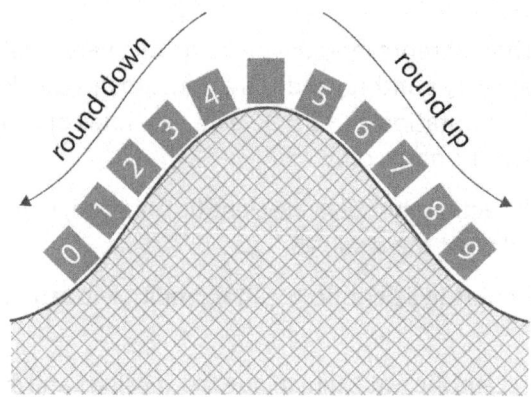

Figure 4.7. Rounding

Practice Question

12. Round the number 138,472 to the nearest thousand.
    A) 138,470
    B) 138,800
    C) 138,000
    D) 139,000

Answer Key

1. A, B, C, D: 72 is a natural number, whole number, and integer. It can be written as a fraction, so it is rational.

$$72 = \frac{72}{1}$$

2. B: Determine the largest square number that is a factor of the radicand 48. Write the radicand as a product using that square number as a factor.

$$\sqrt{48} = \sqrt{16 \times 3} = \sqrt{16}\sqrt{3} = 4\sqrt{3}$$

3. C: Multiply the number of boxes by the number of pencils in each box to find the total number of pencils.

$$10 \times 150 = 1{,}500 \text{ pencils}$$

4. C: Add 15 degrees to −7 degrees.

$$-7°F + 15°F = 8°F$$

5. B: Apply the order of operations by performing the operations inside the parentheses first.

$$2(7-9) + 4 \times 10$$
$$= 2(-2) + 4 \times 10$$

Multiply.

$$= -4 + 4 \times 10$$
$$= -4 + 40$$

Add.

$$= 36$$

6. D: Add the lengths of the three pipe pieces.

$$26.5 + 18.9 + 35.1 = 80.5 \text{ inches}$$

7. D: Write each number as an improper fraction with a common denominator.

A) $2\frac{3}{4} = \frac{(2 \times 4) + 3}{4} = \frac{11}{4}\left(\frac{2}{2}\right) = \frac{22}{8}$

B) $\frac{26}{16} = \frac{13(2)}{8(2)} = \frac{13}{8}$

C) $3\frac{1}{2} = \frac{(3 \times 2)1}{2} = \frac{7}{2}\left(\frac{4}{4}\right) = \frac{28}{8}$

D) $\frac{35}{8}$

8. C: The last value is in the hundredths place. Place 45 over 100 and simplify.

$$0.45 = \frac{45}{100} = \frac{9(5)}{20(5)} = \frac{9}{20}$$

9. C: Find the total number of seats.

$$\text{total seats} = 4{,}500 + 2{,}000 = 6{,}500$$

Find the ratio of lower seats to total seats.

$$\frac{\text{lower seats}}{\text{total seats}} = \frac{4,500}{6,500} = \frac{9}{13}$$

10. C: Set up a proportion and solve.

$$\frac{part}{whole} = \frac{\%}{100}$$

$$\frac{16}{x} = \frac{80}{100}$$

Cross multiply.

$$16(100) = 80(x)$$
$$1,600 = 80(x)$$

Divide by 80.

$$x = 20$$

11. C: Move the decimal point 6 places to the left so that a is between 1 and 10:

4,520,000

$$= 4.52 \times 10^6$$

12. C: The 8 is in the thousands place, and the number to its right is a 4. Because 4 is less than 5, the 8 remains and all numbers to the right become zero.

$$138,472 \approx 138,000$$

Algebra

Algebraic Expressions

Evaluating Algebraic Expressions

The foundation of algebra is the **VARIABLE**, an unknown number represented by a symbol (usually a letter such as x or a). Variables can be preceded by a **COEFFICIENT**, which is a constant in front of the variable, such as $4x$ or $-2a$.

An **ALGEBRAIC EXPRESSION** is any sum, difference, product, or quotient of variables and numbers (such as $2x + 7y - 1$). The value of an expression is found by replacing the variable with a given value and simplifying the result.

Example

Find the value of $x^2 + 3$ when $x = 5$.

$$x^2 + 3$$
$$(5)^2 + 3 = 28$$

Practice Question

1. Evaluate the following expression for $a = -10$:

$$\frac{a^2}{4} - 3a + 4$$

- A) −51
- B) −1
- C) 9
- D) 59

Adding and Subtracting Expressions

TERMS are any quantities that are added or subtracted in an expression. For example, the terms of the expression $x^2 + 5$ are x^2 and 5. **LIKE TERMS** are terms with the same variable part. For example, in the expression $2x + 3xy - 2z + 6y + 2xy$, the like terms are $3xy$ and $2xy$.

Expressions can be added or subtracted by simply adding and subtracting like terms. The other terms in the expression will not change.

$$2x + 3xy - 2z + 6y + 2xy \rightarrow 2x - 2z + 6y + (3xy + 2xy) \rightarrow 2x - 2z + 6y + 5xy$$

Practice Question

2. Evaluate the following expression for $a = xy$ and $b = x^2$:

$$2a + 3b$$

A) $2xy + 3x^2$
B) $3xy + 2x^2$
C) $5xy + 5x^2$
D) $6x^3y$

Distributing and Factoring Expressions

Simplifying expressions may require distributing and factoring, which are opposite processes.

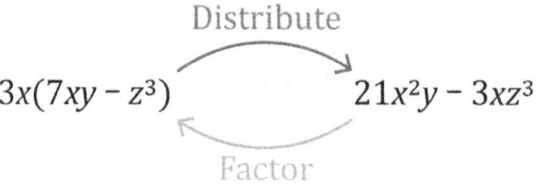

Figure 5.1. Distribution and Factoring

To **DISTRIBUTE**, multiply the term outside the parentheses by each term inside the parentheses. For each term, coefficients are multiplied, and exponents are added (following the rules of exponents).

$$2x(3x^2 + 7) = 6x^3 + 14x$$

FACTORING is the reverse process: it involves taking a polynomial and writing it as a product of two or more factors. The first step in factoring a polynomial is always to "undistribute," or factor out, the greatest common factor (GCF) among the terms. The remaining terms are placed in parentheses.

$$14a^2 + 7a = 7a(2a + 1)$$

To multiply **BINOMIALS** (expressions with two terms), use the acronym *FOIL*: <u>F</u>irst – <u>O</u>uter – <u>I</u>nner – <u>L</u>ast. Multiply the first term in each expression, the outer terms, the inner terms, and the last term in each expression. Then simplify the expression.

$$(2x + 3)(x - 4)$$
$$= (2x)(x) + (2x)(-4) + (3)(x) + 3(-4)$$
$$= 2x^2 - 8x + 3x - 12$$
$$= 2x^2 - 5x - 12$$

Helpful Hint

You can check your factoring by redistributing the term outside the parentheses.

Helpful Hint

When variables occur in both the numerator and the denominator of a fraction, they cancel each other out. So, a fraction with variables in its simplest form will not have the same variable on the top and bottom.

Practice Question

3. Simplify: $2(3x + 4y) + 7(2x - 2y)$
   A) $20x - 6y$
   B) $5x + 2y$
   C) $20x^2 - 6y^2$
   D) $20x + 22y$

Linear Equations

Solving Linear Equations

An **EQUATION** includes an equal sign (e.g., 3x + 2xy = 17) and states that two expressions are equal. Solving an equation means finding the value(s) of the variable(s) that makes the equation true. To do this, isolate the variable on one side of the equation. This can be done by following the same simple steps:

1. Distribute to get rid of parentheses.
2. Use the least common denominator to get rid of fractions.
3. Add/subtract like terms on either side.
4. Add/subtract so that constants appear on only one side of the equation.
5. Multiply/divide to isolate the variable.

$2(2x - 8) = x + 7$	
$4x - 16 = x + 7$	Distribute
$4x - 16 - x = x + 7 - x$	
$3x - 16 = -7$	Subtract x to isolate the variable on one side.
$3x - 16 + 16 = -7y + 16$	
$3x = 9$	Add 16 to both sides.
$\dfrac{3x}{3} = \dfrac{9}{3}$	
$x = 3$	Divide both sides by 3.

Practice Question

4. Solve for x: $5(x + 3) - 12 = 43$.
   A) $x = 3$
   B) $x = 8$
   C) $x = 10.4$
   D) $x = 14$

Helpful Hint

You can perform any operation on an equation as long as you do it to both sides of the equation.

Graphing Linear Equations

A **COORDINATE PLANE** is a plane containing the x- and y-axes. The **x-AXIS** is the horizontal line on a graph where $y = 0$. The **y-AXIS** is the vertical line on a graph where $x = 0$.

The x-axis and y-axis intersect to create four **QUADRANTS**. The first quadrant is in the upper right, and other quadrants are labeled counterclockwise using the roman numerals I, II, III, and IV. **POINTS**, or locations, on the graph are written as **ORDERED PAIRS** (x, y), with the point $(0, 0)$ called the **ORIGIN**. Points are plotted by counting over x places from the origin horizontally and y places from the origin vertically.

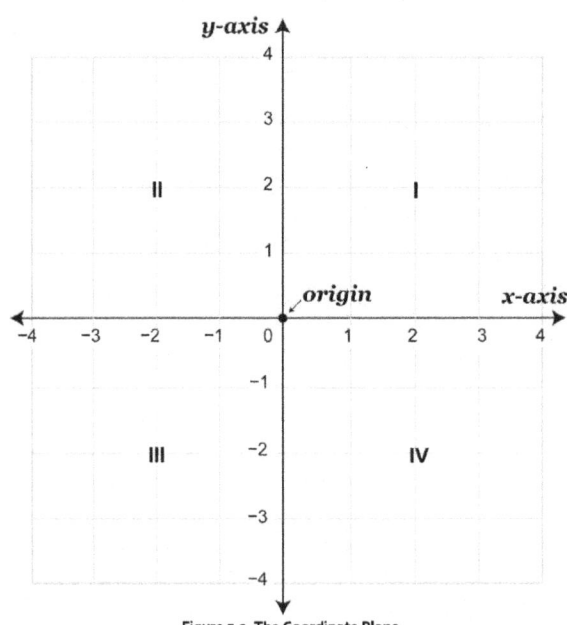

Figure 5.2. The Coordinate Plane

The most common way to write a linear equation is **SLOPE-INTERCEPT FORM**:

$$y = mx + b$$

In this equation, *m* is the slope, and *b* is the *y*-intercept. The **Y-INTERCEPT** is the point where the line crosses the *y*-axis, or where *x* equals zero. **SLOPE** is often described as "rise over run" because it is calculated as the difference in *y*-values (rise) over the difference in *x*-values (run).

$$m = \frac{y_2 - y_1}{x_2 - x_1} = \frac{\text{rise}}{\text{run}}$$

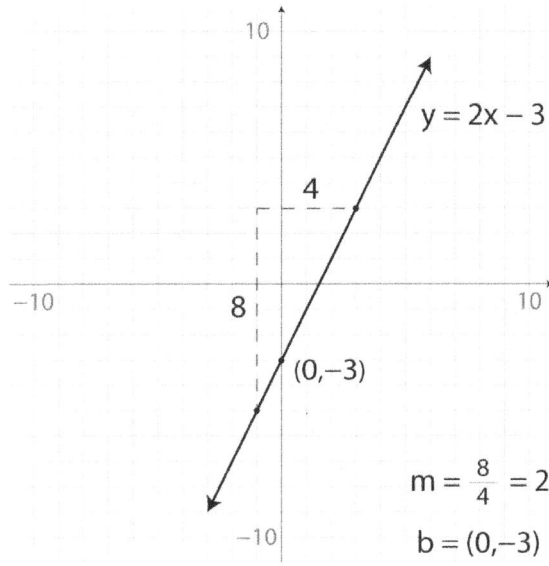

Figure 5.3. Linear Equations

To graph a linear equation, identify the *y*-intercept and place that point on the *y*-axis. Then, starting at the *y*-intercept, use the slope to go "up and over" and place the next point. The numerator of the slope is the number of units to go up (or down if the slope is negative). The denominator of the slope is the number of units to go right. Repeat the process to plot additional points. These points can then be connected to draw the line.

Helpful Hint

Use the phrase begin, move to remember that b is the y-intercept (where to begin) and m is the slope (how the line moves).

To find the equation of a line, identify the *y*-intercept, if possible, on the graph and use two easily identifiable points to find the slope.

Helpful Hint

Two or more parallel lines never intersect, and they have the same or equal slopes. Perpendicular lines intersect to form right angles. The slopes of two perpendicular lines are negative reciprocals of each other.

Helpful Hint

The point-slope equation can be used to find the equation of a line using the slope and one point (x^1, y^1):

$y - y^1 = m(x - x^1)$.

Another way to express a linear equation is in **STANDARD FORM**: $Ax + By = C$. To graph such an equation, it can be converted to slope-intercept form, or the slope and intercepts can be found from the standard form:

▶ $m = -\frac{A}{B}$

▶ x-intercept $= \frac{C}{A}$

▶ y-intercept $= \frac{C}{B}$

It is easy to find the x- and y-intercepts from this form. To find the x-intercept, simply set $y = 0$ and solve for x. Similarly, to find the y-intercept, set $x = 0$ and solve for y. Once these two points are known, a line can be drawn through them.

Practice Questions

5. In which quadrant is the point $(-5, 2)$ located?
    A) I
    B) II
    C) III
    D) IV

6. What is the slope of the line whose equation is $6x - 2y - 8 = 0$?
    A) -3
    B) $-\frac{1}{3}$
    C) 3
    D) 4

Systems of Equations

SYSTEMS OF EQUATIONS are sets of equations that include two or more variables. These systems can only be solved when there are at least as many equations as there are variables.

The solution to the system is the set of values for each variable that satisfies every equation in the system. Graphically, this will be the values where lines intersect:

▶ If the lines intersect at one point, there is **ONE SOLUTION**.

▶ If the lines are parallel (hence, they do not intersect), the system will have **NO SOLUTION**.

▶ If the lines are multiples of each other, meaning they share all coordinates, then the system has **AN INFINITE NUMBER OF SOLUTIONS** because every point on the line is a solution.

| one solution | no solution | infinite solutions |

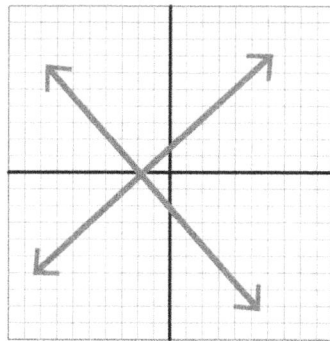 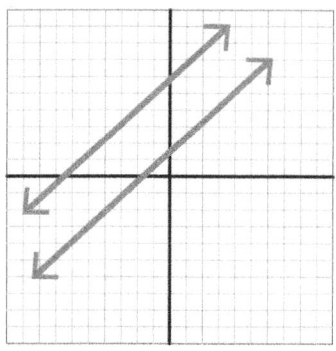 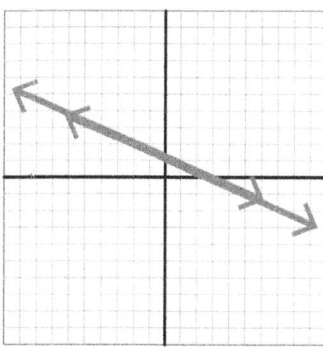

Figure 5.4. Systems of Equations

There are three common methods for solving systems of equations: graphing, substitution, and elimination. To solve by **GRAPHING**, rewrite each equation in slope-intercept form and graph each line individually. The graph will show if the system of equations has one solution, no solution, or infinitely many solutions.

To perform **SUBSTITUTION**, solve one equation for one variable; then, substitute the resulting expression for that variable into the second equation and solve for the variable.

Example

Solve the system of equations:

$$2x - 4y = 28$$
$$4x - 12y = 36$$

Solve one equation for one variable.

$$2x - 4y = 28$$
$$x = 2y + 14$$

Substitute the resulting expression for x in the second equation, and solve for y.

$$4x - 12y = 36$$
$$4(2y + 14) - 12y = 36$$
$$-4y = -20$$
$$y = 5$$

Substitute $y = 5$ into either equation to find the value of x.

$$2x - 4y = 28$$
$$2x - 4(5) = 28$$
$$x = 24$$

The solution is $(24, 5)$.

To solve using **ELIMINATION**, add or subtract two equations so that one or more variables are eliminated. It is often necessary to multiply one or both equations by a scalar (constant) to allow the variables to cancel. Equations can be added or subtracted as many times as necessary to solve for each variable.

Example

Solve the system of equations:

$$6x + 10y = 18$$
$$4x + 15y = 37$$

Multiply each equation so that the *x* variables have opposite coefficients.

$$-2(6x + 10y = 18) \to -12x - 20y = -36$$
$$3(4x + 15y = 37) \to 12x + 45y = 111$$

Add the two equations to eliminate the *x* terms and solve for *y*.

$$25y = 75$$
$$y = 3$$

Replace *y* with 3 in either of the original equations.

$$6x + 10(3) = 18$$
$$6x = -12$$
$$x = -2$$

The solution is $(-2, 3)$.

Practice Question

7. Solve the system of equations:

$$x - 2y = 14$$
$$4x - 8y = 36$$

A) $(18, 2)$
B) $(3, -3)$
C) no solution
D) infinitely many solutions

Linear Inequalities

INEQUALITIES are similar to equations, except both sides of the problem are not necessarily equal ($\neq$). Inequalities may be represented as follows:

▶ greater than (>)

▶ greater than or equal to ($\geq$)

▶ less than (<)

▶ less than or equal to ($\leq$)

Solving Inequalities

Inequalities can be solved by manipulating, just like equations. The only difference is that the direction of the inequality sign must be reversed when the inequality is divided by a negative number.

$$10 - 2x > 40$$
$$-2x > 4$$
$$x < -2$$

The solution to an inequality is a *set* of numbers, not a single value. For example, simplifying $4x + 2 \leq 14$ gives the inequality $x \leq 3$, meaning every number less than or equal to 3 would be included in the set of correct answers.

Practice Question

8. Solve the inequality: $4x + 10 > 58$
    A) $x > 11$
    B) $x > 12$
    C) $x < 12$
    D) $x > 19.5$

Graphing Linear Inequalities

Inequalities with one variable may be represented on a number line, as shown in Figure 5.5. A circle is placed on the end point with a filled circle representing $\leq$ and $\geq$ and an empty circle representing $<$ and $>$. An arrow is then drawn to show either all the values greater than or less than the value circled.

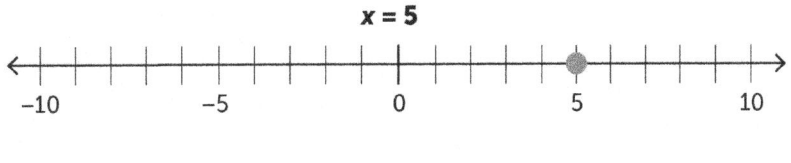

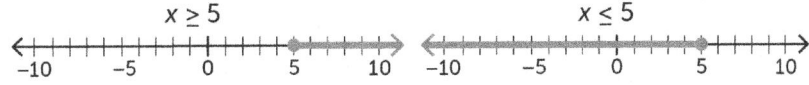

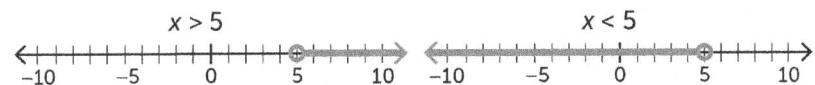

Figure 5.5. Inequality Line Graph

Linear inequalities in two variables can be graphed the same way as linear equations. Start by graphing the corresponding equation of a line (temporarily replace the inequality with an equal sign and then graph). If the inequality is a "greater/less than," a dashed line is used; a solid line is used to indicate "greater/less than or equal to."

Helpful Hint

A dashed line is used for "greater/less than" because the solution may approach that line, but the coordinates on the line can never be a solution.

One side of the boundary line is the set of all points (x, y) that make the inequality true. This side is shaded to indicate that all these values are solutions.

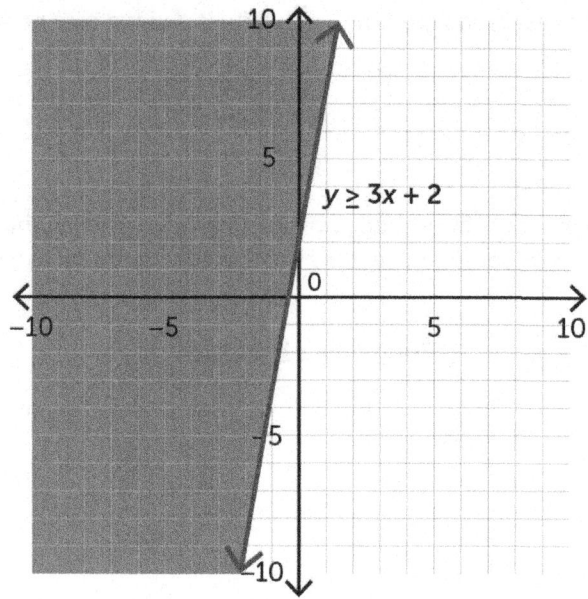

Figure 5.6. Graphing Inequalities

The simplest method to determine which side should be shaded is to choose a point (x, y) on one side of the boundary and evaluate the inequality, substituting these x- and y-values. If the point makes the inequality true, that side is shaded; if it does not, it is not a solution, so the other side is shaded.

Practice Question

9. Solve: $-4x + 2 > -34$
   A) $x > -9$
   B) $x < -8$
   C) $x < 9$
   D) $x > 8$

Quadratic Equations

QUADRATIC EQUATIONS are second-degree polynomials; the highest power on the dependent variable is 2.

Solving Quadratic Equations

Solving the quadratic equation $ax2 + bx + c = 0$ determines the x-intercepts of the parabola (discussed below in "Graphing Quadratic Equations") by making $y = 0$. These are also called the **roots** (or **zeros**) of the quadratic function. A quadratic equation may have zero, one, or two real solutions.

There are several ways to find the roots. One method is to look at the graph of the quadratic. If the graph lies above the x-axis, the quadratic equation has zero roots. If the graph of the vertex is on the x-axis, the quadratic has one root, and if the graph crosses the x-axis at two points, the quadratic has two roots.

Another way to find the roots is to factor the quadratic as a product of two binomials, and then use the zero-product property. (If $m \times n = 0$, then either $m = 0$ or $n = 0$). This can only be used for quadratic equations that can be factored.

Example

Find the root(s) of $z^2 - 4z = -4$.
Factor as a binomial.

$$z^2 - 4z = -4$$
$$z^2 - 4z + 4 = 0$$
$$(z - 2)(z - 2) = 0$$

Set each factor equal to zero and solve for z.

$$(z - 2) = 0$$
$$z = 2$$

All quadratic equations can be solved using the **QUADRATIC FORMULA**:

$$x = \frac{-b \pm \sqrt{b^2 - 4ac}}{2a}$$

The a, b, and c are from the standard form of quadratic equations. (Note: to use the quadratic equation, the right-hand side of the equation must be equal to zero, $ax^2 + bx + c = 0$.)

The part of the formula under the radical ($b^2 - 4ac$) is known as the **DISCRIMINANT**. The discriminant tells how many and what type of roots will result without calculating the roots.

Table 5.1. The Discriminant

If $b^2 - 4ac$ is:	Number of roots:	The parabola:
Zero	Only one real root	Its vertex is on the x-axis (**one** x-intercept since the quadratic equation simplifies to $x = \frac{-b}{2a}$).
Positive	Two real roots	**Two** x-intercepts.
Negative	Zero real roots (but two complex roots)	**No** x-intercepts (never touches the x-axis).

Example

Solve: $3x^2 + 16x = -5$

Write the equation in standard form.

$$3x^2 + 16 + 5 = 0$$

Solve using the quadratic formula.

$$a = 3, b = 16, c = 5$$

$$x = \frac{-b \pm \sqrt{b^2 - 4ac}}{2a}$$

$$\frac{-16 \pm \sqrt{16^2 - 4(3)(5)}}{2(3)}$$

$$-16 \pm \frac{\sqrt{256 - 60}}{6}$$

$$\frac{-16 \pm \sqrt{196}}{6}$$

$$\frac{-16 \pm 14}{6}$$

$$x = \frac{-16 + 14}{6} = -\frac{1}{3} \text{ or } x = \frac{-16 - 14}{6} = -5$$

The solutions are -5 and $-\frac{1}{3}$.

Practice Question

10. What are the solutions to the equation $2x^2 - 5x + 2 = 0$?
    A) $x = 2, 4$
    B) $x = 2, 3$
    C) $x = \frac{9}{4}, 2$
    D) $x = \frac{1}{2}, 2$

Graphing Quadratic Equations

The graph of a quadratic function is a **PARABOLA**, which is U-shaped and has three important components:

▶ The **VERTEX** is where the graph changes direction.

▶ The **AXIS OF SYMMETRY** is the vertical line that cuts the graph into two equal halves; it always passes through the vertex.

▶ The **ZEROS** or **ROOTS** of the quadratic are the x-intercepts of the graph.

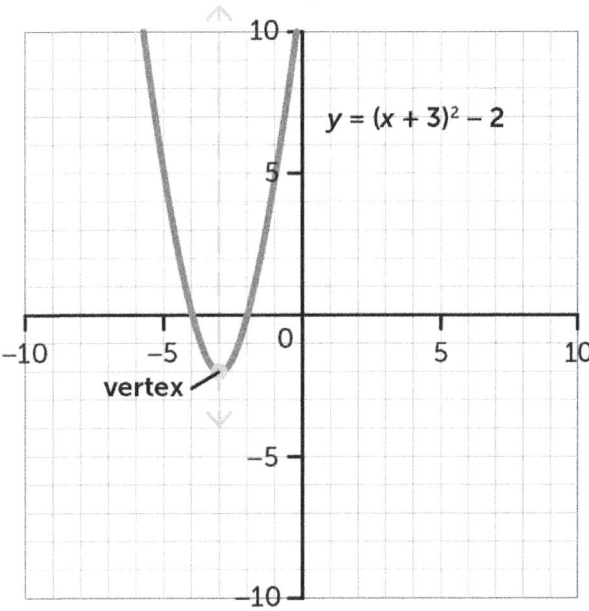

Figure 5.7. Parabola

Quadratic equations can be expressed in standard form or vertex form.

Standard form: $y = ax^2 + bx + c$	Vertex form: $y = a(x - h)^2 + k$
Axis of symmetry: $x = -\frac{b}{2a}$	Vertex: (h, k)
Vertex: $(-\frac{b}{2a}, f(-\frac{b}{2a}))$	Axis of symmetry: $x = h$

Helpful Hint

In both equations, the sign of a determines which direction the parabola opens: if a is positive, it opens upward; if a is negative, it opens downward.

Equations in vertex form can be converted to standard form by squaring $(x - h)$ using FOIL, distributing the a, adding k, and simplifying the result.

Example

Write $y = 2(x - 6)^2 - 14$ in standard form.
Square the $(x - h)$ component:

$$y = 2(x - 6)^2 - 14$$
$$y = 2(x - 6)(x - 6) - 14$$
$$y = 2(x^2 - 12x + 36) - 14$$

Distribute the a and simplify:

$$y = 2x^2 - 24x + 72 - 14$$
$$y = 2x^2 - 24x + 58$$

Equations can be converted from standard form to vertex form by **COMPLETING THE SQUARE**.

Standard form: $y = ax^2 + bx + c$

1. Move c to the left side of the equation by subtracting it from both sides.
2. Divide the entire equation by a (so the coefficient of x^2 is 1).
3. Take half of the coefficient of x, square it, and add the quantity to both sides of the equation.
4. Convert the right side of the equation to a perfect binomial squared, $(x + m)^2$.
5. Isolate y to put the equation in proper vertex form.

Example

Write $y = -3x^2 + 24x - 27$ in vertex form.
Move c to the other side of the equation.

$$y = -3x^2 + 24x - 27$$
$$y + 27 = -3x^2 + 24x$$

Divide by $a = -3$.

$$-\frac{y}{3} - 9 = x^2 - 8x$$

Take half of the new b, square it, and add that quantity to both sides:

$$\frac{1}{2}(-8) = -4 \text{ and } (-4)^2 = 16$$

$$-\frac{y}{3} - 9 + 16 = x^2 - 8x + 16$$

Write the right side as a squared binomial and simplify.

$$-\frac{y}{3} + 7 = (x - 4)^2$$

Rewrite the equation in vertex form.

$$y = -3(x - 4)^2 + 21$$

Practice Question

11. Find the zero(s) of the quadratic equation: $x^2 + 6x + 9 = 0$
    A) $x = 3$
    B) $x = -3$
    C) $x = -3, 3$
    D) no real solutions

Functions

A **FUNCTION** is a relationship between two quantities: for every value of the independent variable (usually x), there is exactly one value of the dependent variable (usually y). Functions can be thought of as a process: when a value is put in, an action (or operation) is performed and a different value comes out.

In a function, each input has *exactly one* output. Graphically this means the graph passes the **VERTICAL LINE TEST**: anywhere a vertical line is drawn on the graph, the line intersects the curve at exactly one point.

Helpful Hint:

On the GRE you may see functions represented as a symbol.

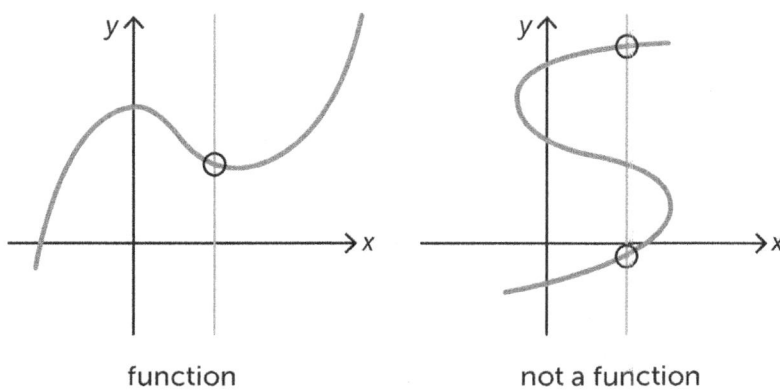

Figure 5.8. Vertical Line Test

The notation $f(x)$—called **FUNCTION NOTATION**—is often used to write functions. The input value is x and the output value (y) is $f(x)$. The output value can be determined by substituting the given input value into the function.

Example

Find $f(2)$ if $f(x) = x + 3$.
Substitute 2 for x and solve.

$$f(x) = x + 3$$
$$f(2) = 2 + 3$$
$$f(2) = 5 \leftrightarrow (2, 5)$$

Every function has an input domain and an output range. The **DOMAIN** is the set of all the possible x-values that can be used as input values. The **RANGE** includes all the y-values or output values that result from applying $f(x)$.

INVERSE FUNCTIONS (written as f^{-1}) switch the inputs and the outputs of a function. If point (a, b) is on the graph of $f(x)$, then point (b, a) will be on the graph of $f^{-1}(x)$. The domain of a function will be the range of its inverse function, and vice versa.

To find the inverse of a function, swap the x and y, and then solve for y.

Example

Find the inverse of $f(x) = 5x + 5$.

Replace $f(x)$ with y:

$$y = 5x + 5$$

Replace every x with a y and replace every y with an x.

$$x = 5y + 5$$

Solve for y:

$$y = \frac{x}{5} - 1$$

$$f^{-1}(x) = \frac{x}{5} - 1$$

COMPOUND FUNCTIONS take two or more functions and combine them using operations or composition. Functions can be combined using addition, subtraction, multiplication, or division.

Helpful Hint

Inverse graphs can be tested by taking any point on one graph and exchanging coordinates to see if that new point is on the other curve. For example, the coordinate point (5, −2) is on the graph of the function and (−2, 5) is a point on its inverse.

Table 5.2. Compound Functions

Operation	Notation	Example
Addition	$(f + g)(x) = f(x) + g(x)$	If $f(x) = x$ and $g(x) = x - 3$, find $f(x) + g(x)$. $x + (x - 3)$ $2x - 3$
Subtraction	$(f - g)(x) = f(x) - g(x)$	If $f(x) = x^2$ and $g(x) = x + 2$, find $f(x) - g(x)$. $x^2 - (x + 2)$ $x^2 - x - 2$
Multiplication	$(fg)(x) = f(x)g(x)$	If $f(x) = x + 3$ and $g(x) = x - 2$, find $f(x)g(x)$. $(x + 3)(x - 2)$ $x^2 - 2x + 3x - 6$ $x^2 + x - 6$

Table 5.2. Compound Functions

Operation	Notation	Example
Division	$\left(\dfrac{f}{g}\right)(x) = \dfrac{f(x)}{g(x)}$ (note that $g(x) \neq 0$)	If $f(x) = x^2 + 3x$ and $g(x) = x$, find $\dfrac{f(x)}{g(x)}$. $\dfrac{x^2 + 3x}{x}$ $\dfrac{x(x+3)}{x}$ $x + 3$
Composition	$(f \circ g)(x) = f(g(x))$	If $f(x) = x^2$ and $g(x) = x + 5$, find $(f \circ g)(x)$. $f(g(x)) = f(x+5)^2$ $= x^2 + 10x + 25$

Practice Question

12. Find the inverse function of $f(x) = \frac{1}{4}x - 9$.
    A) $f^{-1(x)} = \frac{1}{4}x + \frac{9}{4}$
    B) $f^{-1(x)} = \frac{1}{4}x + 36$
    C) $f^{-1(x)} = 4x + 36$
    D) $f^{-1(x)} = 4x - 9$

Arithmetic and Geometric Sequences

A **SEQUENCE** is a string of numbers (called terms) that follow a specific pattern. The terms in a sequence are numbered (meaning there is a first term, a second term, and so on) and are generally described with the notation a_n where n is the number of the term.

In an **ARITHMETIC SEQUENCE**, the difference between each term is the same (a value called the **COMMON DIFFERENCE**). For example, the sequence {20, 30, 40, 50} is arithmetic because the difference between the terms is 10. To find the next term in an arithmetic sequence, add the common value to the previous term.

$$an = a1 + (n-1)d$$

where d is the common difference

In a **GEOMETRIC SEQUENCE**, the ratio between consecutive terms is constant (a valued called the **COMMON RATIO**). For example, the sequence {2, 4, 8, 16, 32, 64} is geometric with a common ratio of 2. To find the common ratio, choose any term in the sequence and divide it by the previous term. To find the next term in the sequence, multiply the previous term by the common ratio.

$$an = a_1 r^{n-1}$$

where r is the common ratio

Practice Question

13. In the sequence below, each term is found by determining the difference between the previous two numbers and multiplying the result by –3. What is the sixth term of the sequence?

$$3, 0, -9, -27$$

- A) –81
- B) –135
- C) 135
- D) 81

Solving Word Problems

Mathematic expressions and equations can be used to model real-life situations. Often these situations are presented as **WORD PROBLEMS** that can be translated into mathematical terms and solved. No matter the problem, this process can be completed using the same steps:

1. Read the problem carefully and identify the value to be solved for.
2. Identify the known and unknown quantities in the problem. Assign variables to represent the unknowns.
3. Translate the problem to an equation.
4. Solve the equation.
5. Check the solution: Is the question answered? Does it make sense?

The table below gives some common phrases and their translations into mathematical terms.

Table 5.3. Translating Word Problems		
Words	**Math Translation**	**Example**
equals, is, will be, yields, the same as	=	a is the same as b $a = b$
add, increase, added to, sum, combined, more than	+	2 more than x $x + 2$
minus, decreased, less than, subtracted, take away, difference between	−	3 less than n $n - 3$
multiplied by, times, product of	×	the product of a and b $a \times b$
divided by, per, out of	÷	x divided by y $x \div y$

Practice Question

14. To determine the amount of a customer's bill, the electric company uses the formula $0.057k + 23.50$, where k represents the number of kilowatt-hours used by the customer. Find the bill amount for a customer who uses 1,210 kilowatt-hours.
    A) $30.40
    B) $68.97
    C) $92.47
    D) $713.20

Distance Word Problems

Distance word problems involve something traveling at a constant or average speed. Whenever you read a problem that involves *how fast*, *how far*, or *for how long*, you should think of the distance equation, where d stands for distance, r for rate (speed), and t for time.

These problems can be solved by setting up a grid with d, r, and t along the top and each moving object on the left. When setting up the grid, make sure the units are consistent. For example, if the distance is in meters and the time is in seconds, the rate should be meters per second.

Practice Question

15. Will drove from his home to the airport at an average speed of 30 mph. He then boarded a helicopter and flew to the hospital at an average speed of 60 mph. The entire distance was 150 miles, and the trip took 3 hours. Find the distance from the airport to the hospital.
    A) 100 miles
    B) 120 miles
    C) 150 miles
    D) 180 miles

Work Problems

WORK PROBLEMS involve situations where several people or machines are doing work at different rates. Your task is usually to figure out how long it will take these people or machines to complete a task while working together. The trick to doing work problems is to figure out how much of the project each person or machine completes in the same unit of time. For example, you might calculate how much of a wall a person can paint in 1 hour, or how many boxes an assembly line can pack in 1 minute.

The next step is to set up an equation to solve for the total time. This equation is usually similar to the equation for distance, but here *work = rate × time*.

Practice Question

16. Ben takes 2 hours to pick 500 apples, and Frank takes 3 hours to pick 450 apples. How long will they take, working together, to pick 1,000 apples?
    A) 1 hour
    B) 1.5 hours
    C) 2 hours
    D) 2.5 hours

Answer Key

1. D: Substitute the value −10 for a in the expression and simplify.

$$\frac{a^2}{4} - 3a + 4$$
$$= \frac{(-10)^2}{4} - 3(-10) + 4$$
$$= \frac{100}{4} + 30 + 4$$
$$= 25 + 30 + 4 = 59$$

2. A: Substitute the given terms for a and b and simplify.

$$2a + 3b$$
$$= 2(xy) + 3(x^2)$$
$$= 2xy + 3x^2$$

3. A: Distribute the 2 by multiplying it by the expression in the first set of parentheses. Distribute the 7 by multiplying it by the expression in the second set of parentheses.

$$2(3x + 4y) + 7(2x - 2y)$$
$$= 6x + 8y + 14x - 14y$$

Combine like terms.

$$= (6x + 14x) + (8y - 14y)$$
$$= 20x - 6y$$

4. B: Distribute the 5 and combine like terms.

$$5(x + 3) - 12 = 43$$
$$5x + 15 - 12 = 43$$
$$5x + 3 = 43$$

Subtract 3 from both sides.

$$5x + 3 - 3 = 43 - 3$$
$$5x = 40$$

Divide both sides by 5.

$$\frac{5x}{5} = \frac{40}{5}$$
$$x = 8$$

5. B: Starting at the origin, move 5 units to the left and then up 2 units. The point is located in the top left quadrant, which is quadrant II.

6. C: Rearrange the equation into slope-intercept form by solving the equation for y.

$$6x - 2y - 8 = 0$$
$$-2y = -6x + 8$$
$$\frac{-2y}{-2} = \frac{-6x}{-2} + \frac{8}{-2}$$
$$y = 3x - 4$$

The coefficient of x is 3.

7. C: Use the elimination method to solve the system. Multiply the top equation by -4 to eliminate the x terms.

$$x - 2y = 14$$
$$-4[x - 2y = 14]$$
$$-4x + 8y = -56$$

Add the two equations to eliminate the x terms.

$$-4x + 8y = -56$$
$$4x - 8y = 36$$
$$0 \neq -20$$

Because the system reduces to a false statement, it has no solution.

8. B: Subtract 10 from both sides.

$$4x + 10 > 58$$
$$4x + 10 - 10 > 58 - 10$$
$$4x > 48$$

Divide by 4 to isolate x.

$$\frac{4x}{4} > \frac{48}{4}$$
$$x > 12$$

9. C: Subtract 2 from both sides.

$$-4x + 2 > -34$$
$$-4x + 2 - 2 > -34 - 2$$
$$-4x > -36$$

Divide both sides by -4.

$$\frac{-4x}{-4} > \frac{-36}{-4}$$

Reverse the sign of the inequality.

$$x < 9$$

10. D: Use the quadratic equation to find the solutions.

$$2x^2 - 5x + 2 = 0$$

$$a = 2, b = -5, c = 2$$

$$x = \frac{-b \pm \sqrt{b^2 - 4ac}}{2a}$$

$$x = \frac{-(-5) \pm \sqrt{(-5)^2 - 4(2)(2)}}{2(2)} = \frac{5 \pm \sqrt{25 - 16}}{4} = \frac{5 \pm \sqrt{9}}{4} = \frac{5 \pm 3}{4}$$

$$x = \frac{5 + 3}{4} = \frac{8}{4} = 2$$

$$x = \frac{5 - 3}{4} = \frac{2}{4} = \frac{1}{2}$$

11. B: Factor the quadratic.

$$x^2 + 6x + 9 = 0$$

$$(x + 3)(x + 3) = 0$$

Set each factor equal to 0 and solve for x.

$$x + 3 = 0$$

$$x = -3$$

12. C: Replace $f(x)$ with y.

$$f(x) = \frac{1}{4}x - 9 \rightarrow y = \frac{1}{4}x - 9$$

Replace every x with y and every y with x.

$$y = \frac{1}{4}x - 9$$

$$x = \frac{1}{4}y - 9$$

Solve for y.

$$x + 9 = \frac{1}{4}y$$

$$4x + 36 = y$$

Write in function notation.

$$f^{-1}(x) = 4x + 36$$

13. A: Find the fifth term.

$$-9 - (-27) = 18$$

$$18 \times -3 = -54$$

Find the sixth term.
$$-27 - (-54) = 27$$
$$27 \times -3 = -81$$

14. C: Plug the value 1,210 into the expression $0.057k + 23.50$ to find the amount of the bill:
$$0.057k + 23.50$$
$$0.057(1210) + 23.50$$
$$= 68.97 + 23.50$$
$$= \$92.47$$

15. B: The first step is to set up a table and fill in a value for each variable:

	d	r	t
driving	d	30	t
flying	150 − d	60	3 − t

You can now set up equations for driving and flying. The first row gives the equation $d = 30t$ and the second row gives the equation $150 - d = 60(3 - t)$.

Next, solve this system of equations. Start by substituting for d in the second equation:
$$d = 30t$$
$$150 - d = 60(3 - t) \; g \; 150 - 30t = 60(3 - t)$$

Now solve for t:
$$150 - 30t = 180 - 60t$$
$$-30 = -30t$$
$$1 = t$$

Although you have solved for t, you are not done yet. Notice that the problem asks for distance. So, you need to solve for d—what the problem asks for. It does not ask for time, but you need to calculate it to solve the problem.

Driving: $30t = 30$ miles

Flying: $150 - d = 120$ miles

The distance from the airport to the hospital is 120 miles.

16. D: Calculate how many apples each person can pick per hour:

Ben: $\frac{500 \text{ apples}}{2 \text{ hours}} = \frac{250 \text{ apples}}{1 \text{ hour}}$

Frank: $\frac{450 \text{ apples}}{3 \text{ hours}} = \frac{150 \text{ apples}}{1 \text{ hour}}$

Together: $\frac{250 \text{ apples} + 15 \text{ apples}}{1 \text{ hour}} = \frac{400 \text{ apples}}{1 \text{ hour}}$

Now set up an equation to find the time it takes to pick 1000 apples:

$$\text{total time} = \frac{1 \text{ hour}}{400 \text{ apples}} \times 1000$$

$$apples = \frac{1{,}000 \text{ apples}}{400 \text{ hours}} = 2.5 \text{ hours}$$

Geometry

Units of Measurement

The United States uses customary units, sometimes called standard units. In this system, several different units can be used to describe the same variable. These units and the relationships between them are shown in Table 6.1.

Variable Measured	Unit	Conversions
Length	inches, foot, yard, mile	12 inches = 1 foot 3 feet = 1 yard 5,280 feet = 1 mile
Weight	ounces, pound, ton	16 ounces = 1 pound 2,000 pounds = 1 ton
Volume	fluid ounces, cup, pint, quart, gallon	8 fluid ounces = 1 cup 2 cups = 1 pint 2 pints = 1 quart 4 quarts = 1 gallon
Time	second, minute, hour, day	60 seconds = 1 minute 60 minutes = 1 hour 24 hours = 1 day
Area	square inch, square foot, square yard	144 square inches = 1 square foot 9 square feet = 1 square yard

Most other countries use the metric system, which has its own set of units for variables like length, weight, and volume. These units are modified by prefixes that make large and small numbers easier to handle. These units and prefixes are shown in the table below:

Variable Measured	Base Unit
length	meter
weight	gram
volume	liter

Metric Prefix	Conversion
kilo	base unit × 1,000
hecto	base unit × 100
deka (or deca)	base unit × 10
deci	base unit × 0.1
centi	base unit × 0.01
milli	base unit × 0.001

CONVERSION FACTORS are used to convert one unit to another (either within the same system or between different systems). A conversion factor is simply a fraction built from two equivalent values. For example, there are 12 inches in 1 foot, so the conversion factor is $\frac{12\ in}{1\ ft}$ or $\frac{1\ ft}{12\ in}$.

To convert from one unit to another, multiply the original value by a conversion factor. Choose a conversion factor that will eliminate the unwanted unit with the desired unit.

Example

How many inches are in 6 feet?

$$6\ ft \times \frac{12\ in}{1\ ft} = \frac{6\ ft \times 12\ in}{1\ ft} = 72\ in$$

Practice Question

1. How many meters are in 4.25 kilometers?
    A) 0.004215 meters
    B) 0.425 meters
    C) 4,250 meters
    D) 42,500 meters

Lines and Angles

Geometric figures are shapes composed of points, lines, or planes. A **POINT** is simply a location in space; it does not have any dimensional properties such as length, area, or volume. Points are written as single capital letters, such as *A* or *Q*.

A collection of points that extends infinitely in both directions is a **LINE**. A point that extends infinitely in only one direction is a **RAY**. A section of a line with a beginning and end is a **LINE SEGMENT**. A line segment is described by the beginning and end points, such as line segment *AQ*. Lines, rays, and line segments are examples of **ONE-DIMENSIONAL OBJECTS** because they can only be measured in one dimension (length).

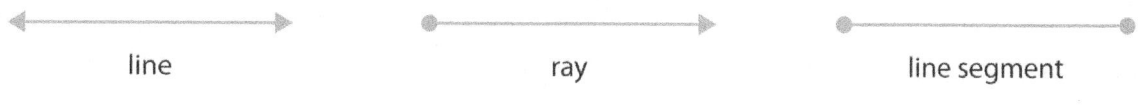

Figure 6.1. Lines and Rays

Lines, rays, and line segments can intersect to create angles, which are measured in degrees or radians. Angles are classified based on the number of degrees:

▶ Angles between 0° and 90° are acute.

▶ Angles between 90° and 180° are obtuse.

▶ An angle of exactly 90° is a right angle.

Two angles with measurements that total to 90° are **COMPLEMENTARY**, and two angles with measurements that total to 180° are **SUPPLEMENTARY**. Two adjacent (touching) angles that are supplementary are called a **LINEAR PAIR**.

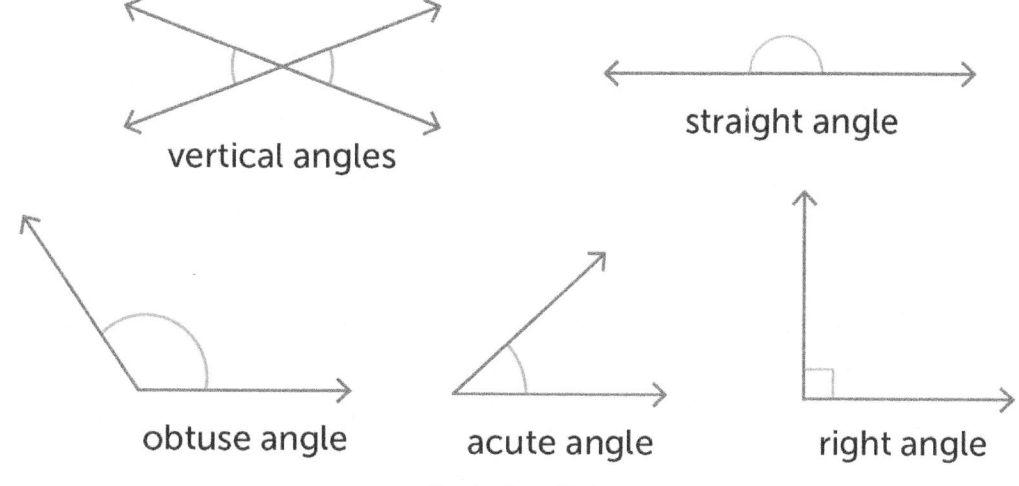

Figure 6.2. Types of Angles

85

Two lines that form right angles are **PERPENDICULAR**. Lines that do not intersect are described as **PARALLEL**.

Figure 6.3. Perpendicular and Parallel Lines

Practice Question

2. Angle *M* measures 36°. What is the measure of an angle supplementary to angle *M*?
    A) 36°
    B) 54°
    C) 144°
    D) 180°

Perimeter and Area

POLYGONS are two-dimensional shapes (e.g., triangles and squares) that have three or more straight sides. Regular polygons are polygons whose sides are all the same length. Angles inside a polygon are **INTERIOR ANGLES**. Angles formed by one side of the polygon and a line extending outside the polygon are **EXTERIOR ANGLES**.

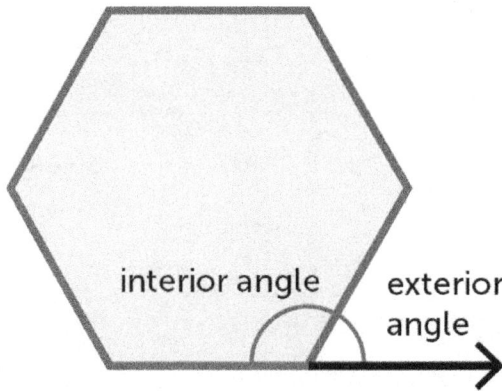

Figure 6.4. Interior and Exterior Angles

The formulas below describe how to find interior and exterior angles of a regular polygon with side *n*:

▶ sum of interior angles = $(n - 2) \times 180°$

▶ measure of interior angle = $\frac{n-2}{n} \times 180°$

▶ sum of exterior angles = 360°

▶ measure of exterior angle = $\frac{360°}{n}$

PERIMETER is the distance around a shape. It can be determined by adding the lengths of all sides of the shape. **AREA** is the amount of space a shape occupies. The area of an object is its length times its width and is measured in square units. For example, if a wall is 3 feet long and 2 feet wide, its area would be 6 square feet (ft²).

Table 6.3. gives the formulas for the area and perimeter of basic shapes. To find the area and perimeter of a circle, use the constant *pi* (π = 3.14).

Shape	Areas	Perimeter
Triangle	$A = \frac{1}{2}bh$	$P = s_1 + s_2 + s_3$
Square	$A = s^2$	$P = 4s$
Rectangle	$A = l \times w$	$P = 2l + 2w$
Circle	$A = \pi r^2$	$C = 2\pi r$ (circumference)

An **EQUILATERAL** figure has sides that are all the same length. In an **EQUIANGULAR** figure, all the angles have the same measurement. To find the length of a side in an equilateral figure, divide the perimeter by the number of sides. To find the measure of each angle, divide the sum of all the interior angles by the number of angles.

Practice Question

3. What is the perimeter of the regular polygon shown below?

A) 6.88 inches
B) 8 inches
C) 10 inches
D) 12 inches

Properties of Two-Dimensional Shapes

TWO-DIMENSIONAL OBJECTS can be measured in two dimensions (length and width). A **PLANE** is a two-dimensional object that extends infinitely in both dimensions.

POLYGONS are two-dimensional shapes, like triangles and squares, that have three or more straight sides. **REGULAR POLYGONS** are polygons with sides that are all equal and angles that are all equal.

Circles

A **CIRCLE** is the set of all the points in a plane that are the same distance from a fixed point (called the **CENTER**). The distance from the center to any point on the circle is the **RADIUS**. The **DIAMETER** is the measurement through the center of the circle and touching two points on the edge. The measure of the diameter is twice the measure of the radius.

A **SECTOR** is the part of the circle formed by two radii (like a pie slice). An **ARC** is the portion of the circle's circumference that forms the side of a sector.

Helpful Hint

Because all the points on a circle are equidistant from the center, all the circle's radii have the same length.

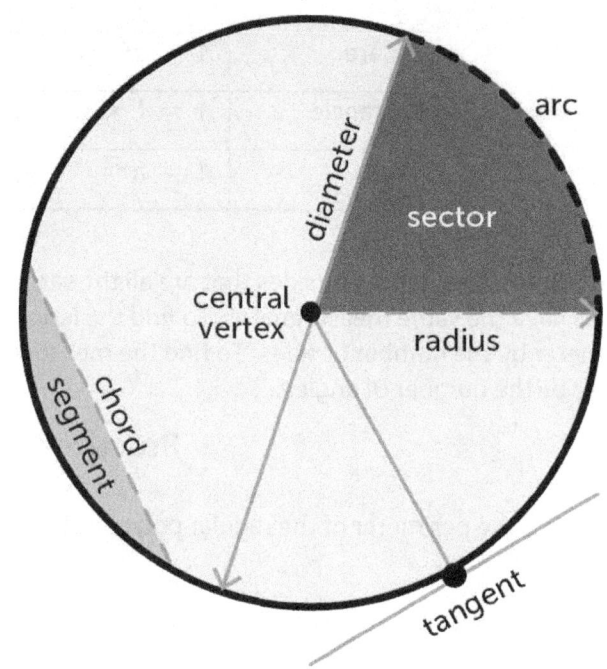

Triangles

TRIANGLES have three sides and three interior angles that always sum to 180°:

▶ A **SCALENE TRIANGLE** has no equal sides or angles.

▶ An **ISOSCELES TRIANGLE** has two equal sides and two equal angles (often called base angles).

▶ In an **EQUILATERAL TRIANGLE**, all three sides are equal, and all angles are 60°.

Triangles Based on Sides

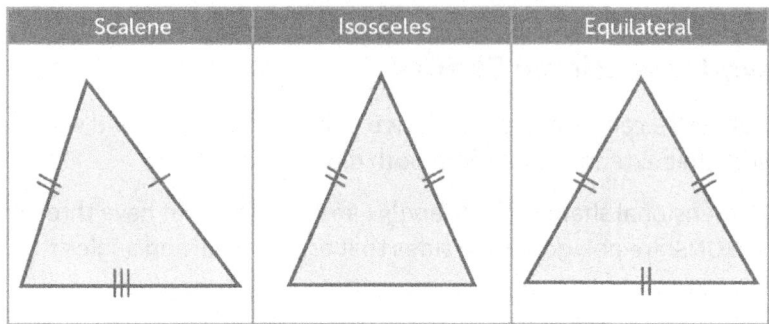

Triangles Based on Angles

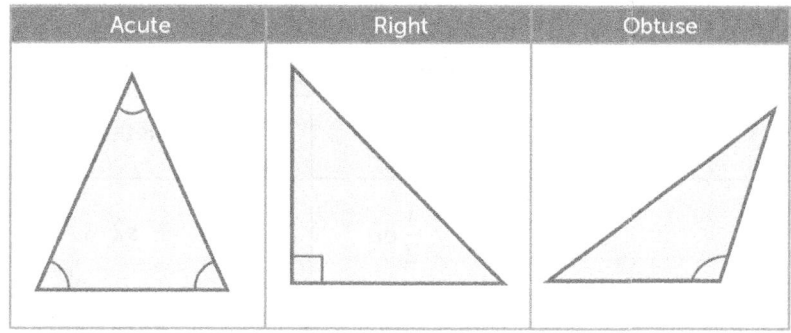

Figure 6.6. Types of Triangles

Quadrilaterals

QUADRILATERALS have four sides and four angles.

▶ In a **RECTANGLE**, each of the four angles measures 90°, and there are two pairs of sides with equal lengths.

▶ A **SQUARE** also has four 90° angles, and all four of its sides are an equal length.

▶ A **RHOMBUS** has four equal sides and two pairs of equal angles.

▶ A **TRAPEZOID** has two parallel sides.

▶ A **PARALLELOGRAM** has two pairs of parallel, equal sides.

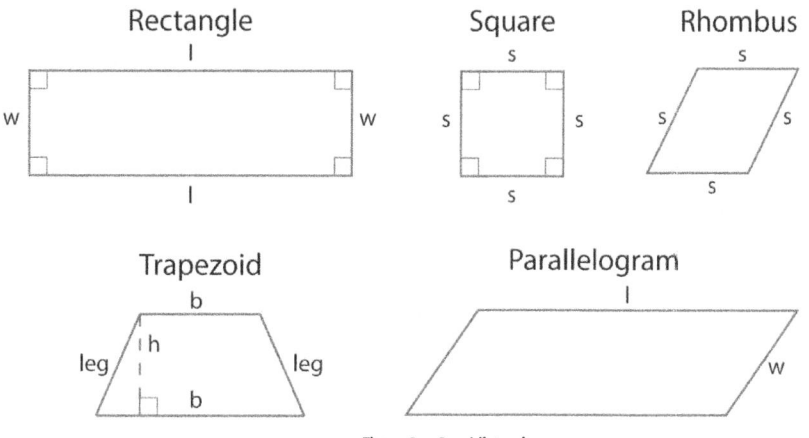

Figure 6.7. Quadrilaterals

Perimeter and Area

The size of the surface of a two-dimensional object is its **AREA**. The distance around a two-dimensional figure is its **PERIMETER**, which can be found by adding the lengths of all the sides.

Shape	Area	Perimeter
Triangle	$A = \frac{1}{2}bh$	$P = s1 + s2 + s3$
Square	$A = s2$	$P = 4s$
Rectangle	$A = l \times w$	$P = 2l + 2w$
Circle	$A = \pi r2$	$C = 2\pi r$
Sector	$A = \frac{x°}{360°}\pi r^2$	$s = \frac{x°}{360°}2\pi r$
Variables	b = base h = height s = side l = length w = width r = radius C = circumference	

Practice Questions

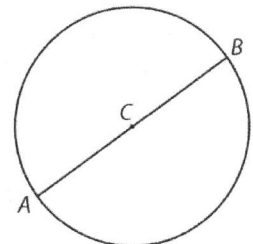

4. The circle above shows a walking path through a park. If the distance from A to B is 4 km, how far will someone travel when they walk along arc AB?
   A) 4 km
   B) 2π km
   C) 8 km
   D) 4π km

5. Which of the following expressions describes the area of the triangle below?

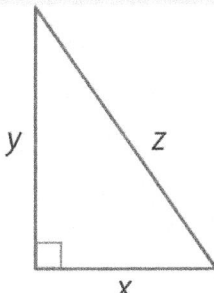

   A) $x + y + z$
   B) $\frac{xy}{2}$
   C) xyz
   D) $\frac{xyz}{2}$

6. The figure below shows a rectangle with 4 square cutouts made to each corner. What is the area of the resulting shape?

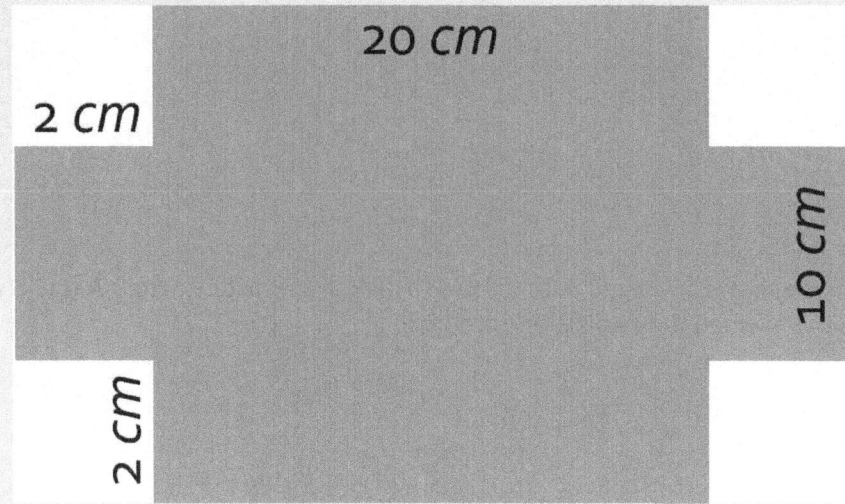

A) 142 cm²
B) 200 cm²
C) 296 cm²
D) 320 cm²

Properties of Three-Dimensional Shapes

THREE-DIMENSIONAL OBJECTS, such as cubes, can be measured in three dimensions (length, width, and height). Three-dimensional objects are also called **SOLIDS**, and the shape of a flattened solid is called a **NET**.

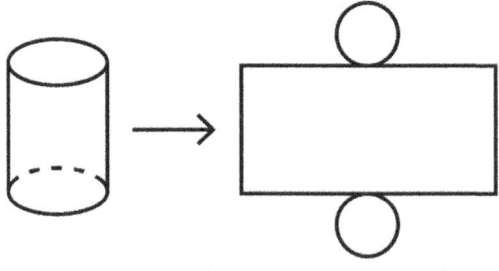

Figure 6.8. Net of a Cylinder

The **SURFACE AREA** (*SA*) of a three-dimensional object can be figured by adding the areas of all the sides. Surface area is measured in square units (e.g., m² or ft²). **VOLUME** (*V*) is the amount of space that a three-dimensional object occupies. Volume is measured in cubic units (e.g., mm³ or ft³).

Shape	Formula	Variables
Prism	$V = Bh$ $SA = 2lw + 2wh + 2lh$ $d2 = a^2 + b^2 + c^2$	B = area of base h = height l = length d = longest diagonal
Cube	$V = s^2$ $SA = 6s^2$	s = cube edge
Sphere	$V = \frac{4}{3}\pi r^2$ $SA = \pi r^2$	r = radius
Cylinder	$V = \pi r2^h$ $SA = 2\pi r^2 + 2\pi rh$	h = height r = radius
Cone	$V = \frac{1}{3}\pi r^2 h$ $SA = 2\pi r^2 + \pi rl$	r = radius h = height l = slant height
Pyramid	$V = \frac{1}{3}Bh$ $SA = B + \frac{1}{2}(p)l$	B = area of base h = height p = perimeter l = slant height

Practice Question

7. What is the surface area of a cube with a side length of 5 mm?
    A) 75 m²
    B) 100 m²
    C) 125 m²
    D) 150 m²

Congruency and Similarity

The term **CONGRUENT** means that two shapes have the same shape and size (but not necessarily the same orientation or location). For example, if the lengths of two lines are equal, the two lines themselves are congruent. Congruence is written using this symbol: ≅. In Figures, congruent parts are denoted with hash marks.

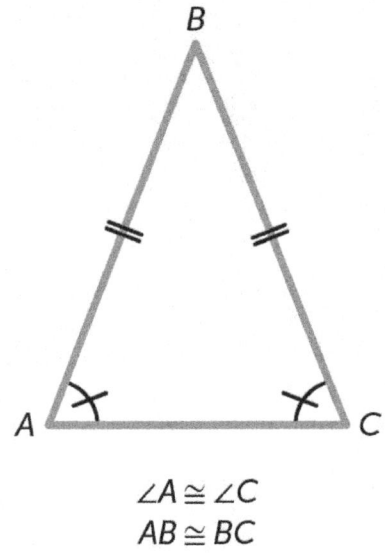

$\angle A \cong \angle C$
$AB \cong BC$

Figure 6.9. Congruent Parts of a Triangle

Shapes that are **SIMILAR** have the same shape but not the same size, meaning their corresponding angles are the same but their lengths are not. For two shapes to be similar, the ratio of their corresponding sides must be a constant (called the scale factor). Similarity is described using this symbol: ~.

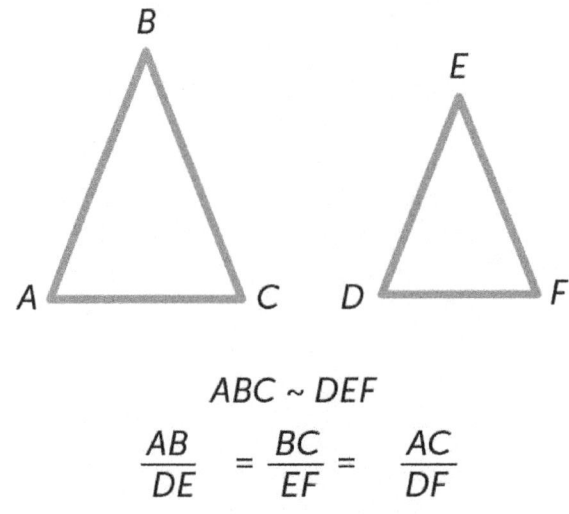

ABC ~ DEF

$$\frac{AB}{DE} = \frac{BC}{EF} = \frac{AC}{DF}$$

Figure 6.10. Similar Triangles

Practice Question

8. The figure below shows similar triangles ABC and DEF.

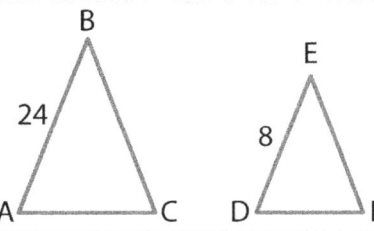

Which of the following statements is true?
 A) $DF = \frac{AC}{3}$
 B) $DF = AC - 16$
 C) $DF = 2AC$
 D) $DF = \frac{2}{3}AB$

Right Triangles and the Pythagorean Theorem

The **PYTHAGOREAN THEOREM** describes the relationship between the three sides (a, b, and c) of a triangle:

$$a^2 + b^2 = c^2$$

Practice Question

9. Erica is participating in a race in which she'll run 3 miles due north and 4 miles due east. She'll then run back to the starting line. How far will she run during this race?
 A) 7 miles
 B) 10 miles
 C) 12 miles
 D) 25 miles

Answer Key

1. C: There are 1,000 kilometers in 1 meter, so use the conversion factor $\frac{1,000 \text{ m}}{1 \text{ km}}$.

$$\frac{4.25 \text{ km}}{1} \times \frac{1,000 \text{ m}}{1 \text{ km}} = 4,250 \text{ meters}$$

2. C: Supplementary angles have a sum of 180°. Subtract the measure of angle M from 180°.

$$180° - 36° = 144°$$

3. C: Add the lengths of all the sides.

$$2 + 2 + 2 + 2 + 2 = 10 \text{ inches}$$

4. B: Find the circle's radius.

$$4 \text{ km} \div 2 = 2 \text{ km}$$

Use the radius to find the circumference of the circle.

$$C = 2\pi r = 2\pi(2) = 4\pi$$

Arc AB is a semicircle, which means its length is half the circumference of the circle.

$$4\pi \div 2 = 2\pi \text{ km}$$

5. B: Use the formula for the area of a triangle. In this triangle, y is the base and x is the height.

$$A = \frac{1}{2}bh = \frac{1}{2}xy = \frac{xy}{2}$$

6. D: Find the area of the complete rectangle.

$$A(rectangle) = lw = (20 + 2 + 2) \times (10 + 2 + 2) = 336 \text{ cm}^2$$

Find the area of the corners.

$$A(corners) = 4(lw) = 4(2 \times 2) = 16 \text{ cm}^2$$

Subtract the area of the missing corners.

$$336 - 16 = 320 \text{ cm}^2$$

7. D: A cube has 6 faces, each of which is a square.

Find the area of each side using the formula for the area of a square.

$$A = s^2 = 5^2 = 25 \text{ m}^2$$

Multiply the area by 6 (because the cube has six faces).

$$SA = 25(6) = 150 \text{ m}^2$$

8. A: Use the given lengths to find the scale ratio for the two triangles.

$$\frac{AB}{DE} = \frac{24}{8} = 3$$

The ratio of *DF* to *AC* will also be equal to 3 because they are corresponding parts of the two triangles. Set up an equation and solve for *DF*.

$$\frac{AC}{DF} = 3$$

$$DF = \frac{AC}{3}$$

9. C: Start by drawing a picture of Erica's route. You will see that it forms a triangle:

One leg of the triangle is missing, but you can find its length using the Pythagorean Theorem:

$$a^2 + b^2 = c^2$$
$$3^2 + 4^2 = c^2$$
$$25 = c^2$$
$$c = 5$$

Adding all 3 sides gives the length of the whole race:

$$3 + 4 + 5 = 12 \text{ miles}$$

Data Analysis

Statistics

Statistics is the study of data. Analyzing data requires using **MEASURES OF CENTRAL TENDENCY** (mean, median, and mode) to identify trends or patterns.

Mean

The **MEAN** is the average; it is determined by adding all values and then dividing by the total number of values.

Find the average of the data set: {16, 19, 19, 25, 27, 29, 75}

$$\text{mean} = \frac{16 + 19 + 19 + 25 + 27 + 29 + 75}{7} = \frac{210}{7} = 30$$

Median

The **MEDIAN** is the number in the middle when the data set is arranged in order from least to greatest.

Find the median of the data set: {16, 19, 19, 25, 27, 29, 75}
$$median = 25$$

When a data set contains an even number of values, finding the median requires averaging the two middle values.

Find the median of the data set: {75, 80, 82, 100}
$$\text{median} = \frac{80 + 82}{2} = 81$$

Mode

The **MODE** is the most frequent outcome in a data set. If several values appear an equally frequent number of times, both values are considered the mode. If every value in a data set appears only once, the data set has no mode.

Find the mode: {16, 19, 19, 25, 27, 29, 75}
$$mode = 19$$

Other useful indicators include range and outliers. The **RANGE** is the difference between the highest and the lowest values in a data set.

Range

Find the range: {16, 19, 19, 25, 27, 29, 75}
$$\text{range} = 75 - 16 = 59$$

Helpful Hint

Mode is most common. Median is in the middle (like a median in the road). Mean is average.

Outliers, or data points that are much different from other data points, should be noted since they can skew the central tendency. In the data set {16, 19, 19, 25, 27, 29, 75}, the value 75 is far outside the other values and raises the value of the mean. Without the outlier, the mean is much closer to the other data points.

$$\text{mean (with outlier)} = \frac{16 + 19 + 19 + 25 + 27 + 29 + 75}{7} = \frac{210}{7} = 30$$

$$\text{mean (without outlier)} = \frac{16 + 19 + 19 + 25 + 27 + 29}{6} = \frac{135}{6} = 22.5$$

Practice Question

1. What is the mean of the following data set?

$$14, 18, 11, 28, 23, 14$$

A) 14
B) 16
C) 18
D) 21.6

Measures of Central Tendency

MEASURES OF CENTRAL TENDENCY identify the center, or most typical, value within a data set. There are three such central tendencies—mean, median, and mode—that describe the "center" of the data in different ways.

Mean

The **MEAN** (μ) is the arithmetic average and is found by dividing the sum of all measurements by the number of measurements:

$$\mu = \frac{x_1 + x_2 + \ldots x_N}{N}$$

Find the mean of the following data set: {75, 62, 78, 92, 83, 90}

$$\mu = \frac{75 + 62 + 78 + 92 + 83 + 90}{6} = \frac{480}{6} = 80$$

Median

The **MEDIAN** divides a set into two equal halves. To calculate the median, place the data set in ascending order. The median is the middle value in a set of data.

Find the median of the following data set: {2, 15, 16, 8, 21, 13, 4}
Place the data in ascending order: {2, 4, 8, 13, 15, 16, 21}

$$\text{median} = 13$$

If the data set has an odd number of values, the median is the exact middle value. If the data set has an even number of data, then the two middle numbers are averaged.

Find the median of the following data set: {75, 62, 78, 92, 83, 91}
Place the data in ascending order: {62, 75, 78, 83, 91, 92}

$$\text{median} = \frac{78 + 83}{2} = 80.5$$

Helpful Hint

Adding a constant to each value in a data set will change both the mean and median by the same constant. Multiplying or dividing each value in a set by a constant will scale the mean and median by the same amount.

OUTLIERS are values in a data set that are much larger or smaller than the other values in the set. Outliers can skew the mean, making it higher or lower than most of the values. The median is not affected by outliers, so it is a better measure of central tendency when outliers are present.

Example

For the set {3, 5, 10, 12, 65}:

$$\text{mean} = \frac{3 + 5 + 10 + 12 + 65}{5} = 19$$

$$\text{median} = 10$$

The **MODE** is simply the value that occurs most often. There can be one, several, or no modes in a data set.

Example

Find the mode: {16, 19, 19, 25, 27, 29, 75}

$$\text{mode} = 19$$

Practice Question

2. What is the median of the following data set?

$$14, 18, 11, 28, 23, 14$$

A) 18
B) 19.5
C) 14
D) 16

Measures of Dispersion

The values in a data set can be very close together (close to the mean) or very spread out. This is called the **SPREAD** or **DISPERSION** of the data. There are a few **MEASURES OF DISPERSION** that quantify the spread within a data set. **RANGE** is the difference between the largest and smallest data points in a set:

$$R = \text{largest data point} - \text{smallest data point}$$

Notice that the range depends on only two data points—the two extremes. For a large data set, relying on only two data points is not an exact tool. For example, the largest or smallest values may be outliers.

To better understand the data set, calculate **QUARTILES**, which divide data sets into four equally sized groups. Use the following steps to calculate quartiles:

1. Arrange the data in ascending order.
2. Find the median of the entire set of data (also called quartile 2 or Q_2).
3. Split the data set into two halves, at Q_2.
4. Find the median of the lower half of the data, called quartile 1 (Q_1).
5. Find the median of the upper half of the data, called quartile 3 (Q_3).

The **INTERQUARTILE RANGE (IQR)** provides a more reliable range that is not as affected by extremes. IQR is the difference between the third quartile data point and the first quartile data point:

$$IQR = Q_3 - Q_1$$

STANDARD DEVIATION (σ) is the average distance of each data point from the mean of the data. The formula is:

$$\sigma = \sqrt{\frac{\sum(x_i - \mu)^2}{N}}$$

In the standard deviation formula, x_i is a data point, μ is the mean, and N is the total number of data points. The **VARIANCE** of a data set is simply the square of the standard deviation:

$$V = \sigma^2$$

Helpful Hint

Variance measures how narrowly or widely the data points are distributed. A variance of zero means every data point is the same; a large variance means there are a relatively small number of data points near the set's mean.

Practice Question

3. What is the standard deviation of the following data set?

$$\{82, 93, 89, 98, 88\}$$

A) 5.33
B) 6.03
C) 28.40
D) 90.00

Data Presentation

BAR GRAPHS present the numbers of an item in different categories. The categories are shown on one axis, and the number of items is shown on the other axis. Bar graphs are used for comparison.

HISTOGRAMS similarly use bars to compare data, but the independent variable is a continuous variable that has been "binned" or divided into categories. For example, the time of day can be broken down from 8:00 a.m. to 12:00 p.m., 12:00 p.m. to 4:00 p.m., and so on. Usually (but not always), a gap is included between the bars of a bar graph but not a histogram.

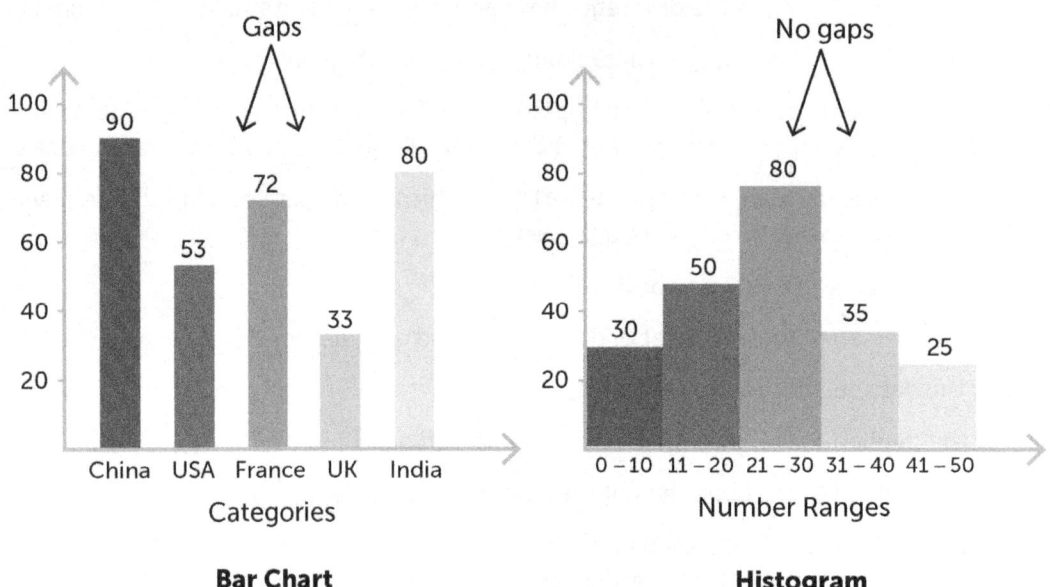

Figure 7.1. Bar Graph versus Histogram

SCATTER PLOTS show the relationship between two sets of data by plotting the data as ordered pairs (x, y). One variable is plotted along the horizontal axis, and the second variable is plotted along the vertical axis.

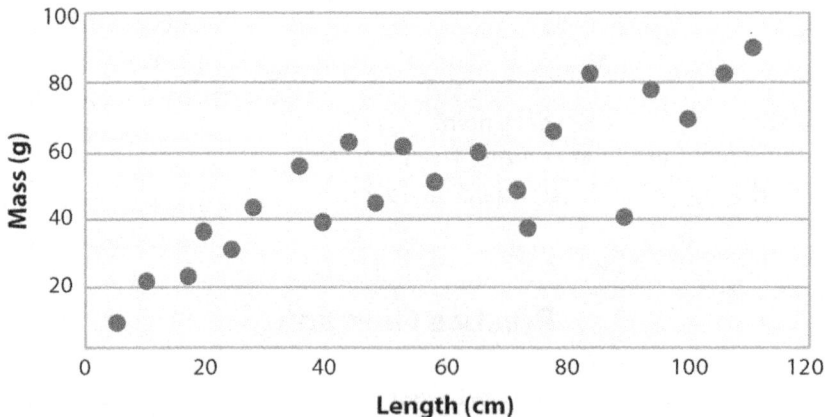

Figure 7.2. Scatter Plot

The data in a scatter plot may show a **LINEAR RELATIONSHIP** between the data sets:

▶ There is a **POSITIVE CORRELATION** (a positive slope) if an increase in one variable corresponds to an increase in the other variable.

▶ A **NEGATIVE CORRELATION** (a negative slope) occurs when an increase in one variable corresponds to a decrease in the other.

▶ If the scatter plot shows no discernible pattern, then there is **NO CORRELATION** (a zero, mixed, or indiscernible slope).

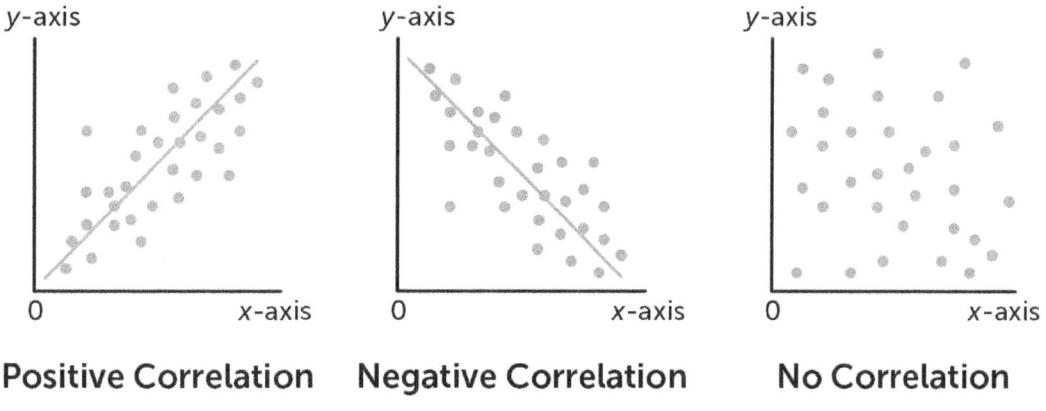

Figure 7.3. Scatter Plots and Correlation

CORRELATION is a mathematical term that describes two variables that are statistically related (meaning one variable can be used to predict the other). The closer the points are clustered together in a scatter plot, the stronger the correlation.

CAUSATION means that one variable directly influences another through a known mechanism. Correlation is not the same as causation: knowing two variables are statistically related does not mean one is directly influencing the other.

LINE GRAPHS are used to display a relationship between two continuous variables, such as change over time. Line graphs are constructed by graphing each point and connecting each point to the next point by a line.

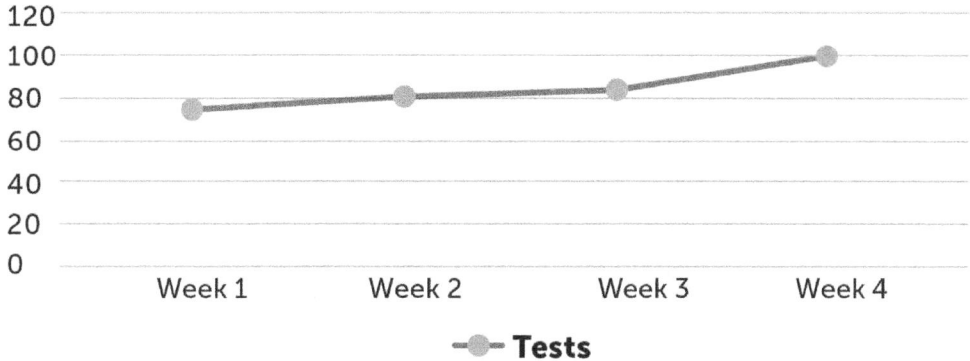

Figure 7.4. Line Graph

PIE CHARTS show parts of a whole and are often used with percentages. Together, all the slices of the pie add up to the total number of items, or 100%.

Helpful Hint

In a line graph, each x-value corresponds to exactly one y-value. A scatter plot may have multiple y-values for one x-value.

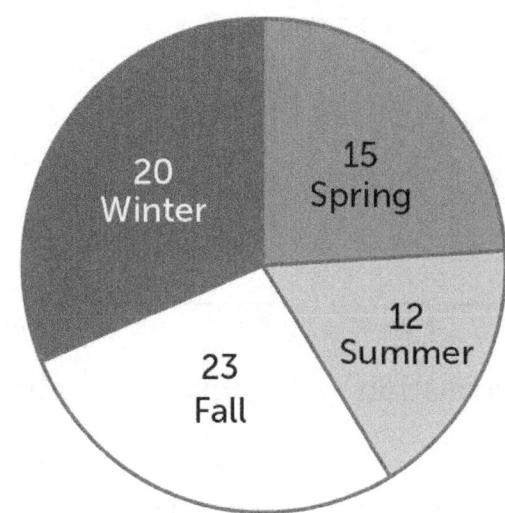

Figure 7.5. Pie Chart

STEM-AND-LEAF PLOTS are ways of organizing large amounts of data by grouping them into rows. All data points are broken into two parts: a stem and a leaf. For instance, the number 81 can be broken down into a stem of 8 and a leaf of 1. All data in the 80s (i.e., that have the same stem) would appear in the same row (this group of data is called a class).

The advantage of this display is that it shows the general density and shape of the data in a compact display, yet all original data points are preserved and available. It is also easy to find medians and quartiles from this display.

Stem	Leaf
8	1 1 1 2 3 4 4 4 5 6 6 6 7 7 8 8 9
9	1 2 2

Figure 7.6. Stem-and-Leaf Plot

Counting Principles

Counting principles are methods used to find the number of possible outcomes for a given situation. The **FUNDAMENTAL COUNTING PRINCIPLE** states that, for a series of independent events, the number of outcomes can be found by multiplying the number of possible outcomes for each event. For example, if a die is rolled (6 possible outcomes) and a coin is tossed (2 possible outcomes), there are $6 \times 2 = 12$ total possible outcomes.

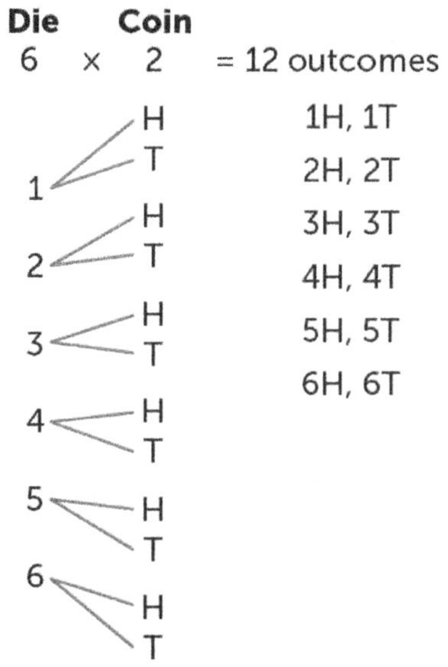

```
       Die    Coin
        6  ×   2    = 12 outcomes
                 H       1H, 1T
              ⟨  T       2H, 2T
         1              
              ⟨  H       3H, 3T
         2       T       4H, 4T
              ⟨  H       5H, 5T
         3       T       6H, 6T
              ⟨  H
         4       T
              ⟨  H
         5       T
              ⟨  H
         6       T
```

Figure 7.7. The Fundamental Counting Principle

Combinations and permutations describe how many ways a number of objects taken from a group can be arranged. The number of objects in the group is written as n, and the number of objects to be arranged is represented by r (or k).

In a **COMBINATION**, the order of the selections does not matter because every available slot to be filled is the same. Examples of combinations include the following:

- ▶ choosing 3 people from a group of 12 to form a committee (220 possible committees)
- ▶ choosing 3 pizza toppings from 10 options (120 possible pizzas)

In a **PERMUTATION**, the order of the selection matters, meaning each available slot is different. Examples of permutations include the following:

- ▶ awarding gold, silver, and bronze medals in a race with 100 participants (970,200 possibilities)
- ▶ selecting a president, vice-president, secretary, and treasurer from a committee of 12 people (11,880 possibilities)

Helpful Hint

The notation $n!$ means to multiply all the whole numbers from the given number n down to 1. For example,

$5! = 5 \times 4 \times 3 \times 2 \times 1 = 120$

The formulas for both calculations are similar. The only difference—the $r!$ in the denominator of a combination—accounts for redundant outcomes. Note that both permutations and combinations can be written in several different shortened notations.

$$\text{Permutation: } P(n,r) = nPr = \frac{n!}{(n-r)!}$$

$$\text{Combination: } C(n,r) = nCr = \binom{n}{r} = \frac{n!}{(n-r)!r!}$$

Practice Question

4. In a class of 20 students, how many conversations must take place so that every student talks to every other student in the class?
    A) 190
    B) 380
    C) 760
    D) 6,840

Set Theory

A **SET** is any collection of items. In mathematics, a set is represented using a capital letter and curly brackets. For example, if S is the set of all integers less than 10, then $S = \{x | x$ is an integer and $x < 10\}$. (The vertical bar | is read "such that.")

The set that contains no elements is called the **EMPTY SET** or the **NULL SET** and is denoted by empty brackets { } or the symbol ∅.

The **UNION** of two sets, denoted $A \cup B$, contains all the data that is in either set A or set B or both sets. The **INTERSECTION** of two sets, denoted $A \cap B$, includes only elements that are in both A and B.

$$A = \{1, 4, 7\} \text{ and } B = \{2, 4, 5, 8\}$$
$$A \cup B = \{1, 2, 4, 5, 7, 8\}$$
$$A \cap B = \{4\}$$

Unions and intersections can be understood in terms of a **VENN DIAGRAM**. The Venn diagram in Figure 7.8. shows two sets, A and B. The union of A and B is the entire area of the diagram; the intersection of sets A and B is the shaded area where they overlap.

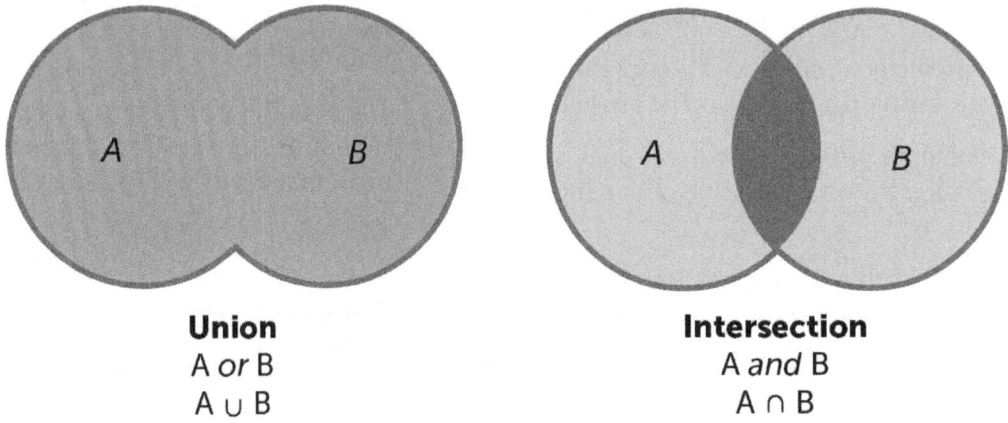

Union
A or B
A ∪ B

Intersection
A and B
A ∩ B

Figure 7.8. Unions and Intersections

Practice Question

5. Which of the following represents the intersection of sets D and E below?

$$D = \{3, 7, 9, 12, 15\}$$

$$E = \{5, 9, 11, 15, 22\}$$

A) $D \cap E = \{15\}$
B) $D \cap E = \{9, 15\}$
C) $D \cap E = \{3, 7, 9, 12, 15\}$
D) $D \cap E = \{3, 5, 7, 9, 11, 12, 15, 22\}$

Probability

Probability of a Single Event

PROBABILITY describes how likely something is to happen. In probability, an **EVENT** is the single result of a trial. An **OUTCOME** is a possible event that results from a trial. The collection of all possible outcomes for a particular trial is called the **SAMPLE SPACE**. For example, when rolling a die, the sample space is the numbers 1 – 6. Rolling a single number, such as 4, would be a single event.

The probability of a single event occurring is the number of outcomes in which that event occurs (called favorable events) divided by the number of total possible outcomes.

$$P \text{ (an event)} = \frac{\text{number of favorable outcomes}}{\text{number of possible outcomes}}$$

The probability of any event occurring will always be a fraction or decimal between 0 and 1. A probability may also be expressed as a percent (e.g., a probability of 0.75 is 75%). An event with 0 probability will never occur, and an event with a probability of 1 is certain to occur.

The probability of an event not occurring is referred to as that event's **COMPLEMENT**. The sum of an event's probability and the probability of that event's complement will always be 1.

Practice Question

6. What is the probability that an even number results when a six-sided die is rolled?

A) $\frac{1}{6}$

B) $\frac{1}{3}$

C) $\frac{1}{2}$

D) $\frac{2}{3}$

Probability of Multiple Events

If events are **INDEPENDENT EVENTS**, the probability of one occurring does not affect the probability of the other event occurring. Rolling a die and getting one number does not change the probability of getting any particular number on the next roll. The number of faces has not changed, so these are independent events.

The probability of two independent events occurring is the product of the two events' probabilities:
$$P(A \text{ and } B) = P(A) \times P(B)$$

Example

A bag contains five marbles: two red, one blue, one green, and one orange. What is the probability of choosing a red marble and rolling an even number on a six-sided die?

Since there are two red marbles and a total of five marbles, there is a $\frac{2}{5}$ chance of choosing a red marble.

There are three even numbers on a die, so the chance of rolling an even number is $\frac{3}{6} = \frac{1}{2}$.

$$\frac{2}{5} \times \frac{1}{2} = \frac{1}{5}$$

The probability of one independent event *or* another occurring event can be found using the following formula:

$$P(A \text{ or } B) = P(A) + P(B) - P(A \text{ and } B)$$

Example

When selecting a single card from a standard deck of 52 cards, what is the probability of drawing either a diamond or a face card?

$$P(A \text{ or } B) = P(A) + P(B) - P(A \text{ and } B)$$

Let A be the event of drawing a diamond $\rightarrow \frac{13}{52}$

Let B be the event of drawing a face card $\rightarrow \frac{12}{52}$

There are three cards that are both a diamond and a face card $\rightarrow \frac{3}{52}$

$$P(A \text{ or } B) = \frac{13}{52} + \frac{12}{52} - \frac{3}{52} = \frac{11}{26}$$

If events are **DEPENDENT EVENTS**, the probability of one event occurring changes the probability of the other event occurring. For example, if cards are drawn from a deck without being replaced, the probability of drawing a specific card changes after each draw.

CONDITIONAL PROBABILITY is the probability of an event occurring *given that* another event has occurred. The notation $P(B|A)$ represents the probability that event B occurs, given that event A has *already* occurred (it is read "probability of B, given A"). Conditional probability is used to find the probability of multiple dependent events:

$$P(A \text{ and } B) = P(A)P(B|A) = P(B)P(A|B)$$

Example

A fish tank contains three red fish and one blue fish. What is the probability of catching two red fish in succession without replacing the first one?

probability of catching one red fish = $\frac{3}{4}$

probability of catching one red fish if one has already been caught = $\frac{2}{3}$

$$P(A \text{ and } B) = \frac{3}{4} \times \frac{2}{3} = \frac{1}{2}$$

Practice Question

7. What is the probability that a coin flipped 4 times in a row will be heads all 4 times?
   A) $\frac{1}{32}$
   B) $\frac{1}{16}$
   C) $\frac{1}{8}$
   D) $\frac{1}{4}$

Answer Key

1. C: The mean is the average. Add the values and divide by 6.

$$\frac{14 + 18 + 11 + 28 + 23 + 14}{6} = \frac{108}{6} = 18$$

2. D: The median is the central number. Since there are an even number of values in this data set, find the two middle numbers and average them.

Place the data in ascending order: $\{11, 14, \mathbf{14}, \mathbf{18}, 23, 28\}$

Average the middle numbers: $\frac{18+14}{2} = \frac{32}{2} = 16$

3. A: First, find the mean.

$$\mu = \frac{82 + 93 + 89 + 98 + 88}{5} = \frac{450}{5} = 90$$

Calculate the standard deviation using the mean.

$$\sigma = \sqrt{\frac{\sum(x_i - \mu)^2}{N}} = \sqrt{\frac{(82 - 90)^2 + (93 - 90)^2 + (89 - 90)^2 + (98 - 90)^2 + (88 - 90)^2}{5}}$$

$$= \sqrt{\frac{(-8)^2 + (-3)^2 + (-1)^2 + (8)^2 + (-2)^2}{5}} = \sqrt{\frac{64 + 9 + 1 + 64 + 4}{5}}$$

$$\sqrt{\frac{142}{5}} = 5.33$$

4. A: Use the combination formula to find the number of ways to choose 2 people out of a group of 20.

$$C(n,r) = \frac{n!}{(n-r)!\,r!}$$

$$C(20,2) = \frac{20!}{(20-18)!\,18!} = \frac{20 \times 19 \times 18!}{2!\,(18!)} = \frac{20 \times 19}{2} = 190$$

5. B: The intersection of two sets of numbers is all the numbers that appear in both sets.

$$D = \{3, 7, 9, 12, 15\}$$
$$E = \{5, 9, 11, 15, 22\}$$
$$D \cap E = \{9, 15\}$$

6. C: $P(\text{rolling even}) = \dfrac{\text{number of favorable outcomes}}{\text{number of possible outcomes}} = \dfrac{3}{6} = \dfrac{1}{2}$

7. B: Find the probability of multiple independent events, and multiply the probability of each separate event.

$$\frac{1}{2} \times \frac{1}{2} \times \frac{1}{2} \times \frac{1}{2} = \frac{1}{16}$$

GRE Practice Test #1

Analytical Writing

1 prompt, 30 minutes

Analyze an Issue

In recent years, catastrophic hurricanes and typhoons around the world have resulted in large-scale destruction and loss of life. However, rapid population growth and the urban development necessary to accommodate the growth have continued in areas vulnerable to storms and flooding, putting millions at risk. Is it possible to allow for economic growth even while keeping people safe?

In your essay, introduce the subject and then either explain the subject you have chosen or take a position about the subject and support that position. At least two evaluators will read and score your essay. Be sure to define your purpose, provide a clear introduction and thesis statement, organize ideas effectively, provide support for your argument, and adhere to Standard English.

Quantitative Reasoning 1

12 questions, 21 minutes

1.

Column A	Column B
the y-intercept of the line $y = 4x$	the slope of the line $y = 4$

   A) The quantity in Column A is greater.
   B) The quantity in Column B is greater.
   C) The two quantities are equal.
   D) The relationship cannot be determined from the information given.

2. For $0 < x < 1$

Column A	Column B
x^2	x^4

   A) The quantity in Column A is greater.
   B) The quantity in Column B is greater.
   C) The two quantities are equal.
   D) The relationship cannot be determined from the information given.

3.

Column A	Column B
the slope of the line $y = -x - 2$	the slope of a line perpendicular to $y = -x - 2$

   A) The quantity in Column A is greater.
   B) The quantity in Column B is greater.
   C) The two quantities are equal.
   D) The relationship cannot be determined from the information given.

4. Given $a > b$

Column A	Column B
3^a	4^b

A) The quantity in Column A is greater.
B) The quantity in Column B is greater.
C) The two quantities are equal.
D) The relationship cannot be determined from the information given.

5. The mean score of a test is 78, the median is 83, the mode is 80, and the range is 37. Ms. Robinson later curves the tests by adding 5 points to each test, and John's new score is 87.

Column A	Column B
John's new test score	the new median test score

A) The quantity in Column A is greater.
B) The quantity in Column B is greater.
C) The two quantities are equal.
D) The relationship cannot be determined from the information given.

6. Given $x \nabla y = 3x - y$,

Column A	Column B
$2 \nabla 3$	$3 \nabla 2$

A) The quantity in Column A is greater.
B) The quantity in Column B is greater.
C) The two quantities are equal.
D) The relationship cannot be determined from the information given.

7. If a student answers 42 out of 48 questions correctly on a quiz, what percentage of questions did she answer correctly?
   A) 82.5%
   B) 85%
   C) 87.5%
   D) 90%

8. Anywhere, USA had 41 inches of rain last year. This year, the area is on track to receive 50 inches of rain. What is the percentage of increase in rainfall, rounded to the nearest percent?
   A) 20 percent
   B) 22 percent
   C) 15 percent
   D) 27 percent

9. What are the roots of the equation $y = 16x^3 - 48x^2$?
   A) $\left\{\frac{3+i\sqrt{5}}{2}, \frac{3-i\sqrt{5}}{2}\right\}$
   B) $\{0, 3, -3\}$
   C) $\{0, 3i, -3i\}$
   D) $\{0, 3\}$

10. In the circle below with center O, the minor arc ACB measures 5 feet. What is the measure of $\angle AOB$?

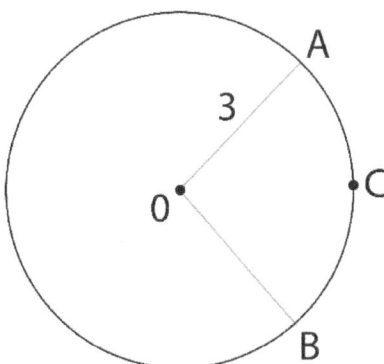

A) 90
B) 90.5
C) 95
D) 95.5

11. In the fall, 425 students pass the math benchmark. In the spring, 680 students pass the same benchmark. What is the percentage increase in passing scores from fall to spring?
A) 37.5%
B) 55%
C) 60%
D) 62.5%

12. A baby weighed 7.5 pounds at birth and gained weight at a rate of 6 ounces per month for the first six months. Which equation describes the baby's weight in ounces, y, after t months?
A) $y = 6t + 7.5$
B) $y = 6t + 120$
C) $y = 7.5t + 120$
D) $y = 6t + 7.5$

Quantitative Reasoning 2

15 questions, 26 minutes

1. For $0 \leq x \leq 1$

Column A	Column B
x^2	x^4

A) The quantity in Column A is greater.
B) The quantity in Column B is greater.
C) The two quantities are equal.
D) The relationship cannot be determined from the information given.

2. Cynthia drives an average of 55 miles per hour. Heather drives an average of 60 miles per hour.

Column A	Column B
the distance driven by Cynthia	the distance driven by Heather

A) The quantity in Column A is greater.
B) The quantity in Column B is greater.
C) The two quantities are equal.
D) The relationship cannot be determined from the information given.

3. Triangles ABC and DFG are equiangular.

Column A	Column B
the area of triangle ABC	the area of triangle DFG

A) The quantity in Column A is greater.
B) The quantity in Column B is greater.
C) The two quantities are equal.
D) The relationship cannot be determined from the information given.

4.

Column A	Column B
0	$\dfrac{x^3}{(x)(x^4)(x^{-2})}$

A) The quantity in Column A is greater.
B) The quantity in Column B is greater.
C) The two quantities are equal.
D) The relationship cannot be determined from the information given.

5. A radio station's playlist consists of 20% rap songs, 30% country songs, 40% rock songs, and 10% easy listening.

Column A	Column B
the probability the station will not play two country songs in succession	50%

A) The quantity in Column A is greater.
B) The quantity in Column B is greater.
C) The two quantities are equal.
D) The relationship cannot be determined from the information given.

6.

Quantity A	Quantity B
the sum of the angles in an obtuse triangle	the sum of the angles in an acute triangle

A) Quantity A is greater.
B) Quantity B is greater.
C) The two quantities are equal.
D) The relationship cannot be determined from the information given.

7. A fruit stand sells apples, bananas, and oranges at a ratio of 3: 2: 1. If the fruit stand sells 20 bananas, how many total pieces of fruit does the fruit stand sell?
    A) 10
    B) 30
    C) 40
    D) 60

8. The given equation represents which type of conic section?

$$x^2 + 2xy + 4y^2 + 6x + 14y = 86$$

    A) circle
    B) ellipse
    C) hyperbola
    D) parabola

9. A person earning a salary between $75,000 and $100,000 per year will pay $10,620 in taxes plus 20% of any amount over $75,000. What would a person earning $80,000 per year pay in taxes?
    A) $10,620
    B) $11,620
    C) $12,120
    D) $12,744

10. A bike store is having a 30%-off sale, and one of the bikes is on sale for $385. What was the original price of this bike?
    A) $253.00
    B) $450.00
    C) $500.50
    D) $550.00

11. Which expression is equivalent to $5^2 \times (-5)^{-2} - (2+3)^{-1}$?
    A) 0
    B) 1
    C) $\frac{5}{4}$
    D) $\frac{4}{5}$

12. Tiffany wants to fence in her backyard. The cost of her chosen fencing is $8.42 per yard. If her backyard measures 20 feet by 40 feet square, how much will the fencing cost?
    A) $336.80
    B) $368.70
    C) $370.20
    D) $372.50

13. Noah makes $18.50 per hour (h) and earns time-and-a-half (t) for any hours he works over 35 in a week. Which equation shows Noah's income (x) if he works 41 hours in a week?
    A) $x = 41h$
    B) $x = 41t$
    C) $x = 35h + 6t$
    D) $x = 35h \times 6t$

14. Using the information in the table, which equation demonstrates the linear relationship between x and y?

x	y
3	3
7	15
10	24

    A) $y = 6x - 6$
    B) $y = 5x - 6$
    C) $y = 4x - 6$
    D) $y = 3x - 6$

15. A chemical experiment requires that a solute be diluted with 4 parts (by mass) water for every 1 part (by mass) solute. If the desired mass for the solution is 90 grams, how many grams of solute should be used?
    A) 15 grams
    B) 16.5 grams
    C) 18 grams
    D) 22.5 grams

Verbal Reasoning 1

12 questions, 18 minutes

1. Because he acted so _____, his friends thought he didn't care about them, so they stopped hanging around with him.
    A) snobbish
    B) inconsequential
    C) skittish
    D) nonchalant

2. The principal was a _____ leader; she showed kindness to all students and staff.
    A) benevolent
    B) tyrannical
    C) laudable
    D) pugnacious

3. The young children teased the boy _____, causing him to cry and leave the party.
   A) benevolently
   B) furiously
   C) maliciously
   D) innocently

Select from the answer options that correspond to the blank sentences in each paragraph. One answer must be selected for each blank. The answer must complete the idea being expressed in the text.

4. Using a variety of sugar, water, food-safe colors, flavorings, and other natural ingredients, confectioners can create delicious candy treats that (i)____ to both young and old alike. Even though the ingredients are often similar among the recipes, the measurements, cooking techniques, temperature, and equipment vary. These differences result in (ii)____ distinct, unique products. Professional candy makers utilize a variety of techniques and equipment to develop and (iii)____ the candy we know and love—everything from chocolate to fudge, lollipops to caramel, marshmallow to toffee.

Question 4 Answer Options		
Blank (i)	Blank (ii)	Blank (iii)
(A) intrigue	(D) greatly	(G) consume
(B) appeal	(E) vastly	(H) taste
(C) satisfy	(F) ferociously	(I) produce

Select TWO answer options that best match the meaning of the sentence. When added to the sentence, the two answers must create complete sentences that have the same meaning.

5. Because of its _____ nature, the dog was constantly returned to the animal shelter.
   A) unchanging
   B) steadfast
   C) whimsical
   D) predictable
   E) erratic
   F) capricious

6. The attorneys had new evidence that seemed to _____ the victim's story, making the case against the defendant airtight.
   A) negate
   B) verify
   C) veto
   D) annul
   E) corroborate
   F) ratify

Use the passages to answer the questions that follow.

The bacteria, fungi, insects, plants, and animals that live together in a habitat have evolved to share a pool of limited resources. They've competed for water, minerals, nutrients, sunlight, and space—sometimes for thousands or even millions of years. As these communities have evolved, the species in them have developed complex, long-term interspecies interactions known as symbiotic relationships.

Ecologists characterize these interactions based on whether each party benefits. In mutualism, both individuals benefit, while in synnecrosis, both organisms are harmed. A relationship where one individual benefits and the other is harmed is known as parasitism. Examples of these relationships can easily be seen in any ecosystem. Pollination, for example, is mutualistic—pollinators get nutrients from the flower, and the plant is able to reproduce—while tapeworms, which steal nutrients from their host, are parasitic.

There's yet another class of symbiosis that is controversial among scientists. As it's long been defined, commensalism is a relationship where one species benefits and the other is unaffected. But is it possible for two species to interact and for one to remain completely unaffected? Often, relationships described as commensal include one species that feeds on another species' leftovers; remoras, for instance, will attach themselves to sharks and eat the food particles they leave behind. It might seem like the shark gets nothing from the relationship, but a closer look will show that sharks in fact benefit from remoras, which clean the sharks' skin and remove parasites. In fact, many scientists claim that relationships currently described as commensal are just mutualistic or parasitic in ways that haven't been discovered yet.

7. What is the meaning of the word *controversial* in the last paragraph?
    A) debatable
    B) objectionable
    C) confusing
    D) upsetting
    E) offensive

8. What is the author's primary purpose in writing this essay?
    A) to argue that commensalism isn't actually found in nature
    B) to describe the many types of symbiotic relationships
    C) to explain how competition for resources results in long-term interspecies relationships
    D) to provide examples of the many different ways individual organisms interact
    E) to explain the differences between commensalism and mutualism

9. Which of the following is NOT a fact stated in the passage?
    A) Mutualism is an interspecies relationship where both species benefit.
    B) Synnecrosis is an interspecies relationship where both species are harmed.
    C) The relationship between plants and pollinators is mutualistic.
    D) The relationship between remoras and sharks is parasitic.
    E) Commensalism is a topic of controversy in the scientific community.

10. Epiphytes are plants that attach themselves to trees and derive nutrients from the air and surrounding debris. Sometimes, the weight of epiphytes can damage the trees on which they're growing. Which term best describes the relationship between epiphytes and their hosts?
    A) mutualism
    B) commensalism
    C) parasitism
    D) synnecrosis
    E) atypical

11. According to the passage, why is commensalism controversial among scientists?
    A) Many scientists believe that an interspecies interaction where one species is unaffected does not exist.
    B) Some scientists believe that relationships where one species feeds on the leftovers of another should be classified as parasitism.
    C) Because remoras and sharks have a mutualistic relationship, no interactions should be classified as commensalism.
    D) Only relationships among animal species should be classified as commensalism.
    E) Some scientists believe animals are incapable of interspecies interaction.

12. What can the reader conclude from this passage about symbiotic relationships?
    A) Scientists cannot decide how to classify symbiotic relationships among species.
    B) The majority of interspecies interactions are parasitic because most species do not get along.
    C) If two species are involved in a parasitic relationship, one of the species will eventually become extinct.
    D) Symbiotic relationships evolve as the species that live in a community adapt to their environments and each other.
    E) Mutualistic relationships are rare and difficult to maintain.

Verbal Reasoning 2

15 questions, 23 minutes

1. Don't be such a _____! Practice what you preach.
    A) traitor
    B) hypocrite
    C) comedian
    D) humanitarian

2. This plant is very _____; it survived through the winter and is now flourishing!
    A) direct
    B) feeble
    C) anemic
    D) robust

3. My guilt was _____ after I found out that I wasn't to blame for the _____ accident.
    A) wasted... devastating
    B) ravaged... harmful
    C) engorged... distressing
    D) assuaged... dreadful

4. The author wrote a _____ sequel; it was completely _____ and no one liked it.
   A) trite... lackluster
   B) banal... inspiring
   C) predictable... original
   D) facile... remarkable

Select from the answer options that correspond to the blank sentences in each paragraph. One answer must be selected for each blank. The answer must complete the idea being expressed in the text.

5. The crew, ten of the best and brightest astronauts from NASA, stared at the sparkling (i)____ of light that (ii)____ from the surrounding stars. Eagerly awaiting an announcement from the captain in the cockpit about their (iii)____ arrival on the alien planet, the astronauts each thought back to the days leading up to the spacecraft's launch and what led them to this once-in-a-lifetime opportunity.

Question 5 Answer Options		
Blank (i)	**Blank (ii)**	**Blank (iii)**
(A) bursts	(D) alluded	(G) impending
(B) orbs	(E) shone	(H) disturbing
(C) sparks	(F) emanated	(I) detrimental

Select TWO answer options that best match the meaning of the sentence. When added to the sentence, the two answers must create complete sentences that have the same meaning.

6. We are required to complete a very _____ set of tests in order to become licensed teachers; many do not pass the first time around.
   A) effortless
   B) rigorous
   C) tedious
   D) painful
   E) arduous
   F) facile

7. Surprisingly, the students rose with ____ and moved excitedly into collaborative groups.
   A) enthusiasm
   B) apathy
   C) disinclination
   D) alacrity
   E) indifference
   F) happiness

Use the passage to answer the questions that follow.

The territories of the state of Ch'in, the present Shensi and eastern Kansu, were from a geographical point of view transit regions, closed off in the north by steppes and deserts and in the south by almost impassable mountains. Only between these barriers, along the rivers Wei (in Shensi) and T'ao (in

Kansu), is there a rich cultivable zone which is also the only means of transit from east to west. All traffic from and to Turkestan had to take this route. It is believed that strong relations with eastern Turkestan began in this period, and the state of Ch'in must have drawn big profits from its "foreign trade." The merchant class quickly gained more and more importance. The population was growing through immigration from the east which the government encouraged. This growing population with its increasing means of production, especially the great new irrigation systems, provided a welcome field for trade which was also furthered by the roads, though these were actually built for military purposes.

The state of Ch'in had never been so closely associated with the feudal communities of the rest of China as the other feudal states. A great part of its population, including the ruling class, was not purely Chinese but contained an admixture of Turks and Tibetans. The other Chinese even called Ch'in a "barbarian state," and the foreign influence was, indeed, unceasing. This was a favourable soil for the overcoming of feudalism, and the process was furthered by the factors mentioned in the preceding chapter, which were leading to a change in the social structure of China. Especially the recruitment of the whole population, including the peasantry, for war was entirely in the interest of the influential nomad fighting peoples within the state. About 250 BC, Ch'in was not only one of the economically strongest among the feudal states, but had already made an end of its own feudal system.

Every feudal system harbours some seeds of a bureaucratic system of administration: feudal lords have their personal servants who are not recruited from the nobility, but who by their easy access to the lord can easily gain importance. They may, for instance, be put in charge of estates, workshops, and other properties of the lord and thus acquire experience in administration and an efficiency which are obviously of advantage to the lord. When Chinese lords of the preceding period, with the help of their sub-lords of the nobility, made wars, they tended to put the newly-conquered [sic] areas not into the hands of newly-enfeoffed [sic] noblemen, but to keep them as their property and to put their administration into the hands of efficient servants; these were the first bureaucratic officials. Thus, in the course of the later Chou period, a bureaucratic system of administration had begun to develop, and terms like "district" or "prefecture" began to appear, indicating that areas under a bureaucratic administration existed beside and inside areas under feudal rule. This process had gone furthest in Ch'in and was sponsored by the representatives of the Legalist School, which was best adapted to the new economic and social situation.

A son of one of the concubines of the penultimate feudal ruler of Ch'in was living as a hostage in the neighbouring state of Chao, in what is now northern Shansi. There he made the acquaintance of an unusual man, the merchant Lü Pu-wei, a man of education and of great political influence. Lü Pu-wei persuaded the feudal ruler of Ch'in to declare this man his successor. He also sold a girl to the prince to be his wife, and the son of this marriage was to be the famous and notorious Shih Huang-ti. Lü Pu-wei came with his protégé to Ch'in, where he became his Prime Minister, and after the prince's death in 247 BC Lü Pu-wei became the regent for his young son Shih Huang-ti (then called Cheng). For the first time in Chinese history a merchant, a commoner, had reached one of the highest positions in the state. It is not known what sort of trade Lü Pu-wei had carried on, but probably he dealt in horses, the principal export of the state of Chao. As horses were an absolute necessity for the armies of that time, it is easy to imagine that a horse-dealer might gain great political influence.

Soon after Shih Huang-ti's accession Lü Pu-wei was dismissed, and a new group of advisers, strong supporters of the Legalist school, came into power. These new men began an active policy of conquest instead of the peaceful course which Lü Pu-wei had pursued. One campaign followed another in the years from 230 to 222, until all the feudal states had been conquered, annexed, and brought under Shih Huang-ti's rule.

"The Ch'in Dynasty (256–207 BC)" in *A History of China* (2004) by Wolfram Eberhard

8. According to the passage, which of the following caused a change in the way power was distributed in China?
   A) Lü Pu-wei
   B) Shih Huang-ti
   C) newly enfeoffed noblemen
   D) the feudal leader of Ch'in
   E) personal servants who were put in charge of properties on behalf of their lords

9. Based on the passage, a primary cause of the disappearance of feudal structure in Ch'in was
   A) the influence of other feudal states in China disappearing.
   B) the new irrigation system that led to greater wealth for the working class.
   C) the foreign influence from Turkestan and Tibet.
   D) the completion of a new road system for the military.
   E) the appearance of terms like *district* and *prefecture*.

10. From the information provided in the first and second paragraphs, it can reasonably be inferred that
    A) other Chinese states did not like Ch'in because it was constantly changing.
    B) outside territories like Turkestan found the Chinese economic system to be backwards and outdated.
    C) Ch'in had no valuable exports except for military strength.
    D) Ch'in was unusual and forward thinking compared to other Chinese states.
    E) Ch'in peoples believed that only the wealthy, ruling classes should have military power.

11. According to paragraph three, which of the following best describes the difference between a bureaucratic official and a nobleman?
    A) An official cares for a district at the charge of a higher lord, while a nobleman owns and administers a piece of land for himself.
    B) An official may be created by a lord, but a lord may not create another nobleman.
    C) An official can only be named from the merchant class, while a nobleman can be created from any class.
    D) An official is better at running a district efficiently, while a nobleman tends to spend excessively.
    E) Servants of feudal lords could easily gain power and move up in social class.

12. The passage indicates that Ch'in became an important leader for other Chinese districts because
    A) the new prime minister for all of China came from Ch'in.
    B) Ch'in was especially successful at replacing its feudal society and obtaining economic success.
    C) Ch'in was a strategic military stronghold, key to winning several wars.
    D) Ch'in joined with neighboring region Chao to annex several feudal states and absorb them.
    E) Ch'in was situated in a fertile land that was near an important transit route.

13. The passage states that the bureaucratic system of rule gained popularity in part because
    A) the feudal serfs rebelled against the feudal leaders and demanded a change.
    B) trading partners for China wanted a more just system of rule and put economic pressure on China.
    C) the lords who conquered new territories preferred to keep the land under the rule of a trusted servant rather than create holdings for new noblemen.
    D) the merchant class became so powerful that they were able to demand a system with more sharing of power.
    E) it allowed servants of lower social classes to easily move up in society.

14. Which of the following is a main idea expressed in the first paragraph?
    A) The lack of cultivable land in Ch'in kept it from growing very quickly.
    B) Several factors contributed to the rapid growth of the trade economy in Ch'in.
    C) The growing merchant class created a problem for the workers by taking their earnings.
    D) The lack of roads was an issue in attracting foreign trade.
    E) The state of Ch'in invested great amounts of money in building roads to facilitate military and trade activity.

15. It can be inferred from the passage that Lü Pu-wei brought his protégé to Ch'in because
    A) he felt that the horse trade in Ch'in would be better than that in Chou.
    B) he thought the child needed to meet his father.
    C) he thought the son would make a better ruler than the father.
    D) he hoped to gain a position of power in the government through the child.
    E) he hoped to change the way power was distributed by uprooting the feudalist system.

GRE Practice Test #1 Answer Key

Analyze and Issue: Sample Essay

Violent storms are a huge risk to human life and property; they also have a strong impact on the economy, interfering with economic activity and sometimes damaging infrastructure. However, natural disasters are a fact of life on our planet, and it is impossible for economic development and growth to cease due to the possibility of a powerful storm. Still, rapid urban development is occurring in particularly storm-prone areas in Asia and even in North America, putting millions of people at risk. While the risks of a calamitous storm should never be underestimated, the solution is not to halt migration and slow economic growth, but to encourage investment in urban planning and public safety instead.

Centers of population in storm-prone areas in Indonesia, the Philippines, the United States East and Gulf Coasts, and elsewhere are indeed growing; natural resources and urban areas in these places are essential to local and national economies and even the global economy. During this time of change, especially in areas that are newly developing, opportunities for proper urban planning abound. Before growing urban areas get even larger, governments must take action to prevent the proliferation of slums, improve existing infrastructure to meet the needs of growing cities (or develop new infrastructure), and put policies into place for good urban management. Given the importance of these urban and industrial areas, especially for billion-dollar sectors like the oil and gas industry, there may even be opportunities for major companies to get involved in sponsoring urban development and safety in the economic zones and cities relevant to their interests around the world.

Furthermore, with economic growth also comes innovation and technology. Today, there are more opportunities than ever to develop products and procedures to ensure safety. From engineering to preparedness to emergency medical treatment, there are a plethora of approaches to storm readiness and flood control. Urban planning can take into account flooding and geographical impediments to emergency response time. There are more products on the market to help families survive for several days without help (for instance, water purifiers and other survival gear). Governments, civic organizations, and NGOs could be involved in emergency preparedness efforts and enlisted to distribute preparedness items during storm seasons, especially to people who are the most likely to be affected and who would most likely be harmed. Using good technology and wise community coordination would ensure that vulnerable workers and their families are as safe as possible during storm season, so that they could benefit year-round from economic growth.

While storms and other natural disasters are and will remain a threat to human life, it is unrealistic to imagine that all economic activity will stop for the sake of safety. Thanks to economic growth and innovation, we can develop planning, technology, policy, and coordination to ensure the safety of communities as they drive the economic growth of those regions affected by major storms. That way, development can continue in as safe an environment as possible.

Quantitative Reasoning 1 Answer Key

1. C: slope-intercept form, $y = mx + b$, with $m =$ slope and $b = y$-intercept

Column A: the y-intercept is 0.

Column B: the slope is 0.

Therefore, the two quantities are equal.

2. A: With fractions, the larger the denominator, the smaller the value of the fraction.

The value of x is between 0 and 1.

For example, let $x = \frac{1}{2}$; $x^2 = \frac{1}{4}$ and $x^4 = \frac{1}{16}$.

$$\frac{1}{4} > \frac{1}{16}$$

The quantity in Column A is greater.

3. B: Both equations are written in slope-intercept form. The coefficient of x is the slope. Column A has a slope of -1. For column B, the slope of a perpendicular line is the opposite reciprocal to the original line, so the slope of a line perpendicular to $y = -x - 2$ would be $+1$. The quantity in Column B is greater.

4. D: Four is greater than three, but the value of the variables is unknown.

If $a = 5$ and $b = 4$, then $3(5) = 15$ and $4(4) = 16$, making Column B greater.

If $a = 7$ and $b = 2$, then $3(7) = 21$ and $4(2) = 8$, making Column A greater.

The relationship cannot be determined from the information given.

5. B: When adding 5 points to each test, the mean, median, and modes will all increase by 5 points.

Mean $= 83$; Median $= 88$; Mode $= 85$

If John's new test score is 87, then it is one point below the median score. Therefore, the quantity in Column B is greater.

6. B: In this function, we are told that $x \nabla y = 3x - y$. Plug in 2 and 3 to solve.

$$2 \nabla 3 = 3(2) - 3 = 6 - 3 = 3$$
$$3 \nabla 2 = 3(3) - 2 = 8 - 2 = 6$$
$$6 > 3$$

Therefore, the quantity in Column B is greater.

7. C: Use the formula for percentages.

$$percent = \frac{part}{whole}$$
$$= \frac{42}{48}$$
$$= 0.875 = 87.5\%$$

8. B: To find the percentage of change, divide the amount of change by the original amount. For this problem, the amount of change is 50 inches − 41 inches = 9 inches of rain. Then divide the result by the original amount: $9 \div 41 = 0.219 = 22$ percent.

9. D: Factor the equation and set each factor equal to 0.

$$y = 16x^3 - 48x^2$$
$$16x^2(x - 3) = 0$$

$x = 0$ and $x = 3$

10. D: Identify the important parts of the circle.

$$r = 3$$

length of ACB = 5

Plug these values into the formula for the length of an arc and solve for θ.

$$s = \frac{\theta}{360°} \times 2\pi r$$

$$5 = \frac{\theta}{360} \times 2\pi(3)$$

$$\frac{5}{6\pi} = \frac{\theta}{360}$$

$$\theta = 95.5°$$

$$m\angle AOB = 95.5°$$

11. C: Use the formula for percent change.

$$\text{percent change} = \frac{\text{amount of change}}{\text{original amount}}$$

$$= \frac{(680 - 425)}{425}$$

$$= \frac{255}{425} = 0.60 = 60\%$$

12. B: There are 16 ounces in a pound, so the baby's starting weight is 120 ounces. He gained 6 ounces per month, or $6t$. So, the baby's weight will be his initial weight plus the amount gained for each month: $y = 6t + 120$.

Quantitative Reasoning 2 Answer Key

1. D: If x is equal to 0 or 1, the two quantities would be equal. If the value of x is between 0 and 1, then in most cases, the quantity in Column A is greater. There is not enough information, so the relationship cannot be determined from the information given.

2. D: The speeds are given, but the time spent driving is not given. The relationship cannot be determined from the information given.

3. D: Equiangular means the two triangles each have the same angle measurement. The triangles have the same angle measures and would therefore be similar; however, the length of the triangles is not given. The relationship cannot be determined from the information given.

4. B: In Column B, simplify the denominator by adding exponents.

$$1 + 4 + (-2) = 3$$

This gives $\frac{x^3}{x^3}$, which simplifies to 1. The quantity in Column B is greater.

5. B: The probability a station plays country music = 30%.

The probability it would not play country music = 70%.

The probability the station would not play two country songs in succession:

$$70\% \times 70\% \text{ or } 0.7 \times 0.7 = 0.49 \rightarrow 49\%$$

$$49\% < 50\%$$

The quantity in Column B is greater.

6. C: Regardless of the types of angles found within a triangle, the angles will always sum up to 180 degrees, so the two quantities are equal.

7. D: Assign variables and write the ratios as fractions. Then, cross multiply to solve for the number of apples and oranges sold.

$$x = apples$$

$$\frac{apples}{bananas} = \frac{3}{2} = \frac{x}{20}$$

$$60 = 2$$

$$x = 30 \text{ apples}$$

$$y = oranges$$

$$\frac{oranges}{bananas} = \frac{1}{2} = \frac{y}{20}$$

$$2y = 20$$

$$y = 10 \text{ oranges}$$

To find the total, add the number of apples, oranges, and bananas together: $30 + 20 + 10 = 60$ pieces of fruit.

8. B: Calculate the discriminant.

$$B^2 - 4AC = 2^2 - 4(1)(4) = -12$$

The discriminant is negative and $A \neq C$, so it is an ellipse.

9. B: Add the base amount and the tax on the extra percentage of the person's income.

$$10{,}620 + 0.2(80{,}000 - 75{,}000) = \$11{,}620$$

10. D: Set up an equation. The original price (p) minus 30% of the original price is $385.

$$p - 0.3p = 385$$

$$p = \frac{385}{0.7} = \$550$$

11. D: Simplify using PEMDAS.

$$5^2 \times (-5)^{-2} - 5^{-1}$$
$$= 25 \times \frac{1}{25} - \frac{1}{5}$$
$$= 1 - \frac{1}{5}$$
$$= \frac{4}{5}$$

12. A: Find the total amount of fencing needed and then convert it to yards (1 yard = 3 feet). If the yard is 20 feet by 40 feet square, then add the length of the 4 sides: $20 + 40 + 20 + 40 = 120$ feet of fencing. Divide this total by 3 to convert to yards: $120 \div 3 = 40$ yards. The fencing costs \$8.42 per yard, so the total needed is $\$8.42 \times 40 = \$336.80$.

13. C: Noah's income is calculated by adding his base pay plus his overtime pay. His base pay is $35h$, and his overtime pay is $6t$. Thus, the equation needed for this problem is $x = 35h + 6t$.

14. D: Substitute one (x, y) pair into each answer choice to find the correct equation.

A)
$$y = 6x - 6; \ (3, 3)$$
$$y = 6(3) - 6$$
$$y = 18 - 6$$
$$y = 12 \neq 3$$

B)
$$y = 5x - 6; \ (3, 3)$$
$$y = 5(3) - 6$$
$$y = 15 - 6$$
$$y = 9 \neq 3$$

C)
$$y = 4x - 6; \ (3, 3)$$
$$y = 4(3) - 6$$
$$y = 12 - 6$$
$$y = 6 \neq 3$$

D)
$$y = 3x - 6; \ (3, 3)$$
$$y = 3(3) - 6$$
$$y = 9 - 6$$
$$y = 3$$

15. C: The ratio of solute to solution is 1:5. Write a proportion and solve.

$$\frac{1}{5} = \frac{x}{90}$$
$$1(90) = x(5)$$
$$18 = x$$

Verbal Reasoning 1 Answer Key

1. D: *Nonchalant* means to be without a care in the world and is the best response. The context clue "he didn't care about them" tells us that he is nonchalant.

2. A: *Benevolent* means kind, so the context clue "kindness" in the second part of the sentence directs us to this answer. *Tyrannical* means oppressive or cruel and is the opposite of kind. *Laudable* means credible, and *pugnacious* means eager to fight.

3. C: *Maliciously* means "unkindly" or "cruelly." Since the children teased the boy so much that he cried and left the party, the teasing must have been extremely unkind or cruel. *Furiously* means "angrily," while *benevolently* and *innocently* act as antonyms.

4. B, E, I: Using a variety of sugar, water, food-safe colors, flavorings, and other natural ingredients, confectioners can create delicious candy treats that appeal to both young and old alike. Even though the ingredients are often similar among the recipes, the measurements, cooking techniques, temperature, and equipment vary. These differences result in vastly distinct, unique products. Professional candy makers utilize a variety of techniques and equipment to develop and produce the candy we know and love—everything from chocolate to fudge, lollipops to caramel, marshmallow to toffee.

5. E (erratic); F (capricious): The key phrase in this sentence is "constantly returned," which indicates a recurring issue. Since things (or, in this case, animals) are returned if they do not work correctly, it is implied that the dog has some sort of problem. Answer option C can be eliminated immediately since the word *whimsical* indicates something fun or amusing. The terms *erratic* and *capricious* both have negative connotations and therefore work best in this sentence.

6. B (verify); E (corroborate): The two key components of this sentence are the words *victim* and *defendant*, which are opposites. Therefore, if the victim has new information that is harmful for the defendant, the correct terms to complete the sentence would be those that imply that the new evidence aligns with the victim's version of events. The best answer options are therefore B and E.

7. A: The author writes that "there's another class of symbiosis that is controversial among scientists" and goes on to say that "many scientists claim the relationships currently described as commensal are just mutualistic or parasitic in ways that haven't been discovered yet." This implies that scientists debate about the topic of commensalism.

8. B: The author writes that "as these communities have evolved, the species in them have developed complex, long-term interspecies interactions known as symbiotic relationships." She then goes on to describe the different types of symbiotic relationships that exist.

9. D: The author writes, "Often, relationships described as commensal include one species that feeds on another species' leftovers; remoras, for instance, will attach themselves to sharks and eat the food particles they leave behind. It might seem like the shark gets nothing from the relationship, but a closer look will show that sharks in fact benefit from remoras, which clean the sharks' skin and remove parasites."

10. C: The author writes, "A relationship where one individual benefits and the other is harmed is known as parasitism."

11. A: The author writes, "But is it possible for two species to interact and for one to remain completely unaffected?..."In fact, many scientists claim that relationships currently described as commensal are just mutualistic or parasitic in ways that haven't been discovered yet."

12. D: The author writes, "The bacteria, fungi, insects, plants, and animals that live together in a habitat have evolved to share a pool of limited resources...As these communities have evolved, the species in them have developed complex, long-term interspecies interactions known as symbiotic relationships."

Verbal Reasoning 2 Answer Key

1. B: A hypocrite is someone who does the opposite of what he or she says.

2. D: The plant is robust: it is sturdy and strong.

3. D: *Assuaged* means "diminished," "alleviated," or "eased." *Dreadful* means "awful" or "horrible."

4. A: *Trite* means "commonplace" or "unoriginal," and *lackluster* means "boring" or "uninteresting."

5. B, F, G: The crew, ten of the best and brightest astronauts from NASA, stared at the sparkling orbs of light that emanated from the surrounding stars. Eagerly awaiting an announcement from the captain in the cockpit about their impending arrival on the alien planet, the astronauts each thought back to the days leading up to the spacecraft's launch and what led them to this once-in-a-lifetime opportunity.

6. B (rigorous); E (arduous): The key clue in the second part of the sentence is, "many do not pass the first time around." This sentence reveals that the tests must not be easy. The best answer choices are therefore B (*rigorous*) and E (*arduous*). While the tests may be *tedious* and even *painful*, these answer options are not ideal. The tests are not *effortless*, and they are definitely not *facile*, both of which are antonyms of the words *rigorous* and *arduous*.

7. A (enthusiasm); D (alacrity): The key words here are *surprisingly*, which indicates a shift from what is expected and *excitedly*, which indicates the mood of the students. The words *apathy*, *disinclination*, and *indifference* are antonyms and can therefore be eliminated. A close answer might be the word *happiness*, but the two best answers are *enthusiasm* and *alacrity*.

8. A: The author writes, "Lü Pu-wei came with his protégé to Ch'in, where he became his Prime Minister, and after the prince's death in 247 BC Lü Pu-wei became the regent for his young son Shih Huang-ti (then called Cheng). For the first time in Chinese history a merchant, a commoner, had reached one of the highest positions in the state."

9. C: The author writes, "The state of Ch'in had never been so closely associated with the feudal communities of the rest of China as the other feudal states. A great part of its population, including the ruling class, was not purely Chinese but contained an admixture of Turks and Tibetans. The other Chinese even called Ch'in a "barbarian state", and the foreign influence was, indeed, unceasing. This was a favourable soil for the overcoming of feudalism."

10. D: The author writes that "About 250 BC, Ch'in was not only one of the economically strongest among the feudal states, but had already made an end of its own feudal system." This implies that Ch'in was ahead of the rest of China in its economic development.

11. A: The author writes, "When Chinese lords of the preceding period…made wars, they tended to put the newly-conquered areas not into the hands of newly-enfeoffed noblemen, but to keep them as their property and to put their administration into the hands of efficient servants; these were the first bureaucratic officials."

12. B: The author writes, "About 250 BC, Ch'in was not only one of the economically strongest among the feudal states, but had already made an end of its own feudal system."

13. C: The author writes, "When Chinese lords of the preceding period…made wars, they tended to put the newly-conquered areas not into the hands of newly-enfeoffed noblemen, but to keep them as their property and to put their administration into the hands of efficient servants; these were the first bureaucratic officials."

14. B: The author indicates that rapid growth of the trade economy was a result of "strong relations with eastern Turkestan," population growth due to immigration, "new irrigation systems," and roads.

15. D: The author writes that "Lü Pu-wei came with his protege to Ch'in, where he became his Prime Minister, and after the prince's death in 247 BC Lü Pu-wei became the regent for his young son Shih Huang-ti (then called Cheng). For the first time in Chinese history a merchant, a commoner, had reached one of the highest positions in the state."

GRE Practice Test #2

Analytical Writing

1 prompt, 30 minutes

Analyze an Issue

Schools and students are embracing technology in service of learning, thanks to modern 1:1 schools (schools that provide computers to all students). However, studies have shown that students who use computers to take notes are distracted and retain less information than those who write their notes by hand. Is technology in the classroom helpful or a distraction?

In your essay, introduce the subject and then either explain the subject you have chosen or take a position about the subject and support that position. At least two evaluators will read and score your essay. Be sure to define your purpose, provide a clear introduction and thesis statement, organize ideas effectively, provide support for your argument, and adhere to Standard English.

Quantitative Reasoning 1

12 questions, 21 minutes

1. A conical cup and a cylindrical cup have the same diameter and height.

Quantity A	Quantity B
the amount of water held in the conical cup	the amount of water held in the cylindrical cup

- A) Quantity A is greater.
- B) Quantity B is greater.
- C) The two quantities are equal.
- D) The relationship cannot be determined from the information given.

2.

Quantity A	Quantity B
the number of unique ways we can arrange the letters in the word *MATH*	the number of unique ways we can arrange the letters in the word *FIRE*

- A) Quantity A is greater.
- B) Quantity B is greater.
- C) The two quantities are equal.
- D) The relationship cannot be determined from the information given.

3. In politics, a state's representation in the House of Representatives is determined by its population, and its representation in the Senate is equal to 2, same as all the other states.

Quantity A	Quantity B
the number of representatives for state X	the number of senators for state X

A) Quantity A is greater.
B) Quantity B is greater.
C) The two quantities are equal.
D) The relationship cannot be determined from the information given.

4.

Quantity A	Quantity B
the number of even prime numbers between 1 and 1,000	the number of odd prime numbers between 1 and 1,000

A) Quantity A is greater.
B) Quantity B is greater.
C) The two quantities are equal.
D) The relationship cannot be determined from the information given.

5. Consider the function $f(x) = 3|x| - 2$

Quantity A	Quantity B
$f(-2)$	$f(0)$

A) Quantity A is greater.
B) Quantity B is greater.
C) The two quantities are equal.
D) The relationship cannot be determined from the information given.

6.

Quantity A	Quantity B
the number of solutions to $|4x - 3| < 6$	the number of solutions to $|4x - 3| \leq 6$

A) Quantity A is greater.
B) Quantity B is greater.
C) The two quantities are equal.
D) The relationship cannot be determined from the information given.

7. What is the value of z in the following system?

$$z - 2x = 14$$
$$2z - 6x = 18$$

A) -7
B) 3
C) 5
D) 24

8. Michael is getting a 7.5 percent raise at work. If he earned $4,280 per month before his raise, what is his new annual salary, to the nearest dollar?
   A) $51,360
   B) $55,212
   C) $52,280
   D) $53,970

9. Which expression is equivalent to $6x + 5 \geq -15 + 8x$?
   A) $x \leq -5$
   B) $x = -5$
   C) $x \leq 10$
   D) $x \geq 10$

10. A theater has 180 rows of seats. The first row has 10 seats. Each row has 4 seats more than the row in front of it. How many seats are in the entire theater?
    A) 18,000
    B) 36,200
    C) 42,500
    D) 66,240

11. What is the equation of the following line?

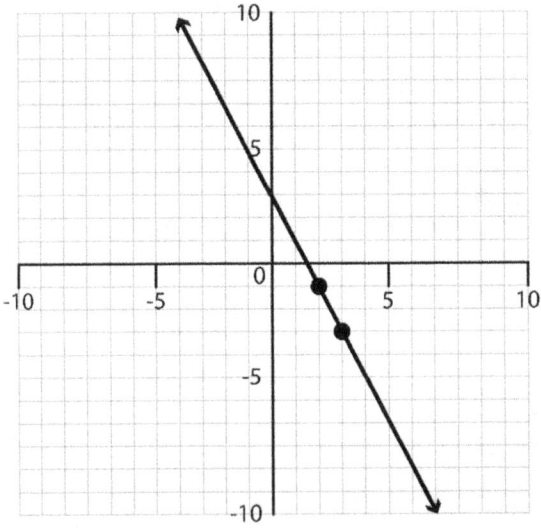

   A) $y = 3x - 2$
   B) $y = -3x + 2$
   C) $y = 2x - 3$
   D) $y = -2x + 3$

12. Which of the following graphs reflects the inequality: $3x + 6y \leq 12$?

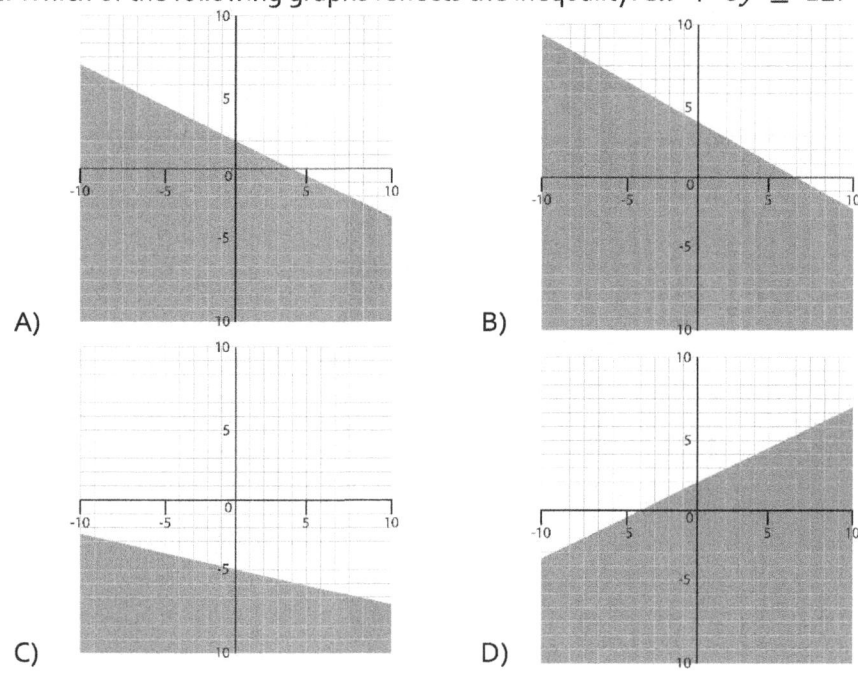

A)

B)

C)

D)

Quantitative Reasoning 2

15 questions, 26 minutes

1.

Quantity A	Quantity B
the number of sides in a trapezoid	the number of sides in a normal kite

A) Quantity A is greater.
B) Quantity B is greater.
C) The two quantities are equal.
D) The relationship cannot be determined from the information given.

2. Most pizzerias determine the sizes of their pizzas by their diameters.

Quantity A	Quantity B
one 16-inch pizza	three 8-inch pizzas

A) Quantity A is greater.
B) Quantity B is greater.
C) The two quantities are equal.
D) The relationship cannot be determined from the information given.

3.

Quantity A	Quantity B
0	$\dfrac{x^5}{x \times x^6 \times x^{-2}}$ if x does not equal 0

- A) Quantity A is greater.
- B) Quantity B is greater.
- C) The two quantities are equal.
- D) The relationship cannot be determined from the information given.

4.

Quantity A	Quantity B
the slope of the line parallel to $y = -x - 3$	the slope of the line perpendicular to $y = -x - 3$

- A) Quantity A is greater.
- B) Quantity B is greater.
- C) The two quantities are equal.
- D) The relationship cannot be determined from the information given.

5. George drives for 3 hours, and Bill drives for 4 hours.

Quantity A	Quantity B
the distance driven by George	the distance driven by Bill

- A) Quantity A is greater.
- B) Quantity B is greater.
- C) The two quantities are equal.
- D) The relationship cannot be determined from the information given.

6. George has $7.24 in coins.

Quantity A	Quantity B
the number of pennies George has	the number of quarters George has

- A) Quantity A is greater.
- B) Quantity B is greater.
- C) The two quantities are equal.
- D) The relationship cannot be determined from the information given.

7. What are the values of a for which $\dfrac{1}{(a-1)} = \dfrac{1}{6} + \dfrac{1}{a}$?
- A) $a = 3$ only
- B) $a = -2$ only
- C) $a = -2$ and $a = 3$
- D) $a = 1$ and $a = 3$

8. A marinade recipe includes 2 tablespoons of lemon juice for $\frac{1}{4}$ cup of olive oil. How many tablespoons of lemon juice would be used with $\frac{2}{3}$ cup olive oil?
   A) $\frac{3}{4}$
   B) $2\frac{1}{3}$
   C) 4
   D) $5\frac{1}{3}$

9. Alex is buying concert tickets for a group of friends. The concert tickets cost $26 each, and he needs to buy tickets for Marsha, Jason, Alejandro, Theresa, Allen, Joanne, and Frederick. Which algebraic property can help him determine how much money he needs to collect from his friends?
   A) Commutative property
   B) Distributive property
   C) Associative property
   D) Identity property

10. Mason is counting the coins that he has saved up in his savings jar to see if he has enough money to buy a concert ticket. He currently has $143.71. He has 325 quarters, 280 dimes, x amount of nickels, and 196 pennies. How many nickels does he have?
    A) 300
    B) 1,300
    C) 325
    D) 650

11. Solve the system of equations for y: $5x + 4y = 20; x = 2y + 1$
    A) $y = \frac{2}{5}$
    B) $y = \frac{4}{5}$
    C) $y = \frac{15}{14}$
    D) $y = \frac{5}{4}$

12. In a theater, there are 4,500 lower-level seats and 2,000 upper-level seats. What is the ratio of lower-level seats to total seats?
    A) $\frac{4}{9}$
    B) $\frac{4}{13}$
    C) $\frac{9}{13}$
    D) $\frac{9}{4}$

13. In parallelogram $ABCD$, the measure of angle m is $m° = 260°$. What is the measure of $n°$?

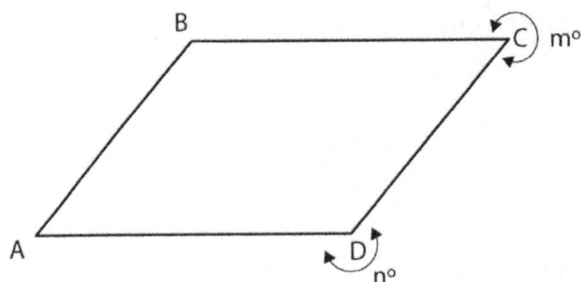

- A) 100°
- B) 180°
- C) 200°
- D) 280°

14. Missy is making her famous strawberry lemonade for the school picnic. She needs 6 gallons of lemonade. Her recipe calls for 2 cans of lemon juice concentrate (8 ounces each) and 16 strawberries for every 2 gallons. The grocery store is out of the 8-ounce cans of juice, so she had to buy 12-ounce cans instead. How many of the 12-ounce cans will Missy need?
- A) 4 cans
- B) 2 cans
- C) 8 cans
- D) 6 cans

15. Noah and Jennifer have a total of $10.00 to spend on lunch. If each buy an order of french fries and a soda, how many orders of chicken strips can they share?

MENU	
Item	Price
Hamburger	$4.00
Chicken Strips	$4.00
Onion Rings	$3.00
French Fries	$2.00
Soda	$1.00
Shake	$1.00

- A) 0
- B) 1
- C) 2
- D) 3

Verbal Reasoning 1

12 questions, 18 minutes

1. The lightning bugs gave off an _____ glow in the evening.
    A) angry
    B) energetic
    C) overwhelming
    D) iridescent

2. Because of the babysitter's reputation for being _____, kids from the neighborhood begged their parents to find someone new to watch them; they didn't want to _____ over their bedtime.
    A) mischievous... debate
    B) intellectual... diverge
    C) stoic... clash
    D) argumentative... squabble

3. After the mountain bike accident, we tried to _____ the bicycle, but we soon realized it was _____ because it would cost more to repair it than it would to buy a new one.
    A) fix... viable
    B) save... easy
    C) salvage... impractical
    D) abandon... effortless

Select from the answer options that correspond to the blank sentences in each paragraph. One answer must be selected for each blank. The answer must complete the idea being expressed in the text.

4. Sleep deprivation, especially on a long-term basis, has terrible (i)_____. From poor academic performance to fatal car crashes, sleep deprivation is just bad for you. Depression is also an effect of sleep deprivation. Lack of sleep is often (ii)____ with (iii)_____ and overeating, making a perfectly healthy person overweight.

Question 4 Answer Options		
Blank (i)	**Blank (ii)**	**Blank (iii)**
(A) issues	(D) compensated	(G) overstimulation
(B) consequences	(E) overproduced	(H) over exaggeration
(C) actions	(F) provided	(I) under

Select TWO options that best match the meaning of the sentence. When added to the sentence, the two answers must create complete sentences that have the same meaning.

5. When the historians uncovered the intact treasure, they realized how ____ they were—dating back to the 1300s.
    A) enduring
    B) obliterated
    C) extinct
    D) destroyed
    E) defunct
    F) extant

6. Because most of the children liked to play in the mud, their parents found it difficult to keep their clothes ____.
    A) slovenly
    B) carefree
    C) fastidious
    D) meticulous
    E) contemptuous
    F) punctilious

7. Because the mother was on the phone, she shouted at her ____ children to be quiet.
    A) loquacious
    B) garrulous
    C) taciturn
    D) reticent
    E) articulate
    F) epicurean

Use the passage to answer the questions that follow.

I have often heard people wonder what Shakespeare would say, could he see Mr. Irving's production of his *Much Ado About Nothing,* or Mr. Wilson Barrett's setting of his *Hamlet.* Would he take pleasure in the glory of the scenery and the marvel of the colour? Would he be interested in the Cathedral of Messina, and the battlements of Elsinore? Or would he be indifferent, and say the play, and the play only, is the thing?

Speculations like these are always pleasurable, and in the present case happen to be profitable also. For it is not difficult to see what Shakespeare's attitude would be; not difficult, that is to say, if one reads Shakespeare himself, instead of reading merely what is written about him.

Speaking, for instance, directly, as the manager of a London theatre, through the lips of the chorus in *Henry V,* he complains of the smallness of the stage on which he has to produce the pageant of a big historical play, and of the want of scenery which obliges him to cut out many of its most picturesque incidents, apologises for the scanty number of supers who had to play the soldiers, and for the shabbiness of the properties, and, finally, expresses his regret at being unable to bring on real horses.

In *A Midsummer Night's Dream*, again, he gives us a most amusing picture of the straits to which theatrical managers of his day were reduced by the want of proper scenery. In fact, it is impossible to read him without seeing that he is constantly protesting against the two special limitations of the Elizabethan stage—the lack of suitable scenery, and the fashion of men playing women's parts, just as he protests against other difficulties with which managers of theatres have still to contend, such as actors who do not understand their words; actors who miss their cues; actors who overact their parts; actors who mouth; actors who gag; actors who play to the gallery, and amateur actors.

And, indeed, a great dramatist, as he was, could not but have felt very much hampered at being obliged continually to interrupt the progress of a play in order to send on someone to explain to the audience that the scene was to be changed to a particular place on the entrance of a particular character, and after his exit to somewhere else; that the stage was to represent the deck of a ship in a storm, or the interior of a Greek temple, or the streets of a certain town, to all of which inartistic devices Shakespeare is reduced, and for which he always amply apologizes. Besides this clumsy method, Shakespeare had two other substitutes for scenery—the hanging out of a placard, and his descriptions. The first of these could hardly have satisfied his passion for picturesqueness and his feeling for beauty, and certainly did not satisfy the dramatic critic of his day. But as regards the description, to those of us who look on Shakespeare not merely as a playwright but as a poet, and who enjoy reading him at home just as much as we enjoy seeing him acted, it may be a matter of congratulation that he had not at his command such skilled machinists as are in use now at the Princess's and at the Lyceum. For had Cleopatra's barge, for instance, been a structure of canvas and Dutch metal, it would probably have been painted over or broken up after the withdrawal of the piece, and, even had it survived to our own day, would, I am afraid, have become extremely shabby by this time. Whereas now the beaten gold of its poop is still bright, and the purple of its sails still beautiful; its silver oars are not tired of keeping time to the music of the flutes they follow, nor the Nereid's flower-soft hands of touching its silken tackle; the mermaid still lies at its helm, and still on its deck stand the boys with their coloured fans. Yet lovely as all Shakespeare's descriptive passages are, a description is in its essence undramatic. Theatrical audiences are far more impressed by what they look at than by what they listen to; and the modern dramatist, in having the surroundings of his play visibly presented to the audience when the curtain rises, enjoys an advantage for which Shakespeare often expresses his desire. It is true that Shakespeare's descriptions are not what descriptions are in modern plays—accounts of what the audience can observe for themselves; they are the imaginative method by which he creates in the mind of the spectators the image of that which he desires them to see. Still, the quality of the drama is action. It is always dangerous to pause for picturesqueness. And the introduction of self-explanatory scenery enables the modern method to be far more direct, while the loveliness of form and colour which it gives us, seems to me often to create an artistic temperament in the audience, and to produce that joy in beauty for beauty's sake, without which the great masterpieces of art can never be understood, to which, and to which only, are they ever revealed.

Excerpt from "Shakespeare on Scenery" by Oscar Wilde

8. Which of the following is a reasonable inference about Elizabethan theater based on paragraph four?
    A) There were no professional actors.
    B) The setting and costumes were not helpful in creating a believable environment.
    C) Female actors were not skillful enough to play major parts.
    D) Playwrights couldn't afford fancy sets because they had to finance the plays themselves.
    E) Theatrical managers were well respected during the time of Elizabethan theater.

9. According to the author's argument, which of the following is true about Shakespeare's plays?
    A) They required elaborate sets to create the appropriate mood for the audience.
    B) They frequently criticized the scenery used by other playwrights.
    C) They lacked enough parts for female actors.
    D) They frequently included complaints about inadequate scenery, actors, or other issues.
    E) Their reliance on descriptions makes them more straightforward and accessible to the audience.

10. Which of the following best summarizes the main problems the author sees for Shakespeare's scenery?
    A) Actors were not always adept at delivering Shakespeare's descriptive lines, and stages were too small to support large sets.
    B) Available materials and artistry did not allow for elaborate sets, and too much description in a play could slow down the action.
    C) Theater-goers did not appreciate elaborate sets, and actors were not willing to help construct them.
    D) Descriptions of scenery were not sufficient for audiences to understand the plays, and theater patrons refused to pay for elaborate sets.
    E) Shakespeare's descriptions were too complicated for set artists to understand and follow.

11. The main idea of the first two paragraphs is best summarized by which of the following statements?
    A) Directors of Shakespearean plays often wonder what Shakespeare might think about a specific version of one of his plays.
    B) Shakespearean plays produced today often look extremely different from those produced in Shakespeare's own time.
    C) Shakespeare's own plays deliver plenty of clues as to how important scenery was to him as a playwright.
    D) Most critics of Shakespeare's plays have not actually read the plays, only what others say about them.
    E) Directors of Shakespearean plays are concerning themselves with the wrong things.

12. Which of the following best describes the two issues addressed by the author?
    A) The Elizabethan theater faced many difficulties in creating scenery, and Shakespeare could address these either with placards or through spoken imagery.
    B) Actors in the Elizabethan period faced many issues, and Shakespeare addressed these by complaining about their acting in interviews.
    C) Elizabethan playwrights faced many rules about what they could write, and Shakespeare addressed this by inserting metaphorical complaints about the rules.
    D) Women in the Elizabethan period were not allowed to act, and Shakespeare addressed this by assigning women's roles to men.
    E) The Elizabethan theater faced many issues, including difficulties in creating scenery and trend of female characters being played by men.

Verbal Reasoning 2

15 questions, 23 minutes

1. The soldiers made a _____ effort throughout the war; their courage and bravery should be rewarded.
    A) diligent
    B) steadfast
    C) valiant
    D) mild

2. The lively, _____ students were wide awake at the beginning of the day. After lunch, however, they became lifeless.
   A) animated
   B) studious
   C) disappointed
   D) bewildered

3. The principal _____ the students who were sent to his office for punishment.
   A) stirred
   B) energized
   C) admonished
   D) condescended

4. The _____ server made the patrons feel welcomed and at home in the restaurant.
   A) spiteful
   B) incompatible
   C) consistent
   D) amiable

Select from the answer options that correspond to the blank sentences in each paragraph. One answer must be selected for each blank. The answer must complete the idea being expressed in the text.

5. He took up a second letter which had (i)_____ unnoticed upon the table while he had been absorbed with the first. This he began to read with a smile of amusement upon his face which gradually (ii)_____ away into an expression of intense interest and concentration. When he had finished he sat for some little time lost in thought with the letter (iii)_____ from his fingers.

Question 5 Answer Options		
Blank (i)	Blank (ii)	Blank (iii)
(A) sat	(D) faded	(G) falling
(B) lain	(E) morphed	(H) dangling
(C) gone	(F) moved	(I) drifting

Select TWO options that best match the meaning of the sentence. When added to the sentence, the two answers must create complete sentences that have the same meaning.

6. Her ____ for running a marathon kept her training even during the pouring rain.
   A) zeal
   B) devotion
   C) trepidation
   D) facility
   E) apathy
   F) lethargy

7. I often _____ when choosing between eating dinner at Italian or Greek restaurants on Friday nights, so my friend must often choose for me.
   A) waffle
   B) decide
   C) settle
   D) vacillate
   E) opt
   F) dodge

8. In the past, certain cultures _____ their elders more than in modern times; older people felt respected.
   A) disesteemed
   B) desecrated
   C) despised
   D) idolized
   E) venerated
   F) abhorred

Use the passages to answer the questions that follow.

In the late 1970s, scientists in the deep-sea bathyscaphe, known as *Trieste II*, discovered something new on the ocean floor: the skeleton of a gray whale. They collected a few bones and brought the vessel back to the surface where they found many small organisms living within the remains. This discovery became known as a *whale fall*, a place on the ocean floor where decomposing whale bodies spawn entire ecosystems. Whale falls can last for a hundred years and attract animals such as giant squids, clams, sharks, and sea cucumbers.

For something discovered within the past 50 years, whale falls are thought to be very common. More than half a million whale carcasses are thought to be in some stage of decomposition at any given time. The cold water of the deep sea, coupled with whales being slightly denser than the surrounding water, allow these havens to exist in the harsh ocean floor conditions.

9. Based on the information provided in the passage, which of the following people would be LEAST helpful on board a bathyscaphe?
   A) A captain
   B) A mechanic
   C) A marine biologist
   D) A submarine pilot
   E) A free-diving specialist

10. Which of the following best describes this passage?
    A) Narrative
    B) Informational
    C) Persuasive
    D) Contemplative
    E) Expository

11. Which of the following best summarizes this passage?
    A) The Trieste II was an important invention in the late 1970s.
    B) Whale falls are very common and attract many animals.
    C) Whale falls are ecosystems built on and surrounding the decomposing carcass of a whale.
    D) The ocean floor is a harsh environment where not many things live.
    E) On deep ocean dives, it is vital to bring back samples of any strange phenomena.

In his treatise on politics, Aristotle wrote, "Man is by nature a social animal; an individual who is unsocial naturally and not accidentally is either beneath our notice or more than human. Society is something in nature that precedes the individual. Anyone who either cannot lead the common life or is so self-sufficient as not to need to, and therefore does not partake of society, is either a beast or a god." For centuries, philosophers have been examining the relationship between man and his social world. It is no wonder, then, that a field of study has arisen to examine just that; the field is referred to as social psychology.

Social psychologists have been studying the effect of societal influences on human behavior for decades, and a number of fascinating findings have been the result. Together, these discoveries have shed light on one clear truth—that human behavior cannot be understood **in a vacuum**; that is, our daily behaviors are inextricably linked with the social context in which they occur.

Why is this important? According to social psychologist Eliot Aronson, it's important because it helps us to understand that the behaviors we witness in others may be as much a result of social influence as they are of the individual's disposition. For example, if you have ever been cut off in the middle of bad city traffic, you may have immediately assumed that the offender was inconsiderate or incompetent. While this may be true, it may be equally likely that the person is dealing with an emergency situation or that they simply did not see you. According to Aronson, this tendency to attribute behaviors, especially negative behaviors, to disposition is risky and can ultimately be detrimental to us and to the other person.

Take, for example, Philip Zimbardo's famous prison experiment, conducted at Stanford University in 1971. At the beginning of the experiment, the participants, all healthy, stable, intelligent male Stanford University students, were classified as either guards or prisoners and told they would be acting their parts in a simulated prison environment for two weeks. However, after just six days, Zimbardo had to terminate the experiment because of the extreme behaviors he was witnessing in both groups: prisoners had become entirely submissive to and resentful of the guards, while the guards had become cruel and **unrelenting** in their treatment of the prisoners. The otherwise healthy, well-adjusted students had experienced dramatic transformations as a result of their assigned roles. Zimbardo's conclusion? Even giving individuals temporary power over others was enough to completely alter the way they viewed and behaved toward each other; indeed, the behaviors he witnessed in each of the groups were not a result of the dispositions of the participants but of the situation in which they had been placed.

Today, social psychologists study the effect of social influence on a number of different behaviors: conformity, obedience, aggression, prejudice, and even attraction and love. The insights these researchers have gained have laid the foundation for further examination of human social behavior and, ultimately, for a refined approach to legal and social policy.

The following passage provides an overview of the purpose and applications of social psychology. Information was drawn from Dr. Elliot Aronson's acclaimed book *The Social Animal*.

12. As used in the passage, the phrase "in a vacuum" most nearly means
    A) without evidence of intention.
    B) in conjunction with other behaviors.
    C) without consideration of the individual's needs.
    D) in isolation.
    E) within its social context.

13. The author indicates that making assumptions about people based on isolated actions is
    A) a prudent way to draw conclusions about one's social world.
    B) recommended when no other information is available.
    C) the most accurate way to assess various personality strengths.
    D) unwise and potentially harmful to all involved.
    E) one of many valid ways to get to know someone new.

14. The author most likely includes the description of the Stanford students in order to
    A) provide a contrast between their normal dispositions and the behavior they displayed during the experiment.
    B) engage the reader through characterization.
    C) illustrate the importance of quality education.
    D) shed light on the characteristics that made them susceptible to social influence.
    E) cast doubt on their fitness for the challenges of college life.

15. The author most likely includes the example of the Stanford Prison Experiment in order to
    A) encourage the reader to participate in social psychology studies.
    B) challenge the reader to question how he or she would behave in the same situation.
    C) illustrate the extent to which social context can influence behavior.
    D) undermine the reader's assumption that the quality of one's education can influence his or her behavior.
    E) cast doubt on the value of an Ivy League education.

GRE Practice Test #2 Answer Key

Analyze an Issue: Sample Essay

Imagine you are a student in a modern high school: At the beginning of your day, you check your phone to remember what assignments are due; you text a friend with a question about the algebra homework; and then you head to school, where you cycle through classes that include using the internet to research local water-use rates versus national, plot points on a graph, create a group presentation using sharing programs, and record all your notes and homework in a digital file. You email teachers and chat with friends, and your phone helps you get text reminders about homework from teachers.

All these actions are possible due to the advent of 1:1 technology in many classrooms, which allows students and teachers to stay connected to the wider world and do many new and exciting things that were not possible before computers became broadly used and available. Putting technology in the classroom gives opportunities to all students, even those who might not be able to afford that technology at home. It provides the chance to learn vital skills for a future job.

Technology in the classroom also prepares students for emergencies and offers flexibility to students, teachers, and families. In 2020, the Covid-19 pandemic forced many schools to begin remote learning. Being familiar with technology enabled many students to continue their education from home, using computers, the internet, and remote interaction.

Schools should embrace technology in the classroom and use every opportunity to inject new learning technology into student work. Student creativity will shine, and students will be well prepared for their futures.

Quantitative Reasoning 1 Answer Key

1. B: The volume of the cylinder is $V = \pi r^2 h$, and the volume of the cone is $V = \frac{1}{3}\pi r^2 h$. If the cone and the cylinder have the same diameter, they also have the same radius. We are told they have the same height, so the cone would hold $\frac{1}{3}$ of the amount of water held in the cylinder, so quantity B is greater.

2. C: Both the words MATH and FIRE have 4 letters, with no letters repeating. In each word, there are 4 slots for the first letter, and then 3 slots for the second letter, and then 2 slots for the third letter, and 1 slot for the last letter. This is mathematically expressed as: $4 \times 3 \times 2 \times 1 = 24$ ways for both words; therefore, the two quantities are equal.

3. D: It is impossible to know the number of representatives for a state without knowing its population size. While all states have an equal number of senators (2), some states have 1 or more representatives, depending on their population sizes. The relationship cannot be determined from the information given.

4. B: A prime number is a number divisible only by 1 and itself. Since all even numbers greater than 2 are divisible by 2, there is only one even prime number, which is 2. On the other hand, there are many odd prime numbers between 1 and 1,000 (167 to be exact), so quantity B is greater.

5. A: To determine the outputs, first plug in -2 for x:
$$f(-2) = 3|-2| - 2$$
$$= 3 \times 2 - 2 = 4$$
$$\text{so } f(-2) = 4$$

Then, plug in 0 for x:
$$f(0) = 3|0| - 2$$
$$= 0 - 2 = -2$$
$$\text{so } f(0) = -2$$

Since $4 > -2$, quantity A is greater.

6. B: Although both absolute value inequalities are similar in appearance, the one in quantity B includes *less than or equal to*, while in quantity A it is just *less than*, so there are two additional solutions in quantity B. Therefore, quantity B is greater.

7. D: Solve the system using substitution.
$$z - 2x = 14 \to z = 2x + 14$$
$$2z - 6x = 18$$
$$2(2x + 14) - 6x = 18$$
$$4x + 28 - 6x = 18$$
$$-2x = -10$$
$$x = 5$$
$$z - 2(5) = 14$$
$$z = 24$$

8. B: To find Michael's new monthly pay rate, multiply his monthly income times the percentage of raise: $\$4,280 \times 0.075 = \$321$ per month, which makes his new monthly income $\$4,280 + \$321 = \$4,601$. To find the annual salary, multiply the monthly income by 12 months: $\$4,601 \times 12 = \$55,212$.

9. C: Isolate the variable on the left side of the inequality. Reverse the direction of the inequality when dividing by a negative number.
$$6x + 5 \geq -15 + 8x$$
$$-2x + 5 \geq -15$$
$$-2x \geq -20$$
$$x \leq 10$$

10. D: Use the formula for the sum of an arithmetic series.
$$S_n = \frac{n}{2}(a_1 + a_n)$$
$$= \frac{n}{2}[2a_1 + (n-1)d]$$
$$= \frac{180}{2}[2(10) + (180-1)4] = 66,240 \text{ seats}$$

11. D: The *y*-intercept can be identified on the graph as $(0, 3)$, so $b = 3$. To find the slope, choose any two points and plug the values into the slope equation. The two points chosen here are $(2, -1)$ and $(3, -3)$:

$$m = \frac{(-3) - (-1)}{3 - 2} = \frac{-2}{1} = -2$$

Replace *m* with -2 and *b* with 3 in $y = mx + b$.

$$y = -2x + 3$$

12. A: The *x*- and *y*-intercepts are $(4, 0)$ and $(0, 2)$. Because of the inequality, the graph must be shaded below the line, making answer option A correct.

$$3x + 6y \leq 12$$
$$3(0) + 6y = 12$$
$$y = 2$$

y-intercept: $(0, 2)$

$$3x + 6(0) \leq 12$$
$$x = 4$$

x-intercept: $(4, 0)$

Quantitative Reasoning 2 Answer Key

1. C: Review the number of sides in a trapezoid and a kite. A trapezoid and a kite are both quadrilaterals, which have 4 sides, so the two quantities are equal.

2. A: Find the area of the pizza in quantity A. A 16-inch pizza has a radius of 8 inches. Use the formula for area of a circle: $A = \pi r^2$

$$A = 8^2 \pi$$
$$A = 64\pi$$

Find the area of the pizzas in quantity B. An 8-inch pizza has a radius of 4 inches.

$$A = 4^2 \pi$$
$$A = 16\pi$$

Add the areas of the three pizzas:

$$16\pi + 16\pi + 16\pi = 48\pi$$

$64\pi > 48\pi$, so quantity A is greater.

3. B: Simplify the denominator in Quantity B: $x \times x^6 \times x^{-2}$

First, add the exponents:

$$1 + 6 + (-2) = 5$$

Simplifying the fraction gives:

$$\frac{x^5}{x^5} = 1$$

Since 1 > 0, quantity B is greater.

4. B: Both equations are written in slope-intercept form, and we know that the coefficient in front of *x* is the slope. For both quantities A and B, the slope is –1. For quantity A, the slope of the parallel line is equal to the slope of the original line, making the slope of that parallel line also –1. For quantity B, the slope of the perpendicular line is the opposite reciprocal of the slope of the original line, so the slope of that perpendicular line would be +1. Quantity B is greater.

5. D: Although we are told how long George and Bill drive, we are not told how fast they are driving, meaning we do not have enough information to find the distances driven. The relationship cannot be determined from the information given.

6. D: It can be inferred that George has at least 4 pennies in order to have $7.24 in pocket change. But there is no additional information regarding the number of pennies, nickels, dimes, quarters, half dollars, or other denominations of change he has, so the relationship cannot be determined from the information given.

7. C: Multiply by the LCD and solve for a.

$$6a(a-1)\left[\frac{1}{a-1} = \frac{1}{6} + \frac{1}{a}\right]$$

$$6a = a(a-1) + 6(a-1)$$

$$6a = (a+6)(a-1)$$

$$0 = a^2 - a - 6$$

$$0 = (a+2)(a-3)$$

$$a = -2 \text{ and } a = 3$$

8. D: Write a proportion and solve.

$$\frac{2}{\left(\frac{1}{4}\right)} = \frac{x}{\left(\frac{2}{3}\right)}$$

$$2\left(\frac{2}{3}\right) = x\left(\frac{1}{4}\right)$$

$$x = \frac{4}{3} \div \frac{1}{4} = \frac{4}{3} \times \frac{4}{1} = \frac{16}{3} = 5\frac{1}{3}$$

9. B: The distributive property states that a term can be distributed, or multiplied, by each number in a term rather than having to be multiplied by the term as a whole. Thus $a(b+c) = ab + ac$. Alex can either multiply the price of the ticket times each friend, or he can add the number of friends together and multiply the total by the cost of the ticket.

10. D: To calculate the value of x, or nickels, create an equation to multiply each number of coins by its value, and then set them equal to the total amount in the jar. $325(0.25) + 280(0.10) + (0.05)x + 196(0.01) = \$143.71$. Then, solve for x to find the number of nickels: $\$81.25 + \$28.00 + 0.05x + \$1.96 = \$143.71 \to \$111.21 + .05x = \$143.71 \to .05x = \$32.50 \to x = 650$.

11. C: Solve the system of equations using substitution:

$$5x + 4y = 20; \quad x = 2y + 1$$
$$5(2y + 1) + 4y = 20$$
$$y = \frac{15}{14}$$

12. C: Find the total seats, then write a proportion to find the ratio.

$$total\ seats = 4,500 + 2,000$$
$$\frac{lower\ seats}{all\ seats} = \frac{4,500}{6,500} = \frac{9}{13}$$

13. D: Find ∠C using the fact that the sum of ∠C and m is 360°.

$$260° + m∠C = 360°$$
$$m∠C = 100°$$

Solve for ∠D using the fact that consecutive interior angles in a quadrilateral are supplementary.

$$m∠C + m∠D = 180°$$
$$100° + m∠D = 180°$$
$$m∠D = 80°$$

Solve for n by subtracting m∠D from 360°.

$$m∠D + n = 360°$$
$$n = 280°$$

14. A: If 2 gallons takes 2 8-ounce cans of juice, then each gallon takes 1 can, or 8 ounces. If she needs to make 6 gallons of juice, she will need 8 × 6 = 48 ounces of juice total. 48 ounces divided by 12 ounces per can means that Missy will need 4 of the 12-ounce cans to make 6 gallons of her lemonade.

15. B: Set up an equation to find the number of orders of chicken strips they can afford:

$$\$10 - 2(\$2.00 + \$1.00) = x$$
$$\$10 - 2(\$3.00) = x$$
$$\$10 - \$6.00 = \$4.00$$

Four dollars is enough money to buy 1 order of chicken strips to share.

Verbal Reasoning 1 Answer Key

1. D: *Iridescent* means dazzling, shimmering, or lustrous.

2. D: *Argumentative* means pugnacious or eager to argue; *squabble* means to bicker or disagree.

3. C: *Salvage* means to repair or fix; *impractical* means unreasonable or unrealistic.

4. B, D, G: Sleep deprivation, especially on a long-term basis, has terrible consequences. From poor academic performance to fatal car crashes, sleep deprivation is just bad for you. Depression is also an effect of sleep deprivation. Lack of sleep is often compensated with overstimulation and overeating, making a perfectly healthy person overweight.

5. A (enduring); F (extant): The important words to consider are *historians*, *intact*, and *1300s*, all of which indicate that something extremely old or ancient has survived over time. The answer cannot be option C since *extinct* indicates that something no longer exists. The answer cannot be option B since the term *obliterated* means "destroyed." The correct words must mean "surviving" and "still in existence"; therefore, options A and F are the best answers.

6. C (fastidious); D (meticulous): The key words here are *mud* and *clothes*. It can be inferred that children who like to play in the mud have a difficult time keeping their clothes clean. The answer options of C and D indicate that something is being kept neat and tidy and are therefore the best choices.

7. A (loquacious); B (garrulous): It can be inferred that a mother on the phone would be upset if she had to shout at her children; therefore, the children must be loud or acting out. Two words—*loquacious* and *garrulous*—both refer to being talkative and are the best answers for this sentence.

8. B: The author writes that "it is impossible to read him [Shakespeare] without seeing that he is constantly protesting against the two special limitations of the Elizabethan stage—the lack of suitable scenery, and the fashion of men playing women's parts."

9. D: The author writes that "it is not difficult to see what Shakespeare's attitude would be [about the use of scenery in the production of his plays]; not difficult, that is to say, if one reads Shakespeare himself, instead of reading merely what is written about him." He then does on the describe examples from *Henry V* and *A Midsummer' Night's Dream* in which Shakespeare laments the shortcomings of the Elizabethan theater.

10. B: The third and fourth paragraphs describe the lack of materials and artistry available to produce elaborate sets; the final paragraph describes the effects of ongoing description on the experience of the audience.

11. C: The author writes, "For it is not difficult to see what Shakespeare's attitude would be; not difficult, that is to say, if one reads Shakespeare himself, instead of reading merely what is written about him."

12. E: The author writes, "In fact, it is impossible to read him [Shakespeare] without seeing that he is constantly protesting against the two special limitations of the Elizabethan stage—the lack of suitable scenery, and the fashion of men playing women's parts."

Verbal Reasoning 2 Answer Key

1. C: *Valiant* means brave.

2. A: The key context clues are "wide awake" and "lively," which are synonyms for the term *animated*.

3. C: The principal would scold or admonish students who are in trouble.

4. D: *Amiable* means likable or friendly.

5. B, D, H: He took up a second letter which had lain unnoticed upon the table while he had been absorbed with the first. This he began to read with a smile of amusement upon his face which gradually faded away into an expression of intense interest and concentration. When he had finished he sat for some little time lost in thought with the letter dangling from his fingers.

6. A (zeal); B (devotion): The words *pouring rain* infer that it would not be pleasant to be outside training for a marathon. Someone who trains even during bad weather must therefore be "devoted" and "zealous," so options A and B are the best answers.

7. A (waffle); D (vacillate): This sentence explains that "I" has an issue making a decision and seems to toggle back and forth on which choice to make. Answer options B and C can therefore be eliminated since they indicate decisiveness, whereas options A and D indicate wavering and are the best answer choices for this sentence.

8. D (idolized); E (venerated): Since the correct words for this sentence would be synonyms for the word *respected*, we can immediately eliminate options A (*disesteemed*), B (*desecrated*), C (*despised*), and F (*abhorred*), leaving options D and E as the only viable answers.

9. E: To begin this question, it is helpful to figure out what a bathyscaphe is. The passage states that the scientists were inside of it when they found the whale bones. It also describes a bathyscaphe as "deep-sea." From these two pieces of information, it can be concluded that a bathyscaphe is a type of submarine. A submarine pilot would be helpful on board a submarine; someone has to steer. A mechanic would be helpful on board a submarine in case there are any mechanical issues. A marine biologist would be useful on a submarine for identifying ocean life and potential dangers. A captain would be useful on a submarine because he or she could keep everyone on task. A free-diving specialist would not be useful. Submarines are used to go places where humans can't safely go, so even in an emergency event, the crew could not free-dive away. Of all the choices, the free-diving specialist would be the least helpful.

10. B: This passage is best described as informational. It delivers a topic and then goes on to describe the topic. It is not narrative because narrative passages focus on telling a story. It is not persuasive because it is not trying to convince the reader of anything. Contemplative is not a type of passage; to contemplate is to think. Although an expository essay does include facts and information, expository essays are a type of persuasive essay; their purpose is to use facts to convince the reader.

11. C: The main idea of this passage is whale falls and what they are. Although the Trieste II may have been an important invention, this passage is not about it. Whale falls are indeed common, but this entire passage is not specifically about just how common they are. Things do live on the ocean floor; whale falls are on the ocean floor, and they host entire ecosystems. Although it may be a good idea to bring back samples of strange phenomena on deep ocean dives, that is not the main idea of this passage.

12. D: The author writes that "our daily behaviors are inextricably linked with the social context in which they occur."

13. D: The author writes that "the behaviors we witness in others may be as much a result of social influence as they are of the individual's disposition" and that the "tendency to attribute behaviors, especially negative behaviors, to disposition is risky and can ultimately be detrimental to us and to the other person."

14. A: The author describes the participants as "healthy, stable, intelligent male Stanford University students" in order to provide a contrast to the "cruel and unrelenting [...]treatment of the prisoners."

15. C: The author writes, "Even giving individuals temporary power over others was enough to completely alter the way they viewed and behaved toward each other; indeed, the behaviors he witnessed in each of the groups were not a result of the dispositions of the participants but of the situation in which they had been placed."

GRE Practice Test #3

Analytical Writing

1 prompt, 30 minutes

Analyze an Issue

Despite humanity's technological advancements, which have led to its mastery of the natural world, people today aren't that different from people in the past. Cultures and lifestyles may vary, but human nature remains unchanged across the centuries. Human nature is a constant that doesn't depend on geography or culture.

In your essay, introduce the subject, and then either explain the subject you have chosen or take a position about the subject and support that position. At least two evaluators will read and score your essay. Be sure to define your purpose, provide a clear introduction and thesis statement, organize ideas effectively, provide support for your argument, and adhere to Standard English.

Analyze an Issue: Sample Essay

Human nature is both a basic and a very complex concept. At its primary definition, human nature refers to how people feel, think, and behave in any given situation. It is our drive to have the basic needs of life, including food, shelter, and companionship. As humans have evolved, however, human nature has become more competitive and selfish, often putting individuals' needs and wants above those of others or the greater community. In that way, humans have become a more selfish and competitive species, particularly when compared with other animals. While human emotion may be the same, our social behaviors and the ways we think about, analyze, and act in response to situations have most definitely changed over time and are impacted by geography, culture, and modern societal advancements.

The most obvious change to human nature can be seen by comparing modern people to our ancient predecessors, such as Neanderthals ("cavemen"), with regard to one of the most basic human needs: food. When people today need food, most of us (particularly those of us living in urban and suburban areas) simply go to the local market or grocery store and buy something to eat. If we can afford it, we might visit a local restaurant and treat ourselves to a hearty meal. The less fortunate among us may panhandle for food or for money to buy food. In more rural areas, people often grow some of their own food and hunt for meat. When they are hungry, they go to their kitchens and prepare a meal from their own gardens and pantries. What we do not do is go out of our caves with a slingshot or spear, kill the first animal we can find, and drag it back to our cave to eat in front of our fire. The basic human nature to feed ourselves has not changed, but our behaviors surrounding how we accomplish this have changed to conform to societal norms and expectations.

While this may seem like an extreme example, how people think about various situations is determined by these societal norms which, in turn, are determined by our geography and culture. Solving another of the basic human needs—shelter—requires analytical thought based on where we live and how we are brought up to meet this need. In modern, urban areas, people generally live in large buildings with many separate residences, such as apartment buildings and condominiums. Moving outward towards suburban areas, people generally seek out single-family homes or more sprawling apartment complexes. When someone needs a place to live, they usually reach out to a realtor or builder to help them find or build a home. Housing in more rural areas is often comprised of homes, homesteads, and farms. In less developed areas, housing may consist of thatched huts, yurts, and other abodes, and the people of the community may come together to build new homes when someone is in need.

While the basics of human nature—our need for food, shelter, and companionship—have not changed, the ways in which we obtain these things have definitely evolved over time and are most decidedly impacted by geography and culture. Gone are the days of hunting and eating huddled in a cave by a fire. Modern society has impacted modern culture and changed how humans think and behave in any given situation. As times change, people evolve and adapt, embracing new technologies, cultures, and societal norms along the way.

Quantitative Reasoning 1

12 questions, 21 minutes

1. Mr. Hawkins receives the AP test scores from his AP microeconomics class. The scores are: 1, 2, 2, 2, 3, 3, 3, 3, 3, 3, 4, 4, 4, 5, 5.

Quantity A	Quantity B
the median test score	the mode test score

A) Quantity A is greater.
B) Quantity B is greater.
C) The two quantities are equal.
D) The relationship cannot be determined from the information given.

2. Use the following relation: (2, 5), (5, 2), (7, 8), (4, 3), and (0, 9).

Quantity A	Quantity B
the sum of the domain values	the sum of the range values

A) Quantity A is greater.
B) Quantity B is greater.
C) The two quantities are equal.
D) The relationship cannot be determined from the information given.

3. A radio station's playlist consists of 20% rap songs, 30% country songs, 40% rock songs, and 10% easy listening.

Quantity A	Quantity B
the probability the station will not play two country songs in succession	50%

A) Quantity A is greater.
B) Quantity B is greater.
C) The two quantities are equal.
D) The relationship cannot be determined from the information given.

4.

Quantity A	Quantity B
the number of pairs of parallel sides in a regular octagon	the number of sides in a rhombus

 A) Quantity A is greater.
 B) Quantity B is greater.
 C) The two quantities are equal.
 D) The relationship cannot be determined from the information given.

5. The mean score of a test is 78, the median is 83, the mode is 80, and the range is 37. Ms. Robinson later curves the tests by adding 5 points to each test, and John's new score is 87.

Quantity A	Quantity B
John's new test score	the new median test score

 A) Quantity A is greater.
 B) Quantity B is greater.
 C) The two quantities are equal.
 D) The relationship cannot be determined from the information given.

6.

Quantity A	Quantity B
the sum of the exterior angles of a heptagon	the sum of all central angles of a circle

 A) Quantity A is greater.
 B) Quantity B is greater.
 C) The two quantities are equal.
 D) The relationship cannot be determined from the information given.

7. At a bake sale, muffins are priced at $1.50 each and cookies are priced at $1 for 2 cookies. If 11 muffins are sold, and the total money earned is $29.50, how many cookies were sold?

 A) 12
 B) 13
 C) 23
 D) 26

8. Yvonne ran 4.6 miles, 4.8 miles, 5.3 miles, 5.2 miles, and 6 miles on five consecutive days. What was her average distance over the five days?

 A) 4.1 mi
 B) 25.9 mi
 C) 5.18 mi
 D) 4.975 mi

9. The number of chairs in the front row of a movie theater is 14. Each subsequent row contains 2 more seats than the row in front of it. If the theater has 25 rows, what is the total number of seats in the theater?

 A) 336
 B) 350
 C) 888
 D) 950

10. Students board a bus at 7:45 a.m. and arrive at school at 8:20 a.m. How long are the students on the bus?
    A) 30 minutes
    B) 35 minutes
    C) 45 minutes
    D) 60 minutes

11. Using the table, which equation demonstrates the linear relationship between x and y?

x	y
3	−18
7	−34
10	−46

   A) $y = -6x - 6$
   B) $y = -5x - 6$
   C) $y = -4x - 6$
   D) $y = -3x - 6$

12. A car traveled at 65 miles per hour for $1\frac{1}{2}$ hours and then traveled at 50 miles per hour for $2\frac{1}{2}$ hours. How many miles did the car travel?
    A) 190.5 miles
    B) 215.0 miles
    C) 222.5 miles
    D) 237.5 miles

Quantitative Reasoning 2

15 questions, 26 minutes

1.

Quantity A	Quantity B
the number of diagonals in a pentagon	5

   A) Quantity A is greater.
   B) Quantity B is greater.
   C) The two quantities are equal.
   D) The relationship cannot be determined from the information given.

2. Rectangles A and B each have an area of 60 square feet.

Quantity A	Quantity B
the perimeter of rectangle A	the perimeter of rectangle B

   A) Quantity A is greater.
   B) Quantity B is greater.
   C) The two quantities are equal.
   D) The relationship cannot be determined from the information given.

3.

Quantity A	Quantity B
the number of real zeroes in a quadratic equation with a discriminant of −12	the number of real zeroes in a quadratic equation with a discriminant of −7

A) Quantity A is greater.
B) Quantity B is greater.
C) The two quantities are equal.
D) The relationship cannot be determined from the information given.

4.

Quantity A	Quantity B
$\sqrt[3]{12^4}$	$12^{\frac{4}{3}}$

A) Quantity A is greater.
B) Quantity B is greater.
C) The two quantities are equal.
D) The relationship cannot be determined from the information given.

5.

Quantity A	Quantity B
the value of sine in Quadrant IV	the value of cosine in Quadrant IV

A) Quantity A is greater.
B) Quantity B is greater.
C) The two quantities are equal.
D) The relationship cannot be determined from the information given.

6. For the function $f(x) = x^2 + 5x + 6$

Quantity A	Quantity B
the number of x-intercept(s) of the function	the number of y-intercept(s) of the function

A) Quantity A is greater.
B) Quantity B is greater.
C) The two quantities are equal.
D) The relationship cannot be determined from the information given.

7. Out of 1,560 students at Ward Middle School, 15% want to take French. Which expression represents how many students want to take French?
   A) 1,560 ÷ 15
   B) 1,560 × 15
   C) 1,560 × 0.15
   D) 1,560 ÷ 0.15

8. What is the percent increase in an employee's salary if it is raised from $57,000 to $60,000?
   A) 0.3%
   B) 3%
   C) 4%
   D) 5%

9. $3x^3 + 4x - (2x + 5y) + y =$
   A) $11x - 4y$
   B) $29x - 4y$
   C) $3x^3 + 2x - 4y$
   D) $3x^3 + 2x + y$

10. A group of 20 friends is planning a road trip. They have 3 cars that seat 4 people, 3 cars that seat 5 people, and 1 car that seats 6 people. What is the fewest number of cars they can take on the trip if each person needs his or her own seat?
    A) 3 cars
    B) 4 cars
    C) 5 cars
    D) 6 cars

11. Justin has a summer lawn care business and earns $40 for each lawn he mows. He also pays $35 per week in business expenses. Which of the following expressions represents Justin's profit after x weeks if he mows m number of lawns?
    A) $40m - 35x$
    B) $40m + 35x$
    C) $35x(40 + m)$
    D) $35(40m + x)$

12. Which of the following is equivalent to $z^3(z + 2)^2 - 4z^3 + 2$?
    A) 2
    B) $z^5 + 4z^4 + 4z^3 + 2$
    C) $z^6 + 4z^3 + 2$
    D) $z^5 + 4z^4 + 2$

13. What is the domain of the inequality $\left|\frac{x}{8}\right| \geq 1$?
    A) $(-\infty, \infty)$
    B) $[8, \infty)$
    C) $(-\infty, -8]$
    D) $(-\infty, -8] \cup [8, \infty)$

14. A cube with volume 27 cubic meters is inscribed within a sphere such that all of the cube's vertices touch the sphere. What is the length of the sphere's radius?
    A) 2.6 meters
    B) 3 meters
    C) 5.2 meters
    D) 9 meters

15. Which of the following is equivalent to $54z^4 + 18z^3 + 3z + 3$?
    A) $18z^4 + 6z^3 + z + 1$
    B) $3z(18z^3 + 6z^2 + 1)$
    C) $72z^7 + 3z$
    D) $3(18z^4 + 6z^3 + z + 1)$

Verbal Reasoning 1

12 questions, 18 minutes

1. By Saturday, the snow and wind is expected to _____; it should be sunny and warm on Sunday.
    A) multiply
    B) diminish
    C) duplicate
    D) increase

2. Clara hoped to _____ the nasty rumor by passing out cupcakes and compliments to everyone who had called her mean.
    A) exaggerate
    B) attract
    C) dispel
    D) start

3. The mother was _____ with her son when he refused to get off of his electronics.
    A) happy
    B) placated
    C) exasperated
    D) energized

Select from the answer options that correspond to the blank sentences in each paragraph. One answer must be selected for each blank. The answer must complete the idea being expressed in the text.

4. True, night by night, through century after century, they rise, and cross the sky, and set. But those are only (i)_____ movements. (ii)_____ as the turning round of Earth upon her axis, once in every twenty-four hours, makes the sun (iii)____ to rise and cross the sky and set, in the daytime; so also the same turning of Earth makes the stars appear to do the same in the night-time.

Question 4 Answer Options		
Blank (i)	**Blank (ii)**	**Blank (iii)**
(A) gradual	(D) Similarly	(G) appear
(B) small	(E) Precisely	(H) attempt
(C) seeming	(F) Exactly	(I) begin

Select TWO answer options that best match the meaning of the sentence. When added to the sentence, the two answers must create complete sentences that have the same meaning.

5. The wealthy entrepreneur avoided being _____ by owning a small cottage and riding a plain bicycle to work.
    A) understated
    B) ostentatious
    C) extravagant
    D) unpretentious
    E) somber
    F) inconspicuous

6. Let's take a more ___ approach to this whole situation and focus on what really matters.
    A) pragmatic
    B) impractical
    C) unrealistic
    D) logical
    E) idealistic
    F) dogmatic

A new NASA-led study shows that tropical forests may be absorbing far more carbon dioxide than many scientists thought, in response to rising atmospheric levels of greenhouse gas. The study estimates that tropical forests absorb 1.4 billion metric tons of carbon dioxide out of a total global absorption of 2.5 billion—more than is absorbed by forests in Canada, Siberia and other northern regions, called boreal forests.

"This is good news, because uptake in boreal forests is already slowing, while tropical forests may continue to take up carbon for many years," said David Schimel of NASA's Jet Propulsion Laboratory, Pasadena, California. Schimel is lead author of a paper on the new research, appearing online today in the Proceedings of National Academy of Sciences.

Forests and other land vegetation currently remove up to 30 percent of human carbon dioxide emissions from the atmosphere during photosynthesis. If the rate of absorption were to slow down, the rate of global warming would speed up in return.

The new study is the first to devise a way to make apples-to-apples comparisons of carbon dioxide estimates from many sources at different scales: computer models of ecosystem processes, atmospheric models run backward in time to deduce the sources of today's concentrations (called inverse models), satellite images, data from experimental forest plots and more. The researchers **reconciled** all types of analyses and assessed the accuracy of the results based on how well they reproduced independent, ground-based measurements. They obtained their new estimate of the tropical carbon absorption from the models they determined to be the most trusted and verified.

"Until our analysis, no one had successfully completed a global reconciliation of information about carbon dioxide effects from the atmospheric, forestry and modeling communities," said co-author Joshua Fisher of JPL. "It is incredible that all these different types of independent data sources start to converge on an answer."

The question of which type of forest is the bigger carbon absorber "is not just an accounting curiosity," said co-author Britton Stephens of the National Center for Atmospheric Research, Boulder, Colorado.

"It has big implications for our understanding of whether global terrestrial ecosystems might continue to offset our carbon dioxide emissions or might begin to exacerbate climate change."

As human-caused emissions add more carbon dioxide to the atmosphere, forests worldwide are using it to grow faster, reducing the amount that stays airborne. This effect is called carbon fertilization. "All else being equal, the effect is stronger at higher temperatures, meaning it will be higher in the tropics than in the boreal forests," Schimel said.

But climate change also decreases water availability in some regions and makes Earth warmer, leading to more frequent and larger wildfires. In the tropics, humans compound the problem by burning wood during deforestation. Fires don't just stop carbon absorption by killing trees; they also spew huge amounts of carbon into the atmosphere as the wood burns.

For about twenty-five years, most computer climate models have been showing that mid-latitude forests in the Northern Hemisphere absorb more carbon than tropical forests. That result was initially based on the then-current understanding of global air flows and limited data suggesting that deforestation was causing tropical forests to release more carbon dioxide than they were absorbing.

In the mid-2000s, Stephens used measurements of carbon dioxide made from aircraft to show that many climate models were not correctly representing flows of carbon above ground level. Models that matched the aircraft measurements better showed more carbon absorption in the tropical forests. However, there were still not enough global data sets to validate the idea of a large tropical-forest absorption. Schimel said that their new study took advantage of a great deal of work other scientists have done since Stephens' paper to pull together national and regional data of various kinds into **robust**, global data sets.

Schimel noted that their paper reconciles results at every scale from the pores of a single leaf, where photosynthesis takes place, to the whole Earth, as air moves carbon dioxide around the globe. "What we've had up till this paper was a theory of carbon dioxide fertilization based on phenomena at the microscopic scale and observations at the global scale that appeared to contradict those phenomena. Here, at least, is a hypothesis that provides a consistent explanation that includes both how we know photosynthesis works and what's happening at the planetary scale."

Excerpt from "NASA Finds Good News on Forests and Carbon Dioxide," published online by the National Aeronautics and Space Administration in December 2014

7. As used in the passage, the term *reconciled* most nearly means
   A) forgave.
   B) studied.
   C) integrated.
   D) gathered.
   E) offered.

8. The passage indicates that wildfires
   A) both result from and contribute to climate change.
   B) are the most significant contributor to climate change.
   C) occur when temperature and humidity are both high.
   D) have little to no effect on carbon dioxide emissions.
   E) are the result of purposeful deforestation processes.

9. According to the passage, what is the relationship between photosynthesis and global warming?
   A) Photosynthesis allows carbon dioxide gas to be released into the atmosphere, exacerbating the issue of global warming.
   B) Carbon dioxide prevents trees from flourishing, thus increasing the amount of greenhouse gas and exacerbating the issue of global warming.
   C) Trees absorb carbon dioxide during photosynthesis, removing much of the carbon dioxide from the atmosphere and slowing the effects of global warming.
   D) Greenhouse gases like carbon dioxide slow the effects of global warming by preventing trees from completing the cycle of photosynthesis.
   E) According to the passage, photosynthesis and global warming are unrelated.

10. The passage indicates that research into carbon dioxide absorption is significant because
    A) it challenges us to question our own opinions on global warming and climate change.
    B) it forces us to recognize that global warming poses a significant threat to our vegetation.
    C) it encourages us to consider whether forests are effective alternatives to carbon dioxide emissions.
    D) it allows us to understand the impact of the earth's forests on climate change.
    E) it generates significant revenues for alternative energy development companies.

11. According to the passage, increased carbon dioxide emissions may result in
    A) increased water availability.
    B) smaller, less frequent wildfires.
    C) faster-growing forests.
    D) decreased oxygen availability.
    E) lower atmospheric temperatures.

12. A student claims that preserving the earth's forests is an essential step in slowing climate change. Which of the following statements from the passage supports this student's claim?
    A) "This is good news, because uptake in boreal forests is already slowing, while tropical forests may continue to take up carbon for many years," said David Schimel of NASA's Jet Propulsion Laboratory, Pasadena, California.
    B) If the rate of absorption [of carbon dioxide] were to slow down, the rate of global warming would speed up in return.
    C) But climate change also decreases water availability in some regions and makes Earth warmer, leading to more frequent and larger wildfires.
    D) That result was initially based on the then-current understanding of global air flows and limited data suggesting that deforestation was causing tropical forests to release more carbon dioxide than they were absorbing.
    E) Fires don't just stop carbon absorption by killing trees, they also spew huge amounts of carbon into the atmosphere as the wood burns.

Verbal Reasoning 2

15 questions, 23 minutes

1. The athletes had a _____ twelve-hour workout; they were exhausted at the end of the day.
    A) grueling
    B) troublesome
    C) moderate
    D) sufficient

2. As the sirens blared, warning us of an _____ tornado, we quickly took shelter in a nearby cellar.
    A) overnight
    B) outlying
    C) ebbing
    D) impending

3. It would be very _____ of you to bring an extra pair of clothes when you go camping, just in case you _____ in the lake.
    A) cautious… cascade
    B) silly… swim
    C) reckless… jump
    D) prudent… plummet

Select from the answer options that correspond to the blank sentences in each paragraph. One answer must be selected for each blank. The answer must complete the idea being expressed in the text.

4. During this unprecedented time in recent history, teachers have been working (i)_____ to create effective virtual classroom experiences for all of their students. In an effort to build up the classroom community—where students feel safe and valued—communication with students, families, and colleagues is (ii)_____. Not only are digital (iii)_____, content knowledge, and literacy skills imperative, but teachers also need to make sure that students are easily able to access their work, understand the objectives of each assignment, and participate in class effectively and appropriately. Having strong remote-learning classroom norms and expectations that help each class to run smoothly are essential as well.

Question 4 Answer Options		
Blank (i)	**Blank (ii)**	**Blank (iii)**
(A) repetitively	(D) crucial	(G) competency
(B) diligently	(E) understood	(H) knowledge
(C) facetiously	(F) needed	(I) effectiveness

Select TWO answer options that best match the meaning of the sentence. When added to the sentence, the two answers must create complete sentences that have the same meaning.

5. The students were so tired and ___ that the teacher made everyone stand up to ensure that they each participated and didn't fall asleep.
    A) voluble
    B) communicative
    C) taciturn
    D) demonstrative
    E) reticent
    F) forthcoming

6. There was a ___ amount of potatoes—enough to last us all winter—all starting from one spud.
    A) barren
    B) fecund
    C) prolific
    D) scant
    E) sterile
    F) rich

7. After she lost her job, Judy realized it would have been ___ to have saved her money instead of spending it all.
    A) nearsighted
    B) improvident
    C) sagacious
    D) reckless
    E) cautious
    F) prudent

What is laughter? It is a spasmodic movement of various muscles of the body, beginning with those which half close the eyes and those which draw backwards and upwards the sides of the mouth, and open it so as to expose the teeth, next affecting those of respiration so as to produce short rapidly succeeding expirations accompanied by sound (called "guffaws" when in excess) and then extending to the limbs, causing up and down movement of the half-closed fists and stamping of the feet, and ending in a rolling on the ground and various contortions of the body. Clapping the hands is not part of the laughter "process," but a separate, often involuntary, action which has the calling of attention to oneself as its explanation, just as slapping the ground or a table or one's thigh has. Laughter is spontaneous, that is to say, the movements are not designed or directed by the conscious will. But in mankind, in proportion as individuals are trained in self-control, it is more or less completely under command, and in spite of the most urgent tendency of the automatic mechanism to enter upon the progressive series of movements which we distinguish as (1) smile, (2) broad smile or grin, (3) laugh, (4) loud laughter, (5) paroxysms of uncontrolled laughter, a man or woman can prevent all indication by muscular movement of a desire to laugh or even to smile. Usually laughter is excited by certain pleasurable emotions, and is to be regarded as an "expression" of such emotion just as certain movements and the flow of tears are an "expression" of the painful emotion of grief and physical suffering, and as other movements of the face and limbs are an "expression" of anger, others of "fear." The Greek gods of Olympus enjoyed "inextinguishable laughter."

It is interesting to see how far we can account for the strange movements of laughter as part of the inherited automatic mechanism of man. Why do we laugh? What is the advantage to the individual or the species of "laughing"? Why do we "express" our pleasurable emotion and why in this way? It is said that the outcast diminutive race of Ceylon known as the Veddas never laugh, and it has even been seriously but erroneously stated that the muscles which move the face in laughter are wanting in them. A planter induced some of these people to camp in his "compound," or park, in order to learn something of their habits, language, and beliefs. One day he said to the chief man of the little tribe, "You Veddas never laugh. Why do you never laugh?" The little wild man replied, "It is true; we never laugh. What is there for us to laugh at?"—an answer almost terrible in its pathetic submission to a joyless life. For laughter is primarily, to all races and conditions of men, the accompaniment, the expression of the simple joy of life. It has acquired a variety of relations and significations in the course of the long development of conscious man—but primarily it is an expression of emotion, set going by the experience of the elementary joys of life—the light and heat of the sun, the approach of food, of love of triumph.

Before we look further into the matter it is well to note some exceptional cases of the causation of laughter. The first of these is the excitation of laughter by a purely mechanical "stimulus" or action from the exterior, without any corresponding mental emotion of joy—namely by "tickling," that is to say, by light rubbing or touching of the skin under the arms or at the side of the neck, or on the soles of the feet. Yet a certain readiness to respond is necessary on the part of the person who is "tickled," for, although an unwilling subject may be thus made to laugh, yet there are conditions of mind and of body in which "tickling" produces no response. I do not propose to discuss why it is that "tickling," or gentle friction of the skin produces laughter. It is probably one of those cases in which a mechanism of the living body is set to work, as a machine may be, by directly causing the final movement (say the turning of a wheel), for the production of which a special train of apparatus, to be started by the letting loose of a spring or the turning of a steam-cock, is provided, and in ordinary circumstance is the regular mode in which the working of the mechanism is started. The apparatus of laughter is when due to "tickling" set at work by a short cut to the nerves and related muscles without recourse to the normal emotional steam-cock.

Excerpt from *More Science from an Easy Chair* by Sir E. Ray (Edwin Ray) Lankester

8. Which of the following best describes the main purpose of this passage?
   A) to describe the difference between voluntary and involuntary laughter
   B) to give an imaginative description of what laughter looks like
   C) to give a physical description of the process of laughing
   D) to offer a philosophical reasoning for why we laugh
   E) to describe various cultural perspectives on laughter and pleasure

9. The main idea of the second paragraph can best be expressed by which of the following statements?
   A) Varied explanations exist for why people laugh, but there is a clear connection to basic emotion.
   B) Because there are some groups of people who never laugh, it is clear that laughter is not a necessary or survival trait for people.
   C) People who do not laugh do not experience important, basic human emotions.
   D) It is impossible to determine why people laugh because most people do not laugh for the same reasons.
   E) Laughter is an important tool of human survival.

10. According to the passage, one physical symptom of laughter is:
    A) long, careful breaths that produce a gasping sound
    B) quick, shallow breaths that lead to sound
    C) creating a downward pull on the facial features
    D) clapping hands to create accompanying sound
    E) widening of the eyes

11. Which of the following best describes the author's purpose for describing laughter in the first paragraph as a group of physical responses or symptoms?
    A) to demonstrate that most people do not understand laughter
    B) to illustrate the grotesqueness of the act of laughing
    C) to isolate the specific causes of laughter
    D) to demonstrate the complex and instinctual physical components of laughter
    E) to make a distinction between genuine laughter and forced laughter

12. Which of the following statements about laughter would the author be LEAST likely to agree with?
    A) Laughter is a complex physical action that is little understood and almost entirely instinctual, though voluntary.
    B) Most people cannot explain why they laugh at a specific joke or occurrence.
    C) By examining the physical attributes of laughter, it is possible to understand the emotional stimulus that causes laughter.
    D) Laughter is a voluntary reaction to either physical or emotional stimulus.
    E) Laughter is an almost universal expression of joy, present across nearly all races and cultures.

13. The last paragraph suggests that tickling
    A) is an expression of joy or happiness.
    B) causes laughter through emotional stimulus.
    C) causes laughter because it is similar to the first physical symptom of laughter.
    D) simulates the final step in the process of laughter.
    E) causes a more involuntary form of laughter that is nearly impossible to control.

14. The phrase "the apparatus of laughter" most nearly means which of the following?
    A) the measurement of intensity of laughter
    B) the process of laughter
    C) the machine of laughter
    D) the body parts affected by laughter
    E) the fakeness of laughter

15. The example of the Veddas serves to reinforce the idea that
    A) laughter is an involuntary action.
    B) joyful emotion is a primary cause of laughter.
    C) there is little in life to laugh about.
    D) no two people laugh about the same things.
    E) laughter is only present in some cultures.

GRE Practice Test #3 Answer Key

Quantitative Reasoning 1

1. C: There are 15 test scores in AP microeconomics and the scores are arranged in ascending order, so the eighth score—3—is the median. The score of 3 appears the most frequently, with six occurrences, which makes 3 the mode as well. The two quantities are equal.

2. B: In a relation, the domain values represent the inputs, or x-values, which are 2, 5, 7, 4, and 0. Add the x-values to find the sum of the domain values:

$$2 + 5 + 7 + 4 + 0 = 18$$

The range values represent the outputs, or y-values, which are 5, 2, 8, 3, and 9. Add the y-values to find the sum of the range values:

$$5 + 2 + 8 + 3 + 9 = 27$$

The sum of the range values is 27, which is greater than the sum of the domain values (18), so quantity B is greater.

3. B: The probability that the station will play country music is 30%, so the probability it will NOT play country music is 70%. Find the probability that the station will not play two country songs in succession by multiplying:

$$70\% \times 70\%$$

$$= 0.7 \times 0.7 = 0.49 = 49\%, \text{ which is less than } 50\%$$

Therefore, quantity B is greater.

4. C: An octagon has 8 sides, and a regular octagon has 4 pairs of parallel sides. A rhombus is a quadrilateral that has 4 sides. The two quantities are equal.

5. B: If Ms. Robinson curves the tests by adding 5 points, then the mean, median, and modes will all increase by 5 points to 83, 88, and 85, respectively. If John's new test score is 87, then it is one point below the median score, 88, so quantity B is greater.

6. C: The sum of the exterior angles of any polygon always equals 360 degrees, the same as the sum of all central angles of a circle. The two quantities are equal.

7. D: Write an equation to represent the problem and solve it. Note: If cookies are $1 for 2, the price of one cookie is $0.50.

$$11(1.50) + 0.50x = 29.50$$
$$16.50 + 0.50x = 29.50$$
$$0.50x = 13.00$$
$$x = 26$$

8. C: Add the values and divide by 5:

$$4.6 + 4.8 + 5.3 + 5.2 + 6 = 25.9$$
$$25.9 \div 5 = 5.18 \text{ mi}$$

9. D: Use the formula for an arithmetic sum.
$$S_n = \frac{n}{2(2a_1 + (n-1)d)}$$

$$\frac{25}{2(2(14) + (25-1)2)} = 950$$

10. B: There are 15 minutes between 7:45 a.m. and 8:00 a.m. and 20 minutes between 8:00 a.m. and 8:20 a.m.
$$15 \text{ minutes} + 20 \text{ minutes} = 35 \text{ minutes}$$

11. C: Substitute one (x, y) pair into each answer choice to find the correct equation.

A)
$$y = -6x - 6; \ (3, -18)$$
$$y = -6(3) - 6$$
$$y = -18 - 6$$
$$y = -24 \neq -18$$

B)
$$y = -5x - 6; \ (3, -18)$$
$$y = -5(3) - 6$$
$$y = -15 - 6$$
$$y = -24 \neq -18$$

C)
$$y = -4x - 6; \ (3, -18)$$
$$y = -4(3) - 6$$
$$y = -12 - 6$$
$$y = -18$$

D)
$$y = -3x - 6; \ (3, -18)$$
$$y = -3(3) - 6$$
$$y = -9 - 6$$
$$y = -15 \neq -18$$

12. C: Multiply the car's speed by the time traveled to find the distance.
$$1.5(65) = 97.5 \text{ miles}$$
$$2.5(50) = 125 \text{ miles}$$
$$97.5 + 125 = 222.5 \text{ miles}$$

Quantitative Reasoning 2

1. C: The formula for the number of diagonals in a polygon with n sides is $n\left(\frac{n-3}{2}\right)$. Calculate for a pentagon:

$$5\left(\frac{5-3}{2}\right)$$

$$= \frac{5(2)}{2}$$

$$= 5$$

So, the two quantities are equal.

2. D: Although we are told that both rectangles have the same area, we are not told the lengths and widths of both. For example, one of the rectangles can have a length of 60 feet and width of 1 foot, making its perimeter $2 \times 60 + 2 \times 1 = 122$ feet, and the other rectangle can have a length of 20 feet and width of 3 feet, making its perimeter $2 \times 20 + 2 \times 3 = 46$ feet. The relationship cannot be determined from the information given.

3. C: The discriminant of a quadratic equation tells us how many real zeroes the equation has. If the discriminant is greater than 0, there are two real zeroes. If the discriminant is equal to 0, there is one real zero; if the discriminant is less than 0, then there are no real zeroes. Because both –12 and –7 are negative numbers, the two equations have no real zeroes, hence the two quantities are equal.

4. C: When expressing fractional exponents with radicals, the denominator of the exponent is the power of the root, and the numerator is the power of the term inside the root. The two quantities are equal.

5. B: In trigonometry, Quadrant IV is located in the southeast part of a coordinate plane. It has positive x-values (positive cosine values) and negative y-values (negative sine values). So, quantity B is greater.

6. A: The number of x-intercepts or zeroes can be determined by the quadratic formula, factoring, or simply by finding the discriminant. To find the discriminant, use $b2 - 4ac$, where $b = 5, a = 1$, and $c = 6$:

$$52 - 4 \times 1 \times 6$$
$$= 25 - 24 = 1$$

Since the discriminant is 1, there are two x-intercepts (in this case $x = -2$ and $x = -3$).
To find the y-intercept, plug in 0 for x:

$$0^2 + 5(0) + 6 = 6$$

There is one y-intercept, so quantity A is greater.

7. C: Use the formula for finding percentages. Express the percentage as a decimal.

$$\text{part} = \text{whole} \times \text{percentage} = 1{,}560 \times 0.15$$

8. D: Use the formula for percent increase.
percent increase=(amount of change)/(original amount)

$$= \frac{3{,}000}{60{,}000} = 0.05 = 5\%$$

9. C: Apply the distributive property, and then combine like terms.

$$3x^3 + 4x - (2x + 5y) + y$$
$$= 3x^3 + 4x - 2x - 5y + y$$
$$= 3x^3 + 2x - 4y$$

10. B: Add together the seats in the cars until there are 20.

$$6 + 5 = 11$$
$$6 + 5 + 5 = 16$$
$$6 + 5 + 5 + 5 = 21$$

They fewest number of cars that will seat 20 people is 4 cars.

11. A: Justin's profit will be his income minus his expenses. He will earn $40 for each lawn, or 40m. He pays $35 is expenses each week, or 35w.

$$\text{profit} = 40m - 35x$$

12. D: Simplify using PEMDAS.
$$z^3(z+2)^2 - 4z^3 + 2$$
$$z^3(z^2 + 4z + 4) - 4z^3 + 2$$
$$z^5 + 4z^4 + 4z^3 - 4z^3 + 2$$
$$z^5 + 4z^4 + 2$$

13. D: Split the absolute value inequality into two inequalities and simplify. Switch the inequality when making one side negative.
$$\frac{x}{8} \geq 1$$
$$x \geq 8$$
$$-\frac{x}{8} \geq 1$$
$$\frac{x}{8} \leq -1$$
$$x \leq -8$$
$$x \leq -8 \text{ or } x \geq 8 \rightarrow (-\infty, -8] \cup [8, \infty)$$

14. A: Since the cube's volume is 27, each side length is equal to $\sqrt[3]{27} = 3$. The long diagonal distance from one of the cube's vertices to its opposite vertex will provide the sphere's diameter:
$$d = \sqrt{3^2 + 3^2 + 3^2} = \sqrt{27} = 5.2$$
Half of this length is the radius, which is 2.6 meters.

15. D: Factor the expression using the greatest common factor of 3.
$$54z^4 + 18z^3 + 3z + 3$$
$$= 3(18z^4 + 6z^3 + z + 1)$$

Verbal Reasoning 1

1. B: *Diminish* means to reduce or weaken. Because it is expected to be sunny and warm the following day, the snow and wind will lessen or diminish.

2. C: To *dispel* means to drive out, chase away, or get rid of.

3. C: *Exasperated* means frustrated, annoyed, or irritated.

4. C, E, G: True, night by night, through century after century, they rise, and cross the sky, and set. But those are only seeming movements. Precisely as the turning round of Earth upon her axis, once in every twenty-four hours, makes the sun appear to rise and cross the sky and set, in the daytime; so also the same turning of Earth makes the stars appear to do the same in the night-time.

5. B, C: The key words in this sentence are *small* and *plain* and are in contrast with the term *wealthy*. This would indicate that words meaning the opposite of the term *noticeable* are needed; however, another key word—*avoided*—indicates that the words should be aligned with extreme wealth or showiness. Options B and C are therefore the best answer choices; the other words are all opposites.

6. A, D: "What really matters" indicates to look for words that focus on something concise and practical. Answer options A (*pragmatic*) and D (*logical*) fit this sentence best; options B (*impractical*), C (*unrealistic*), and F (*dogmatic*) are opposites. The only other possible answer option—E (*idealistic*)—could work, but it focuses more on an optimistic view, which may or may not be practical.

7. C: The use of the word *reconciled* indicates that scientists gathered, compared, contrasted, and integrated data into a comprehensive, global data set.

8. A: The author writes that climate change "decreases water availability in some regions and makes Earth warmer, leading to more frequent and larger wildfires." At the same time, those fires "stop carbon absorption by killing trees" and "spew huge amount of carbon into the atmosphere as the wood burns," contributing to the warming of Earth's atmosphere.

9. C: The author writes, "Forests and other land vegetation currently remove up to 30 percent of human carbon dioxide emissions from the atmosphere during photosynthesis. If the rate of absorption were to slow down, the rate of global warming would speed up in return."

10. D: The author indicates that the research into carbon dioxide absorption "'has big implications for our understanding of whether global terrestrial ecosystems might continue to offset our carbon dioxide emissions or might begin to exacerbate climate change.

11. C: The author writes, "As human-caused emissions add more carbon dioxide to the atmosphere, forests worldwide are using it to grow faster, reducing the amount that stays airborne."

12. B: The author indicates that an inverse relationship between the rate of absorption of global forests and the rate of global warming; therefore, saving forests and increasing the rate of carbon dioxide absorption would slow the effects of climate change.

Verbal Reasoning 2

1. A: *Grueling* means tough, arduous, and tiring.

2. D: *Impending* means imminent, just around the corner, or looming.

3. D: *Prudent* means practical or sensible; *plummet* means to fall.

4. B, D, G: During this unprecedented time in recent history, teachers have been working diligently to create effective virtual classroom experiences for all of their students. In an effort to build up the classroom community—where students feel safe and valued—communication with students, families, and colleagues is crucial. Not only are digital competency, content knowledge, and literacy skills imperative, but teachers also need to make sure that students are easily able to access their work, understand the objectives of each assignment, and participate in class effectively and appropriately. Having strong remote-learning classroom norms and expectations that help each class run smoothly are essential as well.

5. C, E: If the students are tired, they are most likely also quiet; therefore, we can eliminate options A (*voluble*), B (*communicative*), D (*demonstrative*), and F (*forthcoming*) as answers. This leaves options C and E, both of which indicate antisocial, quiet behavior.

6. B, C: Since the potatoes that were produced will last all winter long, the correct word must be synonymous with a large quantity. The words *barren* and *sterile* indicate emptiness and an inability to produce. The term *scant* refers to a very small amount. *Fecund* and *prolific* are synonyms that indicate the ability to create a large amount; therefore, these are the best answer choices for this sentence.

7. C, F: In this sentence, the words that would fit best are those which indicate that it would have been smart for Judy to have saved her money. It was nearsighted (option A) and reckless (option D) of her not to do so, which means those options can be eliminated. The words *sagacious* and *prudent* are the best answer choices for this sentence.

8. C: The author describes laughter as "a spasmodic movement of various muscles of the body, beginning with those which half close the eyes and those which draw backwards and upwards the sides of the mouth, and open it so as to expose the teeth, next affecting those of respiration so as to produce short rapidly succeeding expirations accompanied by sound (called "guffaws" when in excess) and then extending to the limbs, causing up and down movement of the half-closed fists and stamping of the feet, and ending in a rolling on the ground and various contortions of the body."

9. A: The author writes, "It [laughter] has acquired a variety of relations and significations in the course of the long development of conscious man—but primarily it is an expression of emotion, set going by the experience of the elementary joys of life—the light and heat of the sun, the approach of food, of love of triumph."

10. B: The author writes that laughter "affect[s] those [muscles] of respiration so as to produce short rapidly succeeding expirations accompanied by sound (called 'guffaws' when in excess)."

11. D: The author indicates that laughter is a multistep "process" that is "spontaneous," "spasmodic," and "often involuntary."

12. C: The author indicates that both emotional and mechanical stimuli can contribute to laughter and that the process of laughter can occur "without any corresponding mental emotion of joy."

13. D: The author writes, "It is probably one of those cases in which a mechanism of the living body is set to work, as a machine may be, by directly causing the final movement."

14. B: The author indicates that the apparatus of laughter is the process of laughter, which is set in motion either by "the experience of the elementary joys in life" or by "a short cut to the nerves and related muscles."

15. B: The author writes that the Vedda man's response ("It is true; we never laugh. What is there for us to laugh at?") indicates a "pathetic submission to a joyless life."

GRE Practice Test #4

Analytical Writing

1 prompt, 30 minutes

Analyze an Issue

A fundamental flaw of democracy is that it encourages valuing every person's opinion equally. Isn't the opinion of a chemist more useful than that of a banker when discussing complex compounds? Given the value of experts, we should reform our political system to emphasize expertise rather than the opinions of the masses.

In your essay, introduce the subject, and then either explain the subject you have chosen or take a position about the subject and support that position. At least two evaluators will read and score your essay. Be sure to define your purpose, provide a clear introduction and thesis statement, organize ideas effectively, provide support for your argument, and adhere to Standard English.

Analyze an Issue: Sample Essay

There is a lot to be said for referring to experts in many areas of life. We would rather have an experienced cardiologist perform our open-heart surgery, but that is not who we would call when our kitchen sink backs up and overflows or when our car starts making that loud clanking noise again. However, there are areas of life where expertise is not a necessity. We don't need an expert to tell us which television shows we want to watch, how we want to spend our money, or where we want to live. We have our own ideas about what is right and what is wrong, our own values and beliefs, and our own thoughts about what will improve our lives and our communities. People do not need an expert to tell them how they feel about any given issue or how they think that society should be managed. While they won't always agree with the determination of the masses, people can—and should—have a say in how they are governed.

The very idea of democracy is governing of the people, for the people, and by the people. When we all agree to be bound by the rules of society, we should all have a say in what those rules will be or, at the very least, how they will be determined and enforced. People do not generally respond well to being "bossed around." Even children will rebel when they feel like they are not being seen and heard as valued human beings. However, if children are offered explanations and a choice within the rules (such as which color sweater they will wear on a cold day), they will often be more willing to comply with the rules being imposed. Adults understand the need for laws and societal controls, but we, too, will rebel if we are not part of the process that determines how we will be governed. Our nature does not allow us to accept the argument that someone else knows what is "best" for us. Even when we need a heart surgeon or an auto mechanic, we do not simply take their opinions at face value. We often seek second opinions to help us make informed decisions for ourselves. We treasure our autonomy and our beliefs, and we want to see that reflected in the society in which we live.

Expertise is important in many areas of life, and it would be wonderful if everyone were to fully research every issue in society and fully vet every candidate for public office before making a choice and voting. However, freedom and democracy mean accepting that not everyone will do the same things or think the same way we think. Even so, we need to create a society that works for everyone, not a society in which ultimate authoritarians decide what is best for everyone else. In order for society to work for everyone, everyone should have a voice.

Quantitative Reasoning 1

12 questions, 21 minutes

1.

Column A	Column B
the slope of the line $y = -7x$	the slope perpendicular to the line $y = \frac{1}{7}x$

- A) The quantity in Column A is greater.
- B) The quantity in Column B is greater.
- C) The two quantities are equal.
- D) The relationship cannot be determined from the information given.

2. Most pizzerias determine the size of their pizzas by their diameter.

Column A	Column B
the area of one 16-inch circle	the area of two 8-inch circles

- A) The quantity in Column A is greater.
- B) The quantity in Column B is greater.
- C) The two quantities are equal.
- D) The relationship cannot be determined from the information given.

3. Solve with the fact that $x > 1, y > 1,$ and $z < 0$

Column A	Column B
$\left(\dfrac{x^3 \times x^2}{x \times y^2 \times z^{12}}\right)^0$	x^{-2}

- A) The quantity in Column A is greater.
- B) The quantity in Column B is greater.
- C) The two quantities are equal.
- D) The relationship cannot be determined from the information given.

4.

Column A	Column B
the number of days in two weeks	the number of hours in $\frac{2}{3}$ of a day

- A) The quantity in Column A is greater.
- B) The quantity in Column B is greater.
- C) The two quantities are equal.
- D) The relationship cannot be determined from the information given.

5.

Quantity A	Quantity B
The combined radii of two circles with areas of 8 square inches	The radius of one circle with an area of 16 square inches

A) Quantity A is greater.
B) Quantity B is greater.
C) The two quantities are equal.
D) The relationship cannot be determined from the information given.

6.

Quantity A	Quantity B
$\sqrt{x}$	$x^{\frac{1}{3}}$

A) Quantity A is greater.
B) Quantity B is greater.
C) The two quantities are equal.
D) The relationship cannot be determined from the information given.

7. Daniel earned $625 over the summer. He mowed 23 yards and was paid $15 for each yard. He also washed his dad's car 4 times, and his dad paid him $30 for each wash. Finally, he babysat his little sister for $5 per hour. How many hours did Daniel babysit over the summer?
   A) 21 hours
   B) 26 hours
   C) 30 hours
   D) 32 hours

8. Which of the following is a solution to the inequality $2x + y \leq -10$?
   A) $(0, 0)$
   B) $(10, 2)$
   C) $(10, 10)$
   D) $(-10, -10)$

9. Mrs. Jackson has a jar of colorful marbles on her desk. The jar contains blue, green, yellow, red, black, and white marbles. She tells the class that there are 3 blue marbles for every 5 white marbles, and there are 2 red marbles for every 1 white marble. If there are 24 blue marbles, how many red marbles are in the jar?
   A) 48
   B) 40
   C) 80
   D) 72

10. A square-based pyramid has a height of 10 cm. If the length of the side of the square is 6 cm, what is the surface area of the pyramid?

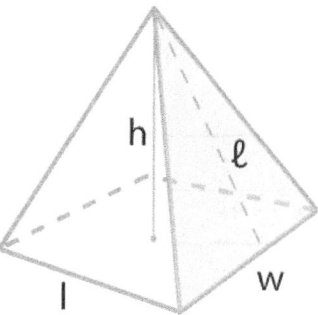

- A) 36 cm
- B) $3\sqrt{109}$ cm
- C) 100 cm
- D) 161.3 cm

11. Josette found an excellent sale on shoes, including boots for 60 percent off the retail price. If she bought three pairs of boots for a total of $252, and all three pairs were the same price, what was the original retail price of each pair of boots?
- A) $140
- B) $84
- C) $168
- D) $125

12. Which equation describes the relationship between x and y shown in the table?

x	y
−4	−9
−1	−3
2	3

- A) $y = -2x - 1$
- B) $y = 3x - 9$
- C) $y = -3x - 8$
- D) $y = 2x - 1$

Quantitative Reasoning 2

15 questions, 26 minutes

1.

Quantity A	Quantity B
the y-intercept of the line $y = 3x$	the slope of the line $y = 3$

A) Quantity A is greater.
B) Quantity B is greater.
C) The two quantities are equal.
D) The relationship cannot be determined from the information given.

2.

Quantity A	Quantity B
the number of solutions to $13 = |x - 4|$	the number of solutions to $-13 = |x + 4|$

A) Quantity A is greater.
B) Quantity B is greater.
C) The two quantities are equal.
D) The relationship cannot be determined from the information given.

3. Solve the expressions, knowing that $x > 0$.

Quantity A	Quantity B
x^2	x^{-2}

A) Quantity A is greater.
B) Quantity B is greater.
C) The two quantities are equal.
D) The relationship cannot be determined from the information given.

4.

Quantity A	Quantity B
40% of 60	60% of 40

A) Quantity A is greater.
B) Quantity B is greater.
C) The two quantities are equal.
D) The relationship cannot be determined from the information given.

5. For $0 < x < 1$

Quantity A	Quantity B
x^3	x^6

A) Quantity A is greater.
B) Quantity B is greater.
C) The two quantities are equal.
D) The relationship cannot be determined from the information given.

6.

Quantity A	Quantity B
$(6 - 2) \times 3$	$6 - (2 \times 3)$

A) Quantity A is greater.
B) Quantity B is greater.
C) The two quantities are equal.
D) The relationship cannot be determined from the information given.

7. Ellen has an employee who seems to be taking too much break time each day. She began keeping an eye on his work time and noted that he spends at least 40 minutes each day chatting with his coworkers, in addition to his allowed 1-hour lunch break and 15-minute afternoon break. He also seems to be taking an additional 15-minute break in the mornings, too. If the employee is at work for 9 hours per day, what percentage of the workday is this employee spending on break?
   A) 18 percent
   B) 20 percent
   C) 24 percent
   D) 28 percent

8. If a car uses 8 gallons of gas to travel 650 miles, how many miles can it travel using 12 gallons of gas?
   A) 870 miles
   B) 895 miles
   C) 915 miles
   D) 975 miles

9. If $y = 2x^2 + 12x - 3$ is rewritten in the form $y = a(x - h)^2 + k$, what is the value of k?
   A) -3
   B) -15
   C) -18
   D) -21

10. If $f(x) = 2x2 + 6$, what is its inverse, $f(x)^{-1}$?
    A) $f(x)^{-1} = \sqrt{\frac{x-6}{2}}$
    B) $f(x)^{-1} = \sqrt{\frac{x+6}{2}}$
    C) $f(x)^{-1} = \frac{\sqrt{x+6}}{2}$
    D) $f(x)^{-1} = \frac{\sqrt{x-6}}{2}$

11. Which of the following equations results in the point shown on the number line?

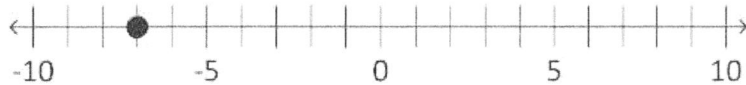

   A) $-2 - 10 \times 2 + 11$
   B) $2 + (10 \times 2) - 11$
   C) $2 + (-10 \times 2) + 11$
   D) $-2 - (-10 \times 2) - 11$
   E) $2 + (10 \times -2) + 11$

12. Juan goes to the grocery store and purchases two avocados for $2.99 each, a package of ground beef for $9.87, and two gallons of milk for $4.89 each. If the tax rate is 3.5%, how much is the total of Juan's purchase?
    A) $26.53
    B) $25.63
    C) $17.75
    D) $18.37
    E) $22.65

13. What is the prime factorization for the number 327?
    A) 1×327
    B) 2×163.5
    C) $2 \times 3 \times 54.5$
    D) 4×81.75
    E) 3×109

14. Simplify the following equation: $7\left(\frac{63}{9}\right) \times (2A) + (4A \times 3)$
    A) $49 \times 14A$
    B) $110A$
    C) $686A$
    D) $49A + 12A$
    E) 49

15. Solve the following equation if $y = 17$: $14(2y) - 76 - (2y)$
    A) 366
    B) 398
    C) 128
    D) 6
    E) 17

Verbal Reasoning 1

12 questions, 18 minutes

1. Jack's friends _____ him after he made an offensive comment in class; they ignored his calls and invitations to a party.
    A) snubbed
    B) invoked
    C) regarded
    D) encouraged

2. The bodybuilder had muscles that were _____ and _____; he won every weight-lifting contest in the country.
    A) strong... feeble
    B) sinewy... brawny
    C) frail... lean
    D) anemic... robust

Select from the answer options that correspond to the blank sentences in each paragraph. One answer must be selected for each blank. The answer must complete the idea being expressed in the text.

3. The game of chess dates back to India in the 6th century A.D. It is seemingly simple, yet offers a wide (i)____ of strategies that players of all ages can implement. In order to play, two opposing players utilize sixteen chess pieces with different pieces having specific ways to move. Using strategy, (ii)____, and skill, each player attempts to capture the king by placing it into what is called "checkmate." Enjoyed by millions of people around the globe, the game continues to (iii)____ even all these centuries later.

Question 3 Answer Options		
Blank (i)	Blank (ii)	Blank (iii)
(A) approach	(D) prediction	(G) insight
(B) supply	(E) foresight	(H) evoke
(C) array	(F) growth	(I) evolve

Select TWO answer options that best match the meaning of the sentence. When added to the sentence, the two answers must create complete sentences that have the same meaning.

4. The series of books for children are ____ and provide specific lessons and morals.
   A) ignorant
   B) didactic
   C) exhortative
   D) preachy
   E) goading
   F) pedagogical

5. Unlike permanent hair dye, semi-permanent sprays are ____ because they will wash away with shampoo.
   A) ephemeral
   B) transient
   C) temporary
   D) eternal
   E) fleeting
   F) stable

6. My best friend came with me to my interview in order to ____ my confidence.
   A) bolster
   B) weaken
   C) strengthen
   D) influence
   E) undermine
   F) deter

Use the passages to answer the questions that follow.

October 29, 1929, was an important day in American history. Known as "Black Tuesday," this was the day that the Wall Street stock market crashed. Investors traded more than 16 million shares in a single day, bringing down the New York Stock Exchange. The drastic plummet that followed **heralded** the beginning of the Great Depression, a period of American history characterized by little food, poor wages, increasing prices, and a steep rise in unemployment.

Part of the cause of this crash was the decade prior, the Roaring Twenties. These were characterized by excessive spending and the expansion of the concept of credit, or buying something with the intention to pay it back later. Debt continued to pile on the average American, most of whom wholly believed that the stock market would rise **indefinitely**. It wasn't until businessmen began to be investigated and arrested for fraudulent activity that the confidence in the market decreased, and within weeks the decade was brought to a bitter end.

7. What is the closest meaning of the word *heralded* in the passage?
    A) Warned of
    B) Mirrored
    C) Was reminiscent of
    D) Signaled
    E) Trumpeted

8. What was the author's purpose for writing this passage?
    A) To voice their opinion about the causes of the Great Depression
    B) To persuade the reader that the stock exchange is broken
    C) To explain the Roaring Twenties
    D) To warn about the dangers of fraudulent business activities
    E) To inform the reader about the causes of the stock market crash

9. What is the main idea of the passage?
    A) The Great Depression could have been stopped by stricter business practices.
    B) Black Tuesday marked the shift of an era.
    C) The average American had too much debt in the twenties.
    D) The crash of the stock exchange is tied to events in the twenties.
    E) The trade of shares should be better regulated.

10. What is the meaning of the word *indefinitely* in the passage?
    A) Without definition
    B) In a controlled manner
    C) Without end
    D) Purposefully
    E) Supposedly

11. Which best summarizes the passage?
    A) The Great Depression was caused by the New York Stock Exchange.
    B) The Roaring Twenties paved the way for the crash of the stock market and the Great Depression.
    C) The crash of the stock market was a result of unchecked optimism.
    D) Lack of temperance among Americans contributed to the stock market crash.
    E) The Roaring Twenties would never have ended if not for fraudulent activity.

12. The popularity of credit directly contributed to the Great Depression in which of the following ways?
    A) Many Americans owed money and therefore had less to spend on themselves.
    B) Americans were forced to give up the possessions they hadn't paid for.
    C) The fraudulent activity was within a credit bureau.
    D) Americans had low credit scores and couldn't buy anything else.
    E) Millions tried to sell stocks on Black Tuesday to pay their debtors.

Verbal Reasoning 2

15 questions, 23 minutes

1. It was clear from the vocabulary used that the essay was _____ and not an _____ piece of writing.
    A) plagiarized... original
    B) commonplace... avoidable
    C) purloined... unoriginal
    D) legal... exemplar

2. After the subway stopped suddenly at the platform, there was a loud _____ coming from the station as workers rushed by.
    A) commotion
    B) quietude
    C) stillness
    D) tranquility

3. The runner started to _____ and lost her energy during the marathon; as a result, she walked the rest of the way.
    A) rile
    B) falter
    C) rally
    D) stabilize

4. We all waited inside for the rain to _____ so that we could go outside and _____ in the sunshine.
    A) replicate... thrive
    B) proliferate... gather
    C) abate... revel
    D) rise... celebrate

Select from the answer options that correspond to the blank sentences in each paragraph. One answer must be selected for each blank. The answer must complete the idea being expressed in the text.

5. There has been a lot of focus on mental health in recent years. One of the biggest (i)_____ in developing and maintaining a positive mental outlook is organization. Staying organized helps reduce stress, improve sleep, (ii)____ self-esteem, increase productivity, and intensify focus and clarity. This is because a tidy, organized space promotes a more relaxed environment, which in turn promote a sense

of calm and control. Using strategies for time-management—a specific form of organization—allow us to feel less overwhelmed by (iii)____ tasks that might otherwise weigh us down.

Question 5 Answer Options		
Blank (i)	**Blank (ii)**	**Blank (iii)**
(A) difficulties	(D) boost	(G) stupid
(B) factors	(E) lower	(H) mundane
(C) problems	(F) inflate	(I) whimsical

Select TWO answer options that best match the meaning of the sentence. When added to the sentence, the two answers must create complete sentences that have the same meaning.

6. The story was full of historical _____, making the author unreliable.
    A) errors
    B) prolepsis
    C) chronologies
    D) anachronisms
    E) accuracy
    F) congruity

7. Do not ____ me simply because I was on television and have become famous; I'm still the same humble person as before.
    A) patronize
    B) adulate
    C) demote
    D) ridicule
    E) lionize
    F) honor

8. The phrasing in some of her poetry was so ___ that no one wanted to read it.
    A) primary
    B) hackneyed
    C) novel
    D) innovative
    E) original
    F) trite

9. Teenagers often get upset over seemingly ___ matters, and parents are often dismissive of these issues.
    A) important
    B) significant
    C) sparse
    D) substantial
    E) trivial
    F) picayune

Use the passages to answer the questions that follow.

The social and political discourse of America continues to be permeated with idealism. An idealistic viewpoint asserts that the ideals of freedom, equality, justice, and human dignity are the truths that Americans must continue to aspire to. Idealists argue that truth is what should be, not necessarily what is. In general, they work to improve things and to make them as close to ideal as possible.

10. Which of the following best captures the author's purpose?
    A) to advocate for freedom, equality, justice, and human rights
    B) to explain what an idealist believes in
    C) to explain what's wrong with social and political discourse in America
    D) to persuade readers to believe in certain truths
    E) to encourage readers to question the truth

Day was fading as they stood above the cliff. All the forest land was blue with shades of approaching night: the river was dull silver: the wooded heights afar mingled their outlines with the towers and banks of turbulent deep blue vapour that hurtled in ceaseless passage through the upper air. Suddenly a window opened in the clouds to a space of clean wan wind-swept sky high above the shaggy hills. Surely Juss caught his breath in that moment, to see those deathless ones where they shone pavilioned in the pellucid air, far, vast, and lonely, most like to creatures of unascended heaven, of wind and of fire all compact, too pure to have aught of the gross elements of earth or water. It was as if the rose-red light of sundown had been frozen to crystal and these hewn from it to abide to everlasting, strong and unchangeable amid the welter of earthborn mists below and tumultuous sky above them. The rift ran wider, eastward and westward, opening on more peaks and sunset-kindled snows. And a rainbow leaning to the south was like a sword of glory across the vision.

Excerpt from *The Worm Ouroboros* E.R. Eddison, 1922

11. What is the meaning of *wan* as used in this passage's third sentence?
    A) Transcendent
    B) Mournful
    C) Pale
    D) Empty
    E) Diseased

12. Which of the following best describes how this passage characterizes nature?
    A) Nature is a great wilderness to be conquered with one's bare hands.
    B) The beauties of nature exceed those of human art.
    C) Different parts of the natural world should be valued independently, not as a unity.
    D) Nature is beautiful because it is useful, not because of an inherent quality.
    E) The elements of nature inspire humanity to see beyond the mundane and imagine the divine.

13. Where is the character Juss positioned in this passage?
    A) Atop a cliff
    B) At a window
    C) On a mountainside
    D) Inside a pavilion
    E) On a river bank

14. What is the purpose of the following sentence in this passage?

"The rift ran wider, eastward and westward, opening on more peaks and sunset-kindled snows."
- A) Describe a rift opening in the land
- B) Expand Juss's vision across a whole landscape
- C) Emphasize the beauty of what Juss saw
- D) Transition to gazing beyond clouds, into the sky
- E) Further describe the "creatures of unascended heaven"

15. What is the main emotion of this passage?
- A) Hubris
- B) Enthusiasm
- C) Trepidation
- D) Awe
- E) Humility

GRE Practice Test #4 Answer Key

Quantitative Reasoning 1

1. C: Slope-intercept form, $y = mx + b$, with $m = slope$ and $b = y$-intercept.

Column A: the slope is -7.

Column B: the slope is perpendicular to $\frac{1}{7}$.

Perpendicular slopes are negative reciprocals. Therefore, the two quantities are equal.

2. A: Determine the area of the pizzas given in each column.

Column A: A 16-inch pizza will have a radius of 8 inches.

$$A = \pi r2 \rightarrow A = \pi(8)2 \rightarrow 64\,\pi$$

Column B: An 8-inch pizza will have a radius of 4 inches.

$$A = \pi r2 \rightarrow A = \pi(4)2 \rightarrow 16\,\pi \times 2\,pizzas = 32\,\pi$$

The quantity in Column A is greater.

3. A: Column A: The fraction is being raised to the power of 0. Any number raised to the power of 0 is equal to 1.

Column B: Since x is greater than 1, the value of x^{-2} is equivalent to $\frac{1}{x^2}$. The value of Column B is between 0 and 1.

The quantity of Column A is greater.

4. B: Column A: 2 weeks $= 14$ days

Column B: The number of hours in $\frac{2}{3}$ of a day is $\frac{2}{3} \times 24 = 16$ hours.

The quantity in Column B is greater.

5. A: The formula for the area of a circle is $A = \pi r^2$. Use this to find the radius of each circle.

Quantity A:

$$8 = \pi r^2$$

$$r = \sqrt{\frac{8}{\pi}}$$

Since there are two circles, Quantity A equals $2 \times \sqrt{\frac{8}{\pi}} \approx 3.19$

Quantity B equals:

$$16 = \pi r^2$$

$$r = \sqrt{\frac{16}{\pi}}$$

Since there is only one circle, Quantity B equals $\sqrt{\frac{16}{\pi}} \approx 2.26$

Quantity A is greater than Quantity B.

6. D: Find the answer by choosing several values for x and substituting them into the expressions for each quantity. For example, if $x = \frac{1}{4}$, then quantity $A = \frac{1}{2}$ while quantity $B = 0.63$. In this case, quantity B is greater than quantity A, but if we substitute a value greater than 1 for x, such as 64, then quantity $A = 8$ and quantity $B = 4$. In this case, quantity A is greater than quantity B. Therefore, the relationship cannot be determined from the information given.

7. D: To solve this problem, first calculate the total Daniel earned for mowing (23 yards at $15 each equals $345). For car washing, Daniel earned 4 × $30 = $120. Together, Daniel earned $345 + $120 = $465 mowing and washing the car. Subtracting $465 from the total earned leaves $160 that Daniel earned from babysitting. $160 ÷ $5 = 32 hours.

8. D: Plug in each set of values and determine if the inequality is true.

$$2(0) + 0 \leq -10 \text{ FALSE}$$
$$2(10) + 2 \leq -10 \text{ FALSE}$$
$$2(10) + 10 \leq -10 \text{ FALSE}$$
$$2(-10) + (-10) \leq -10 \text{ TRUE}$$

9. C: To find the number of red marbles, first solve the ratio for the number of white marbles. The ratio of blue marbles to white marbles is $\frac{\text{blue}}{\text{white}} = \frac{3}{5}$. Plugging in the numbers in the question results in this equation: $\frac{3}{5} = \frac{24}{x}$. Cross-multiply to get $3x = 5 \times 24$. $3x = 120$. Divide both sides by 3, leaving $x = 40$ white marbles. For every white marble, there are 2 red marbles, so the number of red marbles is $40 \times 2 = 80$.

10. D: The surface area will be the area of the square base plus the area of the four triangles. First, find the area of the square ($A = s2$; $62 = 36$). Then, to find the area of the triangles, first find the pyramid's slant height:

$$c^2 = a^2 + b^2$$
$$l^2 = 100 + 9$$
$$l = \sqrt{109}$$

Find the area of the triangle face using the slant height as the height of the triangle face:

$$A = \frac{1}{2} bh$$
$$A = \frac{1}{2} (6)(\sqrt{109})$$
$$A = 3\sqrt{109}$$

Finally, add the area of the square base and the four triangles to find the total surface area:

$$SA = 36 + 4\sqrt{109}$$
$$SA \approx 161.3 \text{ cm}$$

11. A: The first step in solving this equation is calculating the cost of each pair of boots. $252 divided by 3 pairs of boots means that each pair was $84 on sale. 60 percent expressed as a decimal is 0.60, so the equation to find the full price of each pair of boots is $84 = 0.60x$, where x is the original price of the boots. To solve this problem, divide both sides by 0.60, leaving x on its own. $\frac{84}{0.60} = \$140$ per pair.

12. D: The difference between each $f(x)$ value is constant (6), so the function is linear. Find the slope of the line using the formula for slope.

$$m = \frac{y_2 - y_1}{x_2 - x_1} = \frac{-3 - (-9)}{-1 - (-4)} = \frac{6}{3} = 2$$

Use the point-slope equation to find the function.

$$y - y_1 = m(x - x_1)$$
$$y - (-9) = 2(x - (-4))$$
$$y + 9 = 2x + 8$$
$$y = 2x - 1$$

Quantitative Reasoning 2

1. C: The two equations are written in slope-intercept form, $y = mx + b$, with $m =$ slope and $b =$ y-intercept. For quantity A, the slope is 3 and the y-intercept is 0, while for quantity B, the slope is 0 and the y-intercept is 3. Therefore, the two quantities are equal.

2. A: The absolute value of a number is the distance from that number to 0 on a number line, so it must always be a positive number. Solving the equation in quantity A results in two solutions: 17 and –9:

$$13 = |x - 4|$$
$$x - 4 = 13$$
$$x = 17$$
$$x - 4 = -13$$
$$x = -9$$

There are zero solutions for the equation in quantity B because absolute value cannot be a negative number. Thus, quantity A is greater.

3. B: If $x > 1$, then Quantity A will be larger, if $x = 1$, the two quantities will be equal, and if $0 < x < 1$, Quantity B will be larger. This can be seen by the table below:

x	Quantity A (x^2)	Quantity B (x^{-2})	Result
2	$(2)^2 = 4$	$(2)^{-2} = \frac{1}{2^2} = \frac{1}{4}$	Quantity A > Quantity B
1	$(1)^2 = 1$	$(1)^{-2} = \frac{1}{1^2} = \frac{1}{1} = 1$	Quantity A = Quantity B
$\frac{1}{2}$	$\left(\frac{1}{2}\right)^2 = \frac{1}{4}$	$\left(\frac{1}{2}\right)^{-2} = \frac{1}{\left(\frac{1}{2}\right)^2} = 2^2 = 4$	Quantity A < Quantity B

Therefore, the relationship cannot be determined with the information given.

4. C: To determine the value 40% of 60, we multiply $0.4 \times 60 = 24$. For the value 60% of 40, we multiply $0.6 \times 40 = 24$. As both are equal to 24, the two quantities are equal.

5. A: The value of x is between 0 and 1. When comparing fractions, the larger the denominator, the smaller the value of the fraction, so quantity A is greater.

6. A: Use order of operations to solve the problem. Solve the parentheses first.

Quantity A: $(6 - 2) \times 3 = 4 \times 3 = 12$

Quantity B: $6 - (2 \times 3) = 6 - 6 = 0$

We know that 12 is greater than 0, so quantity A is greater.

7. C: First, calculate the total time the employee is on break in minutes: $40 + 15 + 15 + 60 = 130$ minutes. Then divide this by the total time the employee is at work in minutes: $130 \div 9(60) = 130 \div 540 = 0.24 = 24$ percent of the day.

8. D: Set up a proportion and solve.

$$\frac{8}{650} = \frac{12}{x}$$

$$12(650) = 8x$$

$$x = 975 \text{ miles}$$

9. D: Complete the square to put the quadratic equation in vertex form.

$$y = 2x^2 + 12x - 3$$

$$y = 2(x^2 + 6x + \underline{\quad}) - 3 + \underline{\quad}$$

$$y = 2(x^2 + 6x + 9) - 3 - 18$$

$$y = 2(x + 3)^2 - 21$$

10. A: Swap x and y in the equation, then solve for y.

$$f(x) = 2x^2 + 6$$

$$y = 2x^2 + 6$$

$$x = 2y^2 + 6$$

$$y = \sqrt{\frac{x - 6}{2}}$$

11. C: The point on the number line is at -7, which is the solution to Choice C. Using PEMDAS, solve the parenthetical section of the equation first:

$$-10 \times 2 = -20$$

$$2 + (-20) + 11 = -7.$$

12. A: The total of the items before tax is $25.63. To find the tax amount, multiply the total by 3.5%, and then add that to the pre-tax total.

$$\$25.63 \times 3.5\% = 0.897$$
$$\$25.63 = 0.897 = 26.527$$

Round up to $26.53

13. E: $327 \div 3 = 109$; both 3 and 109 are prime numbers.

14. B: Group like numbers using PEMDAS:

$$7\left(\frac{63}{9}\right) = 7(7) = 49$$
$$49 \times 2A + 12A =$$
$$98A + 12A = 110A$$

15. A: Replace y with 17 and solve the equation using PEMDAS:

$$14(2 \times 17) - 76 - (2 \times 17) =$$
$$14(34) - 76 - 34 =$$
$$476 - 76 - 34 = 366$$

Verbal Reasoning 1

1. A: To snub someone is to ignore them.

2. B: *Sinewy* and *brawny* are synonyms that indicate strength.

3. C, E, I: The game of chess dates back to India in the 6th century A.D. It is seemingly simple, yet offers a wide array of strategies that players of all ages can implement. In order to play, two opposing players utilize sixteen chess pieces with different pieces having specific ways to move. Using strategy, foresight, and skill, each player attempts to capture the king by placing it into what is called "checkmate." Enjoyed by millions of people around the globe, the game continues to evolve even all these centuries later.

4. B, C: Because the books teach important lessons, they cannot be described as "ignorant." The books may or may not be preachy, so option D is not the best choice. The term *pedagogical* does indicate something about teaching but is not usually associated with what children would focus on; it is geared more for adults/educators. Finally, the books are likely not "goading," as this often indicates something negative. The best answer options are therefore B and C.

5. A, C: The key phrase is "unlike permanent," which implies that something is temporary. Options A and C are therefore the best answers.

6. A, C: The key term is *best friend*, which indicates someone who would want to help and support someone else. The terms *weaken*, *undermine*, and *deter* can therefore be eliminated as these have negative connotations. The word *influence* does not fit. The best answer options are *bolster* (build up) and *strengthen*.

7. D: In this context, *heralded* means "signaled." Black Tuesday was the beginning of the Great Depression, so the plummet signaled the beginning of it.

8. E: This passage is informational. Its purpose is to explain the stock market crash and what caused it. No opinion is being voiced here, so it cannot be persuasive. Although the Roaring Twenties are mentioned, they are not the entire purpose of this passage. Fraudulent business activities are only mentioned once, so they similarly cannot be the purpose.

9. D: The main idea of this passage is linked to the purpose: to explain the stock market crash and what caused it. Although it's true that Black Tuesday marked a cultural shift, the shift is not the main idea. The Great Depression might have been stopped by stricter business practices, but there is no way to know this for sure; furthermore, the author never states this. The average American likely had too much debt in the twenties, but this is also not the main idea; rather, it's a supporting detail. Whether or not the trade of shares should be better regulated is a matter of opinion, and this is not an opinion piece.

10. C: *Indefinitely* means "without end." Americans expected the stock market to rise forever, as can be deduced by their spending habits and the fact that their confidence in the market decreased later on. This implies they were very confident before that.

11. B: The Great Depression was not caused by the New York Stock Exchange; the author mentions that there were many factors, not just one. Unchecked optimism might have contributed to the stock market crash, but again, this is only briefly mentioned. Lack of temperance, similarly, did contribute, but it is not what the entire passage is about. Whether or not the Roaring Twenties would have continued if it was not for fraudulent activity is not a topic that is discussed in this essay.

12. A: The author states that credit is "buying something with the intention to pay it back later." They also state that the Great Depression was characterized by "little food, poor wages, increasing prices, and a steep rise in unemployment." Combining these facts, Americans owed money in a country where prices were increasing. There was less money left over to spend on themselves. Although they may indeed have been forced to give up possessions, this is not supported by the passage and is just conjecture. The fraudulent activity might have occurred within a credit bureau, but again, this is not supported by the passage in any way. Credit scores are not mentioned in the passage (plus, modern credit scores weren't invented until 1958). The passage states that it was not just any American who was selling stocks; it was investors, specifically.

Verbal Reasoning 2

1. A: *Plagiarized* means stolen or copied without permission; *original* means unique, new, or innovative.

2. A: *Commotion* means uproar or disturbance.

3. B: *Falter* means to hesitate, weaken, or pause.

4. C: *Abate* means to end or stop; *revel* means to bask or delight.

5. B, D, H: There has been a lot of focus on mental health in recent years. One of the biggest factors in developing and maintaining a positive mental outlook is organization. Staying organized helps reduce stress, improve sleep, boost self-esteem, increase productivity, and intensify focus and clarity. This is because a tidy, organized space promotes a more relaxed environment, which in turn promote a sense of calm and control. Using strategies for time-management—a specific form of organization—allows us to feel less overwhelmed by mundane tasks that might otherwise weigh us down.

6. B, D: If an author is unreliable, it means that the author is either not effective or is including information that is not accurate. Answer option E can therefore be eliminated immediately. The other clue in this sentence is the word *historical*, which indicates that the author has made an error somehow. The word *chronologies* indicates accurate timelines while answer option D (*anachronisms*) indicates the opposite. Answer option A (*errors*) could be correct except that it is generic and the sentence clearly indicates history. Answer option B (*prolepsis*) means "chronological error" and is therefore correct.

7. B, E: The key words are *famous* and *humble*. These key words indicate that someone might be viewing "me" as something bigger than what "I" am. Words that glorify or exalt a person would fit best in this sentence; therefore, the correct answer options are B and E.

8. B, F: The key phrase in this sentence is "that no one wanted to read the poetry." This indicates that the poetry must be unappealing or bad in some way. Options D (*innovative*) and E (*original*) can therefore be eliminated since they describe something that someone would most likely want to pay attention to. The best answer options are B and F, each of which have negative connotations.

9. E, F: If parents are dismissive, the answer choices must indicate that something is not important; therefore, options A (*important*) and B (*significant*) can be eliminated immediately. Options E and F are synonyms for the word *insignificant* and work as the best answer choices for this sentence.

10. B: The purpose of the passage is to explain what an idealist believes in. The author does not offer any opinions or try to persuade readers about the importance of certain values.

11. C: *Wan* means pale, with a sickly or frail connotation. It is used in this passage to humanize nature through describing the sky's color. Choice *C* is correct.

12. E: Choice *E* is correct because of the passage's reference to "deathless ones" appearing in Juss's vision as the clouds part. The "rose-red light" is personified to allude to divinity as a quality of the natural world.

13. A: The passage's first sentence positions Juss "above the cliff." Therefore, Choice *A* is correct.

14. B: The sentence describes Juss's vision expanding beyond his initial glimpse through the clouds to "more peaks and sunset-kindled snows." Choice *B* is correct.

15. D: The function of this passage's detailed description is to emphasize Juss's feeling of *awe* at what he sees. This emotion is supported by the description of nature as beautiful and transcendent, as seen in phrases such as "creatures of unascended heaven" and "sword of glory."

GRE Practice Test #5

Analytical Writing

1 prompt, 30 minutes

Analyze an Issue

Claim: It is important for students to study the texts that form the foundation of Western culture as part of their general education.

Reason: Reading the traditional canon helps students understand where their society's values and beliefs come from. Understanding this, students can make insightful choices about whether to retain those values.

In your essay, introduce the subject, and then either explain the subject you have chosen or take a position about the subject and support that position. At least two evaluators will read and score your essay. Be sure to define your purpose, provide a clear introduction and thesis statement, organize ideas effectively, provide support for your argument, and adhere to Standard English.

Analyze an Issue: Sample Essay

It is important to learn from history lest we be doomed to repeat it, as the saying goes. There is absolute value in studying and understanding our past. We need to know what happened, why it happened, and what the results and lasting impacts were in order to understand how we got to where we are now, for better or worse. However, we do not live in the past. We must also learn, grow, and progress as human beings and as a society. It is important, then, that our children both learn from the past and grow into the future, so that they, too, can become productive members of society and carry on where we left off. Thus, a well-rounded education needs to include a thorough study and understanding of our history while also introducing new concepts, beliefs, and ideals. We must learn from history, but we must also continue to grow as a people, making advancements and looking toward the future. We must teach our children how to do that, as well.

We cannot ignore our history. Children must learn where we have been, the good parts as well as the bad, so that they can understand how we got to this point in society. Children, after all, will grow up to be the adults of tomorrow, and society will rely on them to keep it moving forward. To that end, children should read and study the traditional literary canon. The term "literary canon" refers to the books, papers, documents, and other literature that are considered historically and societally important. There is value in the traditional literary canon in that reading these materials gives children an understanding of culture, history, and society. They can see the similarities and differences between the past and the present. They can see themselves in children from the past, and they can compare other cultures and societies with the one in which they live now.

However, the literary canon that is taught in schools should be an ever-expanding, evolving collection of both historical and modern works. The traditional canon gives children a firm foundation to understand history, but they are also looking at that history through a modern lens. Children should be studying more modern texts, as well, because that is where their own frame of reference lies. Children are more likely to engage with texts that make sense to them from their own experiences, where they can see their own lives reflected in the texts. They can relate to and understand those stories on a more personal level.

A truly thorough education should merge the study of the traditional canon with the study of more recent materials. It is important to understand the past, but it is also important to understand society's movement through time and how life evolved from then until now. Reading a variety of literary works throughout that period is what really helps children make "insightful choices" about their own beliefs and values.

Quantitative Reasoning 1

12 questions, 21 minutes

1. Triangles *ABC* and *DFG* are equiangular.

Quantity A	Quantity B
the area of triangle ABC	the area of triangle DFG

A) Quantity A is greater.
B) Quantity B is greater.
C) The two quantities are equal.
D) The relationship cannot be determined from the information given.

2. Triangles ABC and DFG are similar.

Quantity A	Quantity B
the measure of angle ABC	the measure of angle DFG

A) Quantity A is greater.
B) Quantity B is greater.
C) The two quantities are equal.
D) The relationship cannot be determined from the information given.

3. Given $a > b$,

Quantity A	Quantity B
$4a$	$6b$

A) Quantity A is greater.
B) Quantity B is greater.
C) The two quantities are equal.
D) The relationship cannot be determined from the information given.

4.

Quantity A	Quantity B
$|7 - 3|$	$|3 - 7|$

A) Quantity A is greater.
B) Quantity B is greater.
C) The two quantities are equal.
D) The relationship cannot be determined from the information given.

5.

Quantity A	Quantity B
the product of the slopes of two parallel, non-vertical lines	the product of the slopes of two perpendicular lines

A) Quantity A is greater.
B) Quantity B is greater.
C) The two quantities are equal.
D) The relationship cannot be determined from the information given.

6. A series of cylinders and cones have the same diameter and height.

Quantity A	Quantity B
the total volume held in two cylinders	the total volume held in five cones

A) Quantity A is greater.
B) Quantity B is greater.
C) The two quantities are equal.
D) The relationship cannot be determined from the information given.

7. What are the roots of the function $f(x) = 4x^2 - 6x + 7$?

A) $\left\{\frac{3+i\sqrt{19}}{4}, \frac{3-i\sqrt{19}}{4}\right\}$

B) $\{0, 2\}$

C) $\left\{\frac{(6+\sqrt{-7})}{4}, \frac{6-\sqrt{76}}{4}\right\}$

D) $\left\{\frac{3+i\sqrt{5}}{4}, \frac{3-i\sqrt{5}}{4}\right\}$

8. A company's profit, P, can be modeled by the equation $P = -5x^2 + 8,000x$, where x is the number of items sold. What is the maximum profit the company can earn?
   A) $580,000
   B) $2,608,000
   C) $3,200,000
   D) $3,400,000

9. What transformation is created by the –3 in the graph of $y = -3|x - 2| + 2$?
   A) The –3 moves the vertex down 3 and reflects the graph over the x-axis.
   B) The –3 moves the vertex to the left 3 and widens the graph.
   C) The –3 makes the graph wider and reflects it over the x-axis.
   D) The –3 makes the graph narrower and reflects the graph over the x-axis.

10. In the scatter plot, the x-axis represents hours spent studying per week and the y-axis represents the average percent grade on exams during the school year. Is there a correlation between the amount of studying for a test and test results?
    A) Yes, there is a slight positive correlation.
    B) Yes, there is a very strong correlation.
    C) No, there is no correlation.
    D) The information cannot be determined.

11. A landscaping company charges 5 cents per square foot for fertilizer. How much would it charge to fertilize a 30-foot-by-50-foot lawn?
    A) $7.50
    B) $15.00
    C) $75.00
    D) $150.00

12. Solve for x: $8x + 18y = 93; 2x - 15y - 3y = 47$
    A) 5
    B) 14
    C) 75
    D) 105
    E) 140

Quantitative Reasoning 2

15 questions, 26 minutes

1.

Quantity A	Quantity B
the number of congruent sides in an isosceles triangle	the number of congruent sides in an equilateral triangle

   A) Quantity A is greater.
   B) Quantity B is greater.
   C) The two quantities are equal.
   D) The relationship cannot be determined from the information given.

2.

Quantity A	Quantity B
the sum of two vertical angles	the sum of the supplements of two vertical angles

   A) Quantity A is greater.
   B) Quantity B is greater.
   C) The two quantities are equal.
   D) The relationship cannot be determined from the information given.

3. Betty is older than Jeffrey.

Quantity A	Quantity B
three times Jeffrey's age	twice Betty's age

   A) Quantity A is greater.
   B) Quantity B is greater.
   C) The two quantities are equal.
   D) The relationship cannot be determined from the information given.

4.

Quantity A	Quantity B
the number of times a line with a slope of 0 crosses the y-axis	the number of times a line with undefined slope crosses the x-axis

A) Quantity A is greater.
B) Quantity B is greater.
C) The two quantities are equal.
D) The relationship cannot be determined from the information given.

5.

Quantity A	Quantity B
the number of times a line with a slope of 0 crosses the x-axis	the number of times a line with undefined slope crosses the y-axis

A) Quantity A is greater.
B) Quantity B is greater.
C) The two quantities are equal.
D) The relationship cannot be determined from the information given.

6. In a college class, the final grade is determined only by a midterm and a final, where the final weighs twice as much as the midterm. A passing score is 70, and Patrick scored a 78 on the midterm.

Quantity A	Quantity B
the minimum score that Patrick needs to get on the final in order to pass	64

A) Quantity A is greater.
B) Quantity B is greater.
C) The two quantities are equal.
D) The relationship cannot be determined from the information given.

7. Allison wants to calculate her expected weekly income from her tutoring business. She tutors David for two hours per week at a rate of $15 per hour, Sally for one hour per week at a rate of $20 per hour, and Javier for three half-hour sessions at a rate of $18 per hour. Which of the following equations will correctly calculate Allison's weekly income?
  A) $4.5(\$15 + \$20 + \$18)$
  B) $2 + 1 + 1.5(15 + 20 + 18)$
  C) 4.5×53
  D) $2(15) + 1(20) + 1.5(18)$
  E) $2(15) + 1(20) + 3(18)$

8. What is the circumference of a circle whose diameter is 46 cm?
  A) 92 cm
  B) 72.44 cm
  C) 36.11 cm
  D) 23 cm
  E) 144.44 cm

9. Calculate the length of the hypotenuse of a right triangle if one side is 9 and the other side 12.
    A) 10
    B) 12
    C) 15
    D) 18
    E) 20

10. Alberto is planning on fencing in his backyard. If his yard measures 54 feet by 34 feet square, how many feet of fencing will he need?
    A) 176 feet
    B) 88 feet
    C) 1,836 feet
    D) 150 feet
    E) 1,500 feet

11. What is the approximate volume of a grain silo that has a radius of 15 feet and a height of 45 feet?
    A) 675 cubic feet
    B) 1,350 cubic feet
    C) 1,350 square feet
    D) 31,792 cubic feet
    E) 31,792 square feet

12. What is the mean of the following set of numbers?
19, 27, 35, 42, 42, 63, 88, 98, 110, 126

    A) 42
    B) 107
    C) 53
    D) 63
    E) 126

13. In a bag of marbles, there are 50 red marbles, 25 blue marbles, 15 green marbles, and 10 white marbles. What is the probability of drawing a green marble?
    A) 50%
    B) 15%
    C) 25%
    D) 10%
    E) 4%

14. Beatrice is ordering a sub sandwich at a local deli. She can choose from 2 sizes of sandwich and 5 types of bread. She can also pick one of 3 types of meats and one of 4 kinds of cheese. How many different ways can she create a sandwich?
    A) 17
    B) 62
    C) 120
    D) 24
    E) 70

15. If $6x - 26 = 28 - 3x$, what is the value of x?
    A) 12
    B) 8
    C) 13
    D) 4
    E) 6

Verbal Reasoning 1

12 questions, 18 minutes

1. At the end of the movie, the robotic aliens _____ the planet, causing all _____ life to disappear.
    A) created… inanimate
    B) annihilated… dead
    C) obliterated… sentient
    D) abolished… unresponsive

2. Let's settle this _____ and peacefully; there's no reason for us to continue our _____.
    A) tranquilly… ambiguity
    B) amicably… dispute
    C) disagreeably… brutality
    D) aggressively… intenseness

For questions 3-6, select TWO answer options that best match the meaning of the sentence. When added to the sentence, the two answers must create complete sentences that have the same meaning.

3. The simplicity of the recipe was so ___ that the judges of the cooking show instantly walked to the next contestant without a backwards glance.
    A) pedestrian
    B) dazzling
    C) imaginative
    D) prosaic
    E) stimulating
    F) creative

4. The _____ song instantly put me to sleep.
    A) soporific
    B) rousing
    C) stimulating
    D) somnolent
    E) energizing
    F) invigorating

5. A scientific statement's _____ depends on the ability to compare it to observable phenomena.
   A) descriptiveness
   B) veracity
   C) prevarication
   D) evaluation
   E) experiment
   F) accuracy

6. To riff on an old phrase, pet owners might declare "to err is human, to forgive _____."
   A) canine
   B) divine
   C) sublime
   D) equine
   E) prime
   F) ursine

Select from the answer options that correspond to the blank sentences in each paragraph. One answer must be selected for each blank. The answer must complete the idea being expressed in the text.

7. Despite the (i)_____ losses on Omaha Beach during the D-Day landings, the most (ii)_____ deaths during Operation Overlord took place not on the beaches but in the villages of Normandy.

Question 7 answer options	
Blank (i)	**Blank (ii)**
(A) heroic	(D) appalling
(B) tragic	(E) desperate
(C) inconsequential	(F) morbid

8. The most (i)_____ aspect of the inability of our political system to protect the environment is the immediacy of the crisis. Each year we waste with frivolous arguing brings us closer to (ii)_____ disaster.

Question 8 answer options	
Blank (i)	**Blank (ii)**
(A) resolvable	(D) geological
(B) perplexing	(E) ecological
(C) vexing	(F) developmental

Use the passages to answer the questions that follow.

I recently visited the sister ship of the Titanic, viz., the Olympic, at her dock in New York harbor. This was for the purpose of still further familiarizing myself with the corresponding localities which were the scene of my personal experiences on the Titanic, and which are referred to in this narrative. The only difference in the deck plan of the sister ship which I noted, and which the courteous officers of the Olympic mentioned, is that the latter ship's Deck A is not glass-enclosed like the Titanic's; but one of the principal points of discovery that I made during my investigation concerns this matter of the alleged breaking in two of this magnificent ship. The White Star Line officers pointed out to me what they called the ship's "forward expansion joint," and they claimed the Titanic was so constructed that she must have split in two at this point, if she did so at all.

Excerpt from *The Truth About the Titanic* Archibald Gracie, 1913

9. The author uses the phrase "corresponding localities" to indicate which of the following?
    A) He was at the *Olympic*'s dock in New York.
    B) He recognized sections of the *Olympic* based on the *Titanic*.
    C) He was on Deck A when the *Titanic* sank.
    D) He had not seen the "forward expansion joint" while on the *Titanic*.
    E) The White Star Line officers pointed out the location where the *Titanic* broke.

10. Does the author of this passage believe the *Titanic* split in two during the disaster? Why?
    A) Yes, because the officers pointed out the weakness of the "forward expansion joint" to the author.
    B) Yes, because the author believes the *Titanic*'s Deck A was built more weakly than the *Olympic*'s.
    C) No, because the author reports that White Star Line officers said the *Titanic* did not break in two.
    D) No, because the author's language about the *Titanic*'s split is skeptical.
    E) The passage is a neutral account and does not indicate the author's opinion one way or another.

11. What is the main emotion of this passage?
    A) Inquisitive
    B) Hesitant
    C) Confident
    D) Aloof
    E) Contemptuous

12. What is the rhetorical function of this passage's point of view?
    A) It establishes the author as an independent expert on the *Titanic*.
    B) It throws doubt on those who hold opinions opposed to the author's.
    C) It strengthens the author's position by evoking empathy for his personal experience.
    D) It establishes the author's motive for investigating.
    E) It helps conceal personal biases in the author's work.

Verbal Reasoning 2

15 questions, 23 minutes

Select from the answer options that correspond to the blank sentences in each paragraph. One answer must be selected for each blank. The answer must complete the idea being expressed in the text.

1. The night was quiet, and the (i)_____ danced together in the sky over Jon's head. He lay back on the scratchy wool blanket, (ii)_____, and relaxed.

Question 1 answer options	
Blank (i)	**Blank (ii)**
(A) constellations	(D). tapped his fingers
(B) moon	(E) closed his eyes
(C) birds	(F) massaged his forehead

2. When considering the best way to (i)_____ New York's subways, it's important we account for the schedule's impact on daily (ii)_____.

Question 2 answer options	
Blank (i)	**Blank (ii)**
(A) ameliorate	(D) traffic
(B) optimize	(E) revenue
(C) iterate	(F) commuters

3. Many beginner musicians develop a bad habit of keeping (i)_____ by tapping their foot to the beat—which leads to excess noise once they have a chance to perform on stage.

Question 3 answer options
Blank (i)
(A) rhythm
(B) tempo
(C) meter
(D) pace
(E) cadence

4. Hold the bow in your left hand, perpendicular to the ground, with the grip pointed downward. Nock the arrow so that the index (i)_____ points away from your body and the arrow rests on the grip. Lift the bow until it is upright, and extend your left arm, with your right hand keeping the arrow nocked.

Pull back your right arm. Keep your elbow high and your right hand near your cheek. Otherwise, your arrow will (ii)_____ from the target.

Question 4 answer options	
Blank (i)	**Blank (ii)**
(A) fletching	(D) deviate
(B) finger	(E) derivate
(C) guard	(F) evade

5. Each new (i)_____ on Ellis Island had to be processed by the Bureau of Immigration. This included medical inspection by the Public Health Service to (ii)_____ the risk of contagious diseases (such as cholera), followed by (iii)_____ with inspectors to determine occupation, literacy, and self-sufficiency.

Question 3 Answer Options		
Blank (i)	**Blank (ii)**	**Blank (iii)**
(A) delegate	(D) fumigate	(G) arguments
(B) arrival	(E) exacerbate	(H) interviews
(C) delivery	(F) mitigate	(I) quizzes

Select TWO answer options that best match the meaning of the sentence. When added to the sentence, the two answers must create complete sentences that have the same meaning.

6. _____ is the quintessential element that elevates text into poetry; without it, you're just chopping sentences into stanzas.
   A) Meter
   B) Prosody
   C) Musicality
   D) Tempo
   E) Aesthetics
   F) Prose

7. When discussing theology from the perspective of _____, it's important to also consider how this stance impacts ethical theory.
   A) utilitarianism
   B) pantheism
   C) deontology
   D) atheism
   E) realism
   F) psychology

8. Yielding to a rival out of fear for social consequences is a _____ flaw for an academic.
   A) pedestrian
   B) fatal
   C) abstruse
   D) tenured
   E) critical
   F) integral

9. The local _____ all share the same beliefs about what constitutes a fair race.
   A) equestrians
   B) mechanics
   C) contestants
   D) ergonomics
   E) judges
   F) spectators

10. Humans rarely recognize extraordinary times while living through them; nonetheless, there must have been _____ excitement and fear about the changes taking place for those who lived in the first half of the sixteenth century.
    A) consequential
    B) humongous
    C) palpable
    D) unquantifiable
    E) discernible
    F) unjustifiable

Use the passages to answer the questions that follow.

Trust in Athens as a leader, however, we could no longer feel, judging by the examples already given; it being unlikely that she would reduce our fellow confederates, and not do the same to us who were left, if ever she had the power.

Had we all been still independent, we could have had more faith in their not attempting any change; but the greater number being their subjects, while they were treating us as equals, they would naturally chafe under this solitary instance of independence as contrasted with the submission of the majority; particularly as they daily grew more powerful, and we more destitute. Now the only sure basis of an alliance is for each party to be equally afraid of the other; he who would like to encroach is then deterred by the reflection that he will not have the odds in his favor. Again, if we were left independent, it was only because they thought they saw their way to empire more clearly by specious language and by the paths of policy than by those of force.

Excerpt from History of the Peloponnesian War Thucydides, trans. Crawley, 1874

11. Which of the following statements best infers the purpose of this passage?
    A) The speaker is justifying breaking their alliance with Athens.
    B) The speaker is condemning the Athenians as tyrants.
    C) The speaker is explaining why their listeners should fear Athens.
    D) The speaker is arguing that their listeners should submit to Athens.
    E) The passage accuses the Athenians of conspiracy to conquer the speaker's people.

12. How might the speaker describe Athens's current relationship with other cities in its confederation of city-states?
    A) First among equals
    B) Monarch and subjects
    C) Governor and citizens
    D) Tyrant and oppressed
    E) Leader and confederates

13. Why does the speaker claim that alliances are based on fear, not trust?
    A) Fear is a more powerful motivation than trust, if it's a rational fear.
    B) If both sides fear one another, neither will dare to break the alliance.
    C) It's only worth allying with someone if their military is strong enough to be a threat.
    D) Seeking to dominate other states is a natural human urge.
    E) You should fear your ally because then they'll never be able to betray you.

14. Which of the following words best describes this passage's tone?
    A) Placating
    B) Groveling
    C) Defiant
    D) Conniving
    E) Measured

15. Which of the following seems most likely to be one of the "paths of policy" used against the speaker's people?
    A) Economic subjugation through controlling trade
    B) Drafting citizens into Athens's army
    C) Denying participation in their own government
    D) Instituting an Athenian governor over the city
    E) Mandating religious sacrifices to Athenian deities

GRE Practice Test #5 Answer Key

Quantitative Reasoning 1

1. D: Equiangular triangles have equal angles; however, there is no information regarding the lengths of the sides of the triangles, so there is not enough information to determine their areas. The relationship cannot be determined from the information given.

2. C: Similar figures always have the same angle measurements, but they may have different side lengths. Within two similar figures, all corresponding angles are congruent and side lengths are proportional, so the two quantities are equal.

3. D: We know that a is greater than b, but there is no information regarding the values of these two numbers. If $a = 5$ and $b = 4$, then $4a = 4 \times 5 = 20$ and $6b = 6 \times 4 = 24$, which would make quantity B greater; however, if $a = 7$ and $b = 2$, then $4a = 4 \times 7 = 28$ and $6b = 6 \times 2 = 12$, which would make quantity A greater. The relationship cannot be determined from the information given.

4. C: Both expressions are absolute value expressions, so solve each:

$$|7 - 3| = |4| = 4$$
$$|3 - 7| = |-4| = 4$$

Solving the expressions reveals that the two quantities are equal.

5. A: Parallel lines will always have the same slope, making the product of their slopes either 0 (if horizontal) or positive. The product of the slopes of two perpendicular lines will always be −1, as they will be opposite reciprocals, therefore quantity A is greater.

6. A: The volume of a cylinder is V=πr^2 h, and the volume of a cone is V=1/3 πr^2 h. If the cone and the cylinder have the same diameter, they have the same radius. They also have the same height, so the cone's volume is 1/3 of the cylinder's volume. Therefore, it would take six cones to hold the same volume as two cylinders, hence quantity A is greater.

7. A: Use the quadratic formula.

$$f(x) = 4x^2 - 6x + 7$$
$$x = \frac{-(-6) \pm \sqrt{(-6)^2 - 4(4)(7)}}{2(4)}$$
$$x = \frac{3 \pm i\sqrt{19}}{4}$$

8. C: The equation is a parabola, so the maximum profit will be the y-value at the vertex. For a parabola $y = ax^2 + bx + c$, the x-coordinate of the vertex is $-\frac{b}{2a}$, and the y-coordinate is found by plugging the x-coordinate into the equation.

$$-\frac{b}{2a} = -\frac{8,000}{-10} = 800$$
$$P = -5x^2 + 8,000x$$
$$= -5(800)^2 + 8,000(800) = \$3,200,000$$

9. D: For the function $y = a|x - h| + k$:

When $|a| > 1$, the graph will narrow.

When a is negative, the graph is reflected over the x-axis.

10. A: Yes, there is a slight positive correlation. As the number of hours spent studying increases, the average percent grade also generally increases.

11. C: Multiply the area by the charge per square foot.

$$\text{area} = 50 \times 30 = 1{,}500 \text{ square feet}$$
$$1{,}500 \times 0.05 = \$75.00$$

12. B: Combine the like terms on each side of the equals sign in both equations to eliminate one of the variables:

$$8x + 18y = 93$$
$$2x - 15y - 3y = 47$$
$$8x + 2x + 18y - 18y = 93 + 47$$
$$10x = 140$$
$$X = 14$$

Quantitative Reasoning 2

1. D: By definition, an isosceles triangle has at least two congruent sides, and an equilateral triangle has three congruent sides; however, all equilateral triangles can also be considered isosceles, meaning that the number of congruent sides in an isosceles triangle may be two or three, so the relationship cannot be determined from the information given.

2. D: Two vertical angles are always congruent. But the angle measurements of the two vertical angles are unknown, so we cannot determine the measures of their supplements.

For example, imagine two vertical angles, each measuring 120 degrees. Their sum would equal 240 degrees: 120 + 120 = 240. The sum of their supplements would equal 120 degrees: 2 × (180 − 120).

On the other hand, two vertical angles could each measure 50 degrees. Their sum would equal 100 degrees: 50 + 50 = 100. The sum of their supplements would equal 260 degrees: 2 × (180 − 50).

Therefore, the relationship cannot be determined from the information given.

3. D: Betty is older than Jeffrey, but it is not clear how much older she is than him. If Betty is 10 and Jeffrey is 4, then twice Betty's age would be 20, and three times Jeffrey's age would be 12. However, if Betty is 19 and Jeffrey is 18, then twice Betty's age would be 38, and three times Jeffrey's age would be 54. The relationship cannot be determined from the information given.

4. C: A line with a slope of 0 is written as y = number, with that number representing the y-intercept. A line with undefined slope is written as x = number, with that number representing the x-intercept. In both instances, the lines cross their respective axes once, so the two quantities are equal.

5. D: A line with a slope of 0 is written as y = number, with that number representing the y-intercept. A line with an undefined slope is written as x = number, with that number representing the x-intercept. It may be tempting to infer that a line with a slope of 0 will never cross the x-axis (and, unless the equation is y = 0, it will not) and that a line with undefined slope will not cross the y-axis. But a horizontal line with the equation y = 0 follows the x axis in its entirety, just as a vertical line with the equation x = 0 follows the y-axis in its entirety. So, the relationship cannot be determined from the information given.

6. A: The final exam weighs twice as much as the midterm, which can be expressed mathematically as 2x. Patrick scored a 78 on the midterm, and 70 is the grade for passing. Set up an equation, and solve for x:

$$2x + 78 = 70 \times 3$$
$$2x + 78 = 210$$
$$2x = 132$$
$$x = 66$$

Patrick must score at least 66 on the final to pass, so quantity A is greater.

7. D: Because Allison charges different rates for different students, the hours must be multiplied by the corresponding rate, as shown in equation D.

8. E: The circumference of a circle is calculated using the formula C=2 πr or C= πd. Using C= πd:

$$C = 3.14 \times 23$$
$$C = 144.44$$

9. C: The formula for calculating the sides of a right triangle is $a^2 + b^2 = c^2$ with the hypotenuse, or the longest side, equal to c:

$$9^2 + 12^2 = c^2$$
$$81 + 144 = c^2$$
$$225 = c^2$$
$$\sqrt{225} = c$$
$$15 = c$$

10. A: Fencing requires calculating the perimeter of the area to be fenced. In this case, the perimeter is $54 + 54 + 34 + 34 = 176$ feet.

11. D: The formula for calculating the volume of a cylinder is $V = bh$ or $V = \pi r^2 h$. Since the problem does not provide the area of the base, use the second formula:

$$V = \pi r^2 h$$
$$V = \pi(152)(45)$$
$$V = 3.14 \times 225 \times 45$$
$$V = 31{,}792.5 \text{ cubic feet}$$

The solution is approximate because the number for pi has been rounded to the common 3.14.

12. C: The mean is the average of all of the numbers in the set.

$$19 + 27 + 35 + 42 + 42 + 63 + 88 + 98 + 110 + 126 = 650$$
$$650 \div 10 = 65$$

13. B: There are a total of 100 marbles in the bag, of which 15 are green. The probability of drawing a green marble, then, is 15 out of 100, or 15%.

14. C: Because Beatrice can only choose one from each of the options, the solution is calculated using the rule of product: $2 \times 5 \times 3 \times 4 = 120$ possible combinations for her sandwich.

15. E: Combine like terms to solve for x:

$$6x - 26 = 28 - 3x$$
$$6x + 3x = 26 + 28$$
$$9x = 54$$
$$X = 6$$

Verbal Reasoning 1

1. C: *Obliterated* means to destroy completely; *sentient* refers to all conscious, emotional, animate beings.

2. B: *Amicably* means friendly or harmoniously; *dispute* means an argument or fight.

3. A, D: The clue is in the last part of the sentence, "judges . . . instantly walked . . . without a backwards glance." This indicates something negative and means that options B (*dazzling*), C (*imaginative*), E (*stimulating*), and F (*creative*) can be instantly eliminated, leaving options A and D as the only two possible answers.

4. A, D: The hint in this sentence is the fact that the song "instantly put me to sleep." This indicates that the song is not loud, overly stimulating, or invigorating, which would eliminate answer options B (*rousing*), C (*stimulating*), E (*energizing*), and F (*invigorating*). As a result, the only two possible answers are options A and D.

5. B, F: *Veracity* and *accuracy* complete the sentence by emphasizing the quality of scientific statements to be verifiable with data drawn from observation. This quality allows scientists to determine whether or not a statement is true. Choices *B* and *F* are correct.

6. A, D: The use of "pet owners" is a signpost that this sentence is best completed with a pun using an adjective that can also describe a pet. *Canine* and *equine* both fulfill this requirement. Choices *A* and *D* are correct.

7. B, D: The use of "despite" indicates that the Omaha Beach deaths and the Normandy village deaths are being regarded with the same tone, albeit on a different scale (as demonstrated by "most"). This means the first blank should be completed with *tragic* and the second blank with *appalling*. Choices *B* and *D* are correct.

8. C, E: The tone of this passage is frustrated, as demonstrated by "inability" and "frivolous." This indicates that *vexing* is the best answer for the first blank. The second blank restates the first sentence's claim. Therefore, *ecological* is the best answer, indicating an environmental topic. Choices *C* and *E* are correct.

9. B: The author's use of "corresponding localities" indicates that he recognized a parallel between the *Olympic* and the *Titanic* due to his "personal experiences on the *Titanic*." Choice *B* is correct.

10. D: The use of phrases such as "alleged breaking" and "if she did so at all" indicate that the author doubts the *Titanic* split in two during its sinking. Choice *D* is correct.

11. A: The author expresses his inquisitive mood in this passage through reference to his investigation into the *Titanic*'s sinking and his interviews with the White Star Line officers on the *Olympic*. Choice *A* is correct.

12. C: By referencing his "personal experiences" during the *Titanic*'s sinking, the author builds empathy in the reader. Using the first person establishes pathos, which helps persuade the reader to believe the author. Choice *C* is correct.

Verbal Reasoning 2

1. A, E: "Together" provides a signpost that a plural is needed for the first blank, and *constellations* best fits the text's nocturnal setting. The second blank calls for the phrase that best fits with "relaxed." This is *closed his eyes* because the other choices describe restlessness and tension, not relaxation. Thus, Choices *A* and *E* are correct.

2. B, F: The strongest signpost is "the schedule's impact" in the second half of this sentence. This indicates that the second blank is a passive subject impacted by changes in schedule. *Commuters* is the best choice because it identifies people who use the subway (rather than "traffic" more generally). Determining the second blank helps choose *optimize* for the first blank because this verb indicates perfecting the system. Choices *B* and *F* are correct.

3. B: *Tempo* is the best choice because it is the formal term used in music to describe the beat's rapidity. Choice *B* is correct.

4. A, D: *Fletching* must be the correct answer for the first blank because the sentence requires a part of an arrow. The best choice for the second blank is *deviate* because the verb describes the act of straying from the target. Choices *A* and *D* are correct.

5. B, F, H: *Arrival* is the best choice for the first blank because "new" and "Bureau of Immigration" indicate that a word for an immigrant is needed. The second blank is completed with *mitigate* because it means to reduce or make less severe. *Interviews* is the best choice for the third blank because an interview is a common part of an approval process. Choices *B*, *F*, and *H* are correct.

6. A, B: *Meter* and *prosody* are correct because both words describe the use of rhythmic elements in lines of poetry. Choices *A* and *B* are correct.

7. B, D: Despite *pantheism* and *atheism* having opposed definitions, their use in this sentence is equivalent because both positions make theological claims that may or may not influence an individual's beliefs about ethics. Choices *B* and *D* are correct.

8. B, E: *Fatal* and *critical* both complete the sentence effectively by indicating that this is a major flaw, not a minor flaw. Choices *B* and *E* are correct.

9. A, C: *Equestrians* and *contestants* provide the sentence similar meaning because both words designate a group of people who would participate in a race. Choices *A* and *C* are correct.

10. C, E: *Palpable* and *discernible* provide equivalent meaning in this sentence because each adjective provides a sense of concreteness to the description of abstract emotions. Choices *C* and *E* are correct.

11. A: The speaker's stated lack of trust combined with their use of the past tense indicates that the speaker's people already broke their alliance with Athens and that this speech explains why afterward. Choice *A* is correct.

12. D: The speaker states that their people were left independent only because the Athenians were not yet able to forcefully oppress them. This indicates that the speaker sees Athens as a tyrant and that Choice D is correct.

13. B: As the author writes, "he who would like to encroach is then deterred by the reflection that he will not have the odds in his favor." Mutual fear ensures the allies will not gamble on breaking the alliance. Choice B is correct.

14. E: This tone is best described as *measured* because the speaker presents their argument directly, with little use of emotional rhetoric either to mollify or to condemn the Athenians. Choice E is correct.

15. A: Choice A is most likely because the speaker says that their people were becoming "destitute." This indicates impoverishment, not direct military or political control. Therefore, Choice A is correct.

Made in the USA
Coppell, TX
24 February 2025

46343807R10122